Clergy: The Origin of Species

THIS
BOOK
BELONGS TO
ROBERT
THEWSEY

Boscastle
August 08

Clergy: The Origin of Species

Martyn Percy

continuum

The Continuum International Publishing Group
The Tower Building, 11 York Road, London SE1 7NX
80 Maiden Lane, Suite 704, New York, NY 10038

www.continuumbooks.com

British Library Cataloguing-in-Publication Data
A catalogue record for this book is available from the British Library

Typeset by Data Standards Limited, Frome, Somerset UK
Printed on acid-free paper in Great Britain by MPG Books Ltd, Bodmin, Cornwall

ISBN 0826482872 (hardback)
ISBN 0826482805 (paperback)

To
the students at Ripon College Cuddesdon
and the Oxford Ministry Course

Contents

Foreword

It is very difficult to be prescriptive about what counts as a vocation to the sacred ministry or what is essential to the priestly or ministerial role apart from authorization from the religious community to act as its representative in certain core activities. In my own case the 'call' was initially a friendly remark to the effect that, being rather critical of the Church, I might consider helping it more concretely through a non-stipendiary ministry alongside my other vocation as an academic.

Once embarked on this course I discovered how extraordinarily varied were the motivations and life-experiences of those similarly embarked, but most desired to be 'of service' in every sense of 'service'. The Church is a treasury of meanings, available to all sorts and conditions and we dip into the treasury at different times for various reasons to discover 'things both old and new'.

At that time many ordinands came originally from nonconformist denominations. Those denominations, with their distinctive models of ministry and church, had broken away in quite specific and contingent circumstances and were marked by the character and ethos of their times, whether we think of the Puritans and early capitalism or the Methodists and the industrial revolution. They were, to use the biological analogy that pervades Martyn Percy's book, adaptations of the continuities of Christianity all the way back to the fluid conditions of the earliest Church, but redesigned to 'serve the present age' – as Charles Wesley put it. The biological analogy works in several directions of course: what is temporarily recessive in one generation can be held in trust for the next.

I was able to carry something of Methodism with me in the Anglican ministry, just as others were able to carry something of the medieval Church through a 'Catholic' usage in the enactment of the liturgy. That reinforced my sense of the sheer variety of paths that intersect in any particular ecclesiastical space. I know perfectly well, of course, from my sociological studies as well as my personal acquaintance that even dogmatic churches with clear norms and strong boundaries are in practice very varied, which is indeed part of their ability to be inclusive and 'Catholic'. The Anglican Church is not all that special in being 'broad' and in hosting any number of enclaves.

The core of the Church, expressed in the shared gift of Christ's body or the shared ecstasy of 'tongues' is a point of intersection between the transcendent and the time-bound, the essential and the contingent, and therefore, as Martyn Percy says, a manifestation of the incarnation. It is also a manifestation of Pentecost because however varied our languages and personal accents there is some translatability across times and spaces. Sometimes the translatability fails in a way that is expressed in the imagery of the gospel itself, because the new wine cracks open the old wineskins. Nor is that straightforward loss, because the clash of visions as they arise out of our creaturely locatedness is creative. Again, to quote the gospel, there are 'other sheep not of this fold', and schism can express the intensity of different perspectives on truth. All human life is perspectival, because 'our gaze is submarine', as T.S. Eliot put it.

One perennial problem is the very human tendency to take the part for the whole, which means that we invest the part we know with the inclusive aura of the sacred. Perhaps this is less widespread than it once was for the obvious reason that we now encounter so many alternatives as part of our everyday life-experience. Automatic and untroubled acceptance of a particular faith or of a particular understanding of what it is to be the parish 'person' (or parson), or of what is meant by the parish community, has become fragile and contested. If we are to make choices we have to sort things out, perhaps discarding what once seemed a given or discovering a fresh focus on what we take to be essential. The familiarity engendered by background and usage inevitably shapes our perceptions. My Methodist background made the idea of 'validity' unattractive, and arguments against women priests unimaginable. In a similar way when we talk about 'reception' of a given change that seems to me not much more than a polite way of talking about a change becoming familiar. We are in a profound (and benign) sense creatures of 'habit', and habit refers to the clothes we feel comfortable in as part of our taken-for-granted identity.

Like Martyn Percy I am shaped by two intellectual genealogies, one sociological and the other theological, and that breeds a 'binocular' approach, attempting to relate the lightening that 'strikes' us, perhaps like St Paul almost literally, to the 'earthen vessels' in which it lodges. As sociologists we are by the nature of our trade suspicious of the way contingent practices and structures of power are legitimized by appeal to organizational 'essences' whether based on a particular biblical mode of understanding – liberal or conservative – or based on some notion of the development of tradition. We are sceptical (if hardly surprised) when either the appeal to the Bible or the development of tradition is eked out by further appeal to the Holy Spirit. When St Paul warned Christians to test the 'spirits' carefully he might well have included the Holy Spirit in his warning. None of us, not even liberals, are in receipt of authorized faxes from heaven. Moreover, what some of our representatives, episcopal or presbyteral, take to be 'our' beliefs are in fact not at all representative. Sometimes I wonder whether the Holy Spirit may not be differently located at some distance from his presumed holy office in the Church, and at other times I am dispirited by the way statements from his official office seem to lag behind what has become common knowledge elsewhere. Part of the institutional lag bedevilling the Church has to do with its emphasis on internal forbearance and consensus.

Martyn Percy argues constantly for a situated view of the Church, above all in terms of his preferred analogy of 'adaptation' within the clerical species. One of his most telling examples concerns the Coptic Church which, because isolated, adapted in quite specific ways to its distinctive environment. Of course, when it comes to cultural change the analogy of biological adaptation can only be pushed so far. But there are cultural niches to which the Church adapts, so that the Roman Church may officially modify its teaching on contraception to cope with the problem of AIDS, and thereby conform to an adaptation already achieved by most of its members. That is another instance of 'representatives' not being representative. Once you look at the past history of adaptation, and the different lines time and again drawn in the sand, it is difficult to say what *the* Church has always taught. Indeed, the Church is perfectly capable of teaching quite forcefully what it has forcefully fought against only a century or so previous. (Historical memory does have its uses.) Martyn Percy recalls us to that memory in his dealings with ecclesiastical history, as well as to the repertoire of faith expressed under so many forms, *hic et ubique*.

Martyn Percy has in a plain and scholarly way posed the question of what is relevant 'to serve the present age' from a sociological viewpoint based on our relatedness to our particular time and place. He does so while rejecting the philosophical premises that reduces historical relatedness to moral and theological relativism. His challenge is itself timely, being directed both against the assertion of false 'essences' and the acceptance of relativism and indifference.

David Martin

Acknowledgements

The six main essays in this book represent several years of reflection on theologies of ministry. This process began when I was myself training for ordination, and the essays have, quite naturally, come to the surface now that I find myself as principal of a theological college that trains men and women for ordained ministry in the Church of England. The essays also represent several years of ongoing conversations with friends and colleagues, for which I am profoundly grateful. Some of the material included in this volume has appeared in earlier drafts in journals, or in edited collections of essays, notably *Unmasking Methodist Theology* (edited by Clive Marsh, Brian Beck, Angela Shier-Jones and Helen Wareing; London: Continuum, 2004), *Predicting Religion* (edited by Grace Davie, Paul Heelas and Linda Woodhead; Aldershot: Ashgate, 2003), *Public Faith?* (edited by Paul Avis; London: SPCK, 2003), *Religion, Identity and Change* (edited by Simon Coleman and Peter Collins; Aldershot: Ashgate, 2004) and *The Character of Wisdom* (edited by Stephen Lowe and Martyn Percy; London: Ashgate, 2004). I am also grateful for permission to reproduce 'The Bright Field' by R.S. Thomas (*Collected Poems 1945–1990*, London: Weidenfeld & Nicolson, 1995) and 'Description without Place' by Wallace Stevens (*Collected Poems*, London: Faber, 1955). I also owe a debt of gratitude to conversation partners from whom I have learnt so much, and wish to especially thank Mark Chapman, Tom Keighley, Emma Percy, Mark Cobb, Chris Swift, Andrew Walker, David Martin, Linda Woodhead, Grace Davie, Ian Markham, Gareth Jones, Margaret Cadman and Alastair Redfern. Mention should also be made of friends and colleagues at Continuum, who have encouraged this project from the very beginning, and who have provided much valued support. To all of them, and most especially to friends and colleagues here on 'God's Holy Hill', I gladly dedicate this book.

MWP, Epiphany 2006

Introduction

This book proposes a new way of thinking about theologies of ministry. It argues that ministries need to self-consciously contemplate, critically reflect upon and imagine their occurrence in relation to their context and environment, over and against the typical sense of development that is normally conveyed by theology or ecclesiology. I should confess that the enquiry has been driven by a deep fascination that started long ago, and continues to grow the more one encounters self-referential descriptions and explanations of ecclesiology and ministry. It is not that these accounts are of themselves deficient; many are lucid, theologically rich and spiritually acute. Rather, the concern is with what such theological narratives habitually exclude. On one level, then, this book sets out to radically re-narrate the assumptions that underpin many theologies of ministry, and in so doing, it invites the reader to ponder a new theory of ministry. Of course, I am well aware that the creation of a theory is little more than the articulation of an interest-driven pattern. To discern or impose a pattern is to suggest an order in life that merits attention and deep consideration, because it makes more sense than chaos and randomness, or than previous patterns. This is, in essence, the primary concern of this modest volume.

The patterning of the ecclesiologies with which I take issue often seem to be based upon some (claimed) divine blueprint, which is itself, obviously, contestable. Moreover, such narrations tend to take little account of the contextual features that have actually had a distinctive role in determining the shape of ecclesial or ministerial identity. In some cases, it is almost as though an entirely a-contextual theory is proposed. Whether or not this is intended, the effect is to present a church or ministry in such a way as to commit a kind of apotheosis, in which their origin and development can only be described and explained with reference to the intention and activity of God. This, as I argue, represents a kind of 'creationism' at work in ecclesiology, in which the ordering and functioning of the church is held to be above ordinary critical scrutiny. The apparent 'givens' of this kind of theological approach can operate in a similar manner to certain types of fundamentalism.

The pattern proposed in place of this is a theological reconstruction of ministry that takes the role of the environment and the functioning of the contextual – in relation to shaping theological and ecclesial development – much more seriously. I hold this to be an essential

1

task for ecclesial hermeneutics (i.e., the incorporation of 'theological realism'). But in addition, I also argue that this approach serves as an important corrective to the romanticizing and idealizing tendencies that can be present in many different kinds of ecclesiology, which often remove the church from facing the contingencies and realities that do so much to shape ministerial and ecclesial identity.

Correspondingly, the argument deployed in the book utilizes evolutionary theory as an analogical and analytical lens through which the debate is conducted. In so doing, I am not taking any particular side in the evolution vs. creation debate. Rather, I am merely using the simple, basic essence of Darwinian theories, in a way that draws the readers' attention to socio-historical dynamics and their relation to the shaping of ministerial and ecclesial identity. I am also following something of the morphological style contained within Darwin's *Origin*, insofar as his book, like mine, depends on a kind of 'mosaic' of research, insight, observation, analysis and reflection, pieced together to make a representative pattern that challenges prevailing paradigms. In using the 'mosaic' analogy here, I am consciously signalling to readers that, unlike other more obvious pure or systematic forms of research, the sum that readers encounter here will be greater than the parts. This is a patterned theory that depends on fragments of knowledge being pieced together in a particular way, and for particular ends. It is deliberately artistic, and therefore, inevitably, to an extent, impressionistic. That said, there are three key arenas of enquiry that serve to drive the shape and argument of the book: the changing nature of clerical identity; the role of the environment (or culture as an agent of change); and the function of churches, denominations and congregations as both resistors and accommodators of cultural change, being the main context in which ministers operate.

This task is, arguably, an urgent one, when one considers the gap between ecclesially sponsored accounts of priesthood, the diaconate, episcopacy, or ministry more generally, and their actual operations. Typically, the former kind of account will reach for authoritative traditions to determine and proscribe what ministry is, and, with rare exceptions, indulge either in a simplistic form of biblical functionalism, or in a romanticization about the recovery of a past that is deemed to be neglected or forgotten. But neither is adequate when it comes to illuminating the actuality of ministry. Here is how one fictional (but undoubtedly representative) clergyman describes his ministry:

Lionel: ...I don't think anyone knows quite what the job is. Mostly it's just listening to anger. One reason or another. Lately it's the change in DSS rules. If you're young, setting up home, you can no longer get a loan for a stove, unless you can prove you'll be able to pay the money back. I've had three couples in the last week. They need somewhere to go to express their frustration. They're drawn to a priest. They're furious. At the system. At where they can find themselves. And they come to the Vicar because he's the one man that can never hit back.[1]

The sentiments outlined above, which express part of the deep and unquantifiable emotional dimension of ministry, are in sharp contrast, of course, to the kinds that once found expression in the eighteenth century, where the status, tasks and roles of clergy seemed rather different. As Thomas Hinde suggests of a different era, 'country parsons suggest some sociological experiment: give a reasonably educated middle-class Englishman a modest income, a house in the country, and job security for life, and see what he will do'. Hinde observes that the clergy then evolved in remarkable ways:

> He becomes a world authority on spiders; he invents a theory of history which makes the Druids a tribe of Phoenician pre-Christian Christians; he plants 5,000 rose-bushes in his garden and the surrounding countryside, runs his own foxhound pack, makes his rectory into a monastery and turns Roman Catholic, collects folk-songs, breeds winning racehorses or green mice, rides from Land's End to John O' Groats...There seems no limit to the variety of his interests or to the obsessiveness with which he pursues them.[2]

In recent years there has been a more sustained attempt by churches and pastoral theologians to come to terms with the reality of ministry. This has prompted a continuous stream of writings and reflections, many of which attempt to reaffirm the vitality and sanctity of the sacred office of ordained ministry. To be sure, many of these offerings are welcome, but they also tend to suffer, as a general rule, from being interiorized accounts of ordained ministry that take insufficient account of key cultural drivers and forces that are shaping ministry and contemporary ecclesiology. Inevitably, therefore, such treatments merely tend to address the presenting symptoms that are causing obvious stress or difficulty in clerical identity. Few are prepared to engage in the root causes of environmental change that manifestly have such an impact on the shaping of the church.

This book, therefore, is not only about the changes that have been wrought in clerical identity over several centuries. It also engages seriously with culture as an environmental element that affects the shape and identity of ministry. Because churches, like their ministers, are rooted and grounded in distinctive cultures, it is likely (as well as it might be desirable) for environmental factors to play a part. For instance, recent studies carried out by Gallup in the USA show to what extent the cultural shifts on issues such as sexuality become, in the end,

---

[1] D. Hare, *Racing Demon* (London: Faber & Faber, 1990), p. 31.
[2] T. Hinde, *A Field Guide to the English Country Parson* (London: Heinemann, 1983), p. 4.

a force for change within the churches. In 1977 56 per cent of Americans thought that homosexual people should have equal rights in the workplace; the figure for 2004 is 89 per cent. Support for gay clergy has moved in the same period from 27 per cent to 56 per cent. Some 60 per cent of Americans in the 18–29 age-bracket now support same-sex 'marriage', compared to only 25 per cent of those who are over the age of 65. The statistical surveys of churchgoers repeatedly show that there is growing toleration for same-sex unions in congregations and amongst clergy, across the ecclesial and theological spectra. All of which suggests a church that will adapt and evolve in relation to its context.[3]

There is nothing especially surprising about the idea that religions move with the times. In their need to adapt and survive, they are, like any organic species, conscious of their need to both resist and accommodate their environment. For example, the ancient religion of the Egyptian Pharaohs, which had developed from the pyramids of Giza, and arguably reached its epoch in the time of Rameses II, was deliberately adapted by Alexander, and, subsequently, the conquerors from Rome. Later, as Christianity spread through Egypt in the fourth century CE, what was left of the old Egyptian religion retreated southwards down the Nile, with each generation gradually abandoning its sacred sites: the pyramids at Giza, the Valley of the Kings, and eventually the temples of Luxor. The last evidence we have of functioning ancient Egyptian religion is the remote temple at Philae, where an inscription (a prayer to Horus) can be found on a pillar, dating from about 390 CE. But by then the writings and the rituals are all but extinct – the religious equivalent of the Dodo – extinguished by the growing flames of Coptic Christianity that swept all before it.

The book is also concerned with a further stream of debate, namely the ways in which denominations, congregations and churches function as discrete environments that also have a bearing upon the evolution of theologies of ministry. The country parson and diarist Francis Kilvert, when visiting the university church of Oxford in 1876, where he had worshipped as an undergraduate some decades earlier, was extremely surprised to find that it had changed, almost beyond recognition:

> The clergy and choir entered with a procession, incense bearers and a great gilt cross, the thurifers and acolytes being in short white surplices over scarlet cassocks and the last priest in the procession wearing a biretta and a chasuble stiff with gold...the sermon came after the Third Collect. I was disappointed in it and so I think were many more. After the service there was an offertory and a processional hymn, and then round came the procession down the South aisle and up the nave in the following order. First the thurifer in short white surplice and scarlet cassock swinging a

---

[3] D. Myers and L. Scanzoni, *What God Has Joined Together?* (San Francisco: Harper, 2005), pp. 140ff.

chained censer high in the air and bringing it back with a sudden check and violent jerk which brought the incense out in a stifling cloud. Next an acolyte in a similar dress bearing aloft a great gilt cross. Then three banners waving and moving above the heads of the people in a weird strange ghostly march, as the banner-bearers steered them clear of the gaslights.

As we came out of Church Mayhew said to me, '*Well* did you ever see such a function as that?' No, I never did and I don't care if I never do again. This was the grand function of the Ascension at St Barnabas, Oxford. The poor humble Roman Church hard by is quite plain, simple and Low church in its ritual compared with St Barnabas in its festal days and holidays.[4]

That churches evolve in style, ordering and function will be obvious to most, if not all readers. But it is interesting to note just how little attention theologians pay to the social and contextual realities that shape ecclesiologies. The danger of this is that by ignoring socio-contextual factors, the church that is narrated runs the risk of being a creature of the imagination rather than a reliable description of an authentic Christian community that is rooted in the soil of its environment. This book sets out, therefore, to press a claim for a more radical inculcation of the ambiguous social and historical forces that help to determine and prescribe ecclesial shape and identity. It does so in relation to the emergence of clergy and their distinctive functions, and in so doing, attempts to suggest a different patterning for theologies of ministry.

Finally, readers may appreciate a brief word about content and methodology. Although I write as an Anglican priest, I have tried to draw on examples from several different denominations to ensure that the argument functions more fairly and fully. So readers will find references to mainstream and emerging denominations throughout, contributing to the discussion as a whole. In addition, I have chosen to address a mosaic of concerns that to some extent represent some key features of the clerical paradigm. Readers will therefore encounter meditations and musings that cover such topics as denominational identity, power, authority, confession, professional identity, pastoral offices, gender and polity, youth ministry and parish identity. In terms of methodology, a volume like this naturally pays appropriate attention to sociology and anthropology, but placed within the broader economy of practical theology. There is also, inevitably, some discussion of pastoral theology, as the kind of practical theological critique that materializes here will inevitably have some implications for the understandings of ministry that emerge out of contextual and environ-

---

[4] William Plomer (ed.), *The Diary of Francis Kilvert 1840–1879* (London: Penguin, 1987), pp. 318–20.

mental considerations. The primary focus, as with some of my previous works, is to address the context of the church in its past and present, and to consider its future possibilities in the light of practical theological reasoning.

An analogical *aperitif* might help to hint at the agenda here. Situated in south-east Siberia is Lake Baikal, one of the oldest (25 million years) and deepest (1,700 metres) freshwater lakes in the world. The lake is known as 'the Galapagos of Russia' for its extraordinary range of plant and marine life, including the world's only freshwater seals. It is reasonable to presume that these seals began their life in the saline oceans millions of years ago when the lake itself was part of the sea. But the shifting continental plates, resulting in the creation of new land mass, eventually led to the lake being formed, with the seals gradually evolving as the water slowly lost its salinity. These seals are related to their oceanic cousins, but they adapted to fit their environment. Much like Independent Methodists, perhaps, who having broken their connexional ties with mainstream British Methodism, now find that their proclivities make them more suited to joining the waters of the Baptist Union.

Or consider the development of new, emerging denominations in the twenty-first century. It is mostly the case that of those bodies which began as radical – house churches, and a whole variety of other expressions of Restorationism in the 1960s and 1970s – are now debating their future life. Their leaders, if not dead, are either in retirement or very close to it. Yet almost without exception, no new leader of note has been generated from within any of these movements to take the emerging church to its next phase. No Joshua has been found to replace Moses. These once-new radical expressions of Christianity find themselves, in their second phase of development, led by an emerging system (not a person), bequeathed to them by the original founding Charismatic leader – who *de facto*, could find no equal to replace them. Such is the nature of charisma. Because nature abhors a vacuum, so far as denominations are concerned, it is normally the case that the absence of personalities leads to a consequential rise in levels of bureaucracy. Such is evolution: to survive, the species adapts.

In writing like this, the book offers a kind of weaving together of methods, insights and critiques that suggest a reconsideration of the prevailing patterning for the construction of theologies of ministry and ecclesiology. The choice to not privilege one method or theory over another is therefore a deliberate strategy, in the hope that it will permit the reader to develop his or her own problem-posing stratagem in relation to ecclesial and ministerial identity. Put another way, it is only by daring to pose questions to those answers that are deemed to be given, that theology and ecclesiology can advance in their understanding. Such a path sets its heart on discerning wisdom, its mind on seeking truth, and the risk of being illumined by what is eventually discovered on the journey.

Chapter 1

On Reflection

The genesis of this book lies in an idle moment, when sitting in the study, browsing through some diaries kept by a former incumbent in the vicarage in which I was living at the time. This had been the same study which the Revd Oliver Tomkins, later Bishop of Bristol (1959–1975) had used during the Second World War, and from which he had penned his numerous BBC World Service broadcasts, and had also kept valuable records of his day-to-day activities. According to his diaries, Tomkins would rise early, and would spend the morning in his study reading, writing and preparing sermons or lectures. He would then lunch, before going out each afternoon on a programme of visiting, returning at tea time before devoting the evening to more meetings and other appropriate parochial consultations. It was the uncompromising ordering of Tomkins' diary that struck me most. Each day was meticulously laid out with an almost military precision; the patterning of his time had a logic and order to it that might seem alien to many contemporary clergy, some fifty years later. He seemed to know what he was doing; why and for whom. This was an age of charmed innocence; there were no nagging questions about clerical identity – only horizons of possibility.

At the time of writing this essay, I sit in another study – that of Runcie, Riches, Knapp-Fisher, Houlden and other former Principals of Cuddesdon – who have devoted themselves to the task of training and forming individuals for ordination in the Church of England. That study – which I now find myself occupying as Principal – is infused with the ethos of broad Anglicanism. This is the cradle for a certain type of Anglican polity – of relaxed awareness; of the delicate combination of order and innovation; the probing and affirming of doctrine and tradition. The study is, in many ways, a unique environment; a place (or formative context) that is responsible for the shaping of vocations and the nourishing of ministries. But if the place is more or less the same, the time is most certainly not. For the 'obvious' certainties and givens of clerical identity have given way, over the last half-century or more, to a profound (if implicit) sense of bewilderment.

There are doubtless many reasons for this. But this essay suggests that chief amongst them is the rapid compression of clerical identity during the industrial revolution and post-industrial era, such that the 'clerical profession' has been narrowed and specialized in ways that are both helpful and unhelpful. On the one hand, clergy generally understand themselves to be not merely engaged in a set of ministerial tasks, but also to have been ordained, such that they can be defined by what they are, not merely what they do. On the other hand, it is not wholly unfair to suggest that one consequence of this ontological separatism is that clergy roles have evolved to become so distinctive as to render them potentially problematic: too particular and exclusive, virtually creating a separatist elite. The problem here may not simply be with clergy who are trying harder and harder to carve out a niche for themselves in a world increasingly driven by choice and consumption. It may also be with society itself, that assumes for the most part that it can assemble its own myriad of individual portfolios of meaningful spirituality, each of which no longer requires the services of a full-time religious professional. What are the clergy to do? They might insist on the primacy of religion over spirituality, and of obligation over choice. They might also place a premium on the theological (or revelatory) story that apparently or allegedly privileges holy orders as being 'by God established'. But beyond this, it is hard to be precise about exclusive roles and tasks, and the concrete nature of clerical identity.

Thus was it ever so. The Apostle Paul wrestled with his own identity problem after his Damascus Road conversion. He was a gifted evangelist, church planter and apologist for the Christian faith. But he wasn't an Apostle – at least not in the sense that the other 'twelve' defined the role. (Interestingly, Paul never refers to 'the twelve' as a group, let alone as an authoritative body.) Paul had not seen the risen Jesus prior to the moment of Ascension, because his conversion took place after that. But Paul's giftedness in tasks made his elevation to the role of Apostle as essential as it was desirable. He argues that apostleship cannot be confined to the original twelve disciples. And this is how his claims to be 'one untimely born' – but also an Apostle – must be read (1 Cor. 9.1-2; 1 Cor. 15.9; 2 Cor. 11.5, 13, etc.). He is, in some sense, the original proto-Christian minister, speaking for the new faith, but without the benefit of having had an original encounter with the Jesus of Galilee the others had walked with.

But if Paul sought to establish his apostolic credentials – and he did so on several occasions – he can hardly be said to have had a concrete self-understanding of himself as a full-time (let alone professional) minister. He was an itinerant evangelist, church leader (but not always accepted as such), well-educated teacher, as well as an accomplished manufacturer of tents (Acts 18.3); and he represents one of several approaches of the early church, to both the forming and bonding of emerging ecclesial communities and networks. Moreover, it is not as if the word 'apostle' ever had a precise meaning, other than the one the church (eventually) gave it. The noun from which the word is derived was borrowed from nautical terminology, and can mean 'ambassador', 'delegate' or 'messenger'; Paul is all of these. I make this point for only one reason. Whenever a contemporary crisis in clerical identity emerges, churches are often tempted to look afresh for role models. Some look backwards; others look around them; a few look to the future, and speculate on the quest for the emerging church.

For some groups, such models must, inevitably, lie in the origins of the church. And so the reasoning goes: be like the first disciples – eager, willing, deployable, gifted; evangelists, church-planters and wonder workers – but don't bother too much with formal theological education, which is arguably a hindrance to development. Other groups attempt to reconnect with the past in different ways, and perhaps invoke early Christian tradition; we must somehow be like the believers of the first four centuries, prior to the Constantinian settlement. If the church grew rapidly against a background of pluralism then, so the argument goes, becoming like the early church should work now. Others look more towards their current environment, and find models of ministry in CEOs, or in inspirational patterns of leadership or management drawn from secular spheres; or modes of organization that will lead to new, more maverick forms of ecclesial polity.

Each of these models, and the reasoning behind them, has some merit. And clearly it is the case that somewhere in the first four centuries, ecclesial roles developed and tasks were assigned. The church took a relatively short period of time to develop the offices of deacon, priest and bishop; and of catechist and evangelist. And these titles, to varying degrees, have scriptural warrant. Stephen, the first martyr, was a deacon (Acts 6) – but we have no description of his liturgical role. Paul recites details of the last supper in almost liturgical terms (1 Cor. 11.23ff), but leaves us with few clues as to how or by whom this rite was celebrated. There are persistent references to oversight, overseers and other offices in the New Testament (1 Cor. 12.28ff), but again no obvious indication of how a system of episcopal governance might have worked in the primitive church.

For the Christian theologian, there can be no objection to rooting around in Scripture, tradition and reasoning for models of ministry. But at the heart of this essay is a concern that in the act of such searching, some of the critical aspects and dimensions that form and shape theological constructions of ministry are often neglected. I speak here, of course, about the ways in which the environment, culture and necessity impact clerical identity. Some liturgical vestments, such as copes or chasubles, for example, began their life with a mainly functional purpose – keeping the clergy warm in the colder climes of northern Europe. To point this out, of course, is not to imply that such vestments can now be done away with in all churches which enjoy good heating systems, since over time, the vestments acquired a symbolic purpose that was greater than their original functionality. Nor is it to suggest that the origin of these vestments might well lie in the sphere of the sacred or revealed, rather than the practical. From the perspective of practical theology, both the revelatory and the functional can be affirmed: what we can say is that, historically, the vestments identified particular clergy in particular roles. The garments were and are distinctive markers of office and function; the vestments are vested with meaning and truth. Moreover, as any decent liturgical history will show, some aspects of priestly or diaconal identity have grown out of necessity, as much as they may also have acquired a more mature religious significance during the process of evolution.

To begin thinking like this is, perhaps, simply to make space for considering the social construction of revelation. This is not to suppose that what is 'revealed' (in terms of sacred or theological under-standings) is immediately reducible to some social or scientific account of reality. It is, rather, to signal a proper focus upon the materials or agents of revelation (i.e., texts, ideas, patterns of behaviour, cherished customs, rituals, etc.), which are themselves open to many kinds of analysis, instead of unquestionably postulating a divine origin for what is held to be revealed. So to speak of the social construction of revelation is to have some understanding of how human or social agencies function; how they acquire a mystique, or are sacralized; the delicate and multifarious ways in which the *opus hominum* and *opus dei* combine; how the divine and human pulses, activity and performances are conflated in such a way as to make 'religion'. Put another way, one can adapt the oft-used phrase of Peter Berger and Thomas Luckmann (i.e., 'the social construction of reality') and justifiably speak of the theological construction of reality, whereby events, materials and symbols are given meanings beyond themselves; as must be the case whenever one wishes to speak of the sublime or transcendent.

Two fine but important distinctions, however, are worth making when speaking of the social construction of revelation, and of the theological construction of reality. First, the notion of the social construction of revelation implies that all which is held to be revealed can, in some sense, be analysed or interpreted as a social construct. It can't be *entirely* understood like this, but it can be interpreted faithfully on these grounds, yet without exhausting other possible meanings. I hold that this does not diminish the notion of revelation; rather, it simply owns that revelation itself, to have any meaning socially, must itself be grounded and constructed in valid social concepts. The heavenly city, the new wine and Christ the king come immediately to mind; they have no revelatory value without a prior social grounding. The spiritual meaning only connects by being socially relative.

Second, the idea of the theological construction of reality, whilst not dissimilar, acknowledges that some of the ordinary or extraordinary phenomenon that is encountered in everyday ecclesial or spiritual life requires a language and conceptualization that reaches beyond the secular to the sacred. Here, what one person may describe as catharsis will be, to another, conversion; one person's coincidence will be another person's moment of grace or religious destiny. This will be a moment of supremely divine orchestration that is inadequately explained by other interpretations. In neither case – the social construction of revelation, or theological construction of reality – is there a requirement to capitulate to relativism. It is simply to recognize that in the world, religion, ascription and description are not easily disentangled; and that the grammar of assent is grounded in the dictionary as much as it is in the experience of God. (One should expect nothing less from a faith where the word becomes flesh; the theologically abstract becomes the socially embodied.)

To earth this a little more, we might consider the question of falling in love. Amongst men or women of a certain age or social background, particular expressions of love and prescribed ways of feeling and acting may all be common knowledge. The gestures that symbolize falling in love may all be agreed and understood, and may mark a relationship out as being significant rather than casual. The more the relationship gains in significance, the more stylized the gestures that symbolize love become, perhaps culminating in the ritual of marriage. But even when these rituals and actions are analysed, they are found to only represent a deeper, hidden, and often inexpressible reality – that of being in love. The heart of the dilemma might be said to lie in the following conversation.

> 'I've been in love with you for weeks.' [Vic says]
> 'There's no such thing,' [Robyn says]. 'It's a rhetorical device. It's a bourgeois fallacy.'
> 'Haven't you ever been in love, then?' [he responds]
> 'When I was younger,' [she says], 'I allowed myself to be constructed by the discourse of romantic love for a while, yes.'
> 'What the hell does that mean?' [he says, clearly irritated]
> 'We aren't essences, Vic. We aren't unique individual essences existing prior to language. There is only language.'[1]

Having contended that one can speak of the social construction of revelation and of the theological construction of reality, the rest of this essay is devoted to considering a range of questions that are primarily centred on the issue of clerical identity. Using the concept of evolution as a kind of analytical catalyst for the discussion, and deploying it analogically, we shall consider how ideas of ministry are formed, and the extent to which theology should be dependent on understanding the culture and context in which it arises in order to more fully comprehend the development of ecclesial structures and nuance. I hold that this is an urgent and vital task for theologians and churches, namely gaining some understanding of *where* theology speaks from, and, correspondingly, how it is constructed from its time and place. In the case of churches, it is no less vital to pay attention to the soil and situations in which congregations are immersed; the environment plays a vital part in the

---

[1] David Lodge, *Nice Work* (London: Penguin Books, 1989), p. 293.

shaping of ecclesiology. Relative social affluence will lead to one kind of theology and ecclesiology being shaped; oppression and violence will most likely lead to another form coming to the fore. Churches, like theologies, are culturally relative and culturally produced, as much as they may eventually find the means whereby those very cultures are challenged, transformed, or perhaps resisted.

In a recent short book by Graham Ward, he rightly draws our attention to the relationship between habitus and to the production of the theologian.[2] For example, to talk of (Karl) Barth's theology is also to speak of a time and a place – a Swiss, somewhat apolitical writer whose pre-eminence came to the fore during the Second World War and its aftermath. But in the climate of the Cold War, McCarthyism and post-war affluence, the conditions and atmosphere for this kind of theology are not there in the same way. This is not merely a question of fashion; it is deeper than that, and suggestive of the ways in which environments help to shape and form ideas. Barth's theology could not have emerged out of the context that formed Aquinas or Augustine; the former was a German Protestant, the latter were not. The sharp grit of oppression will produce pearls such as Boff or Sobrino in South America; but you can't write theology like that from the peace and tranquillity of a Swiss canton, puffing on a cigar.

Similarly (and at the risk of engaging in morphological caricatures), it is difficult to imagine the austerity of Scottish Free Presbyterianism surviving well in the sunny, relaxed environs of southern Mediterranean countries. The cold, harsh climate of northern Europe seems to produce varieties of hardy and more disciplined strains of Christianity, which are no doubt partly indebted to the ingrained Protestant work ethic. Southern Europe, for its part, produces forms of Christianity that thrive on a different cultural and environmental diet. One is tea, no sugar – a decidedly dour and monochrome affair; the other is sangria, colour and a seemingly endless procession of festivals.[3]

The gentle suggestion that theology might be culturally produced and shaped by its context (as much as some will claim that it emerges from some kind of 'pure' or divine source that was unsullied by any kind of agency) raises crucial questions about how ministry is to be both studied and understood. Clearly, and from one perspective, one can opt for the accounts that emanate from the centre of the church, and build from there. Purist theological accounts of authority exist in most Christian traditions. A related anecdote may be helpful here. A young child belonging to a sectarian church was taken on a tour of an exquisite English cathedral and was told by the guide all about the history and architecture of the place. At the end of the tour the guide asked him:

---

[2] G. Ward, *Cultural Transformation and Religious Practice*, (Cambridge: Cambridge University Press, 2005), p.16.

[3] See Garrison Keillor, *Lake Wobegon Days* (London: Faber & Faber, 1985), pp. 101ff.

'Who built your church?', to which the youngster replied: 'Jesus'. The child concerned belonged to a tiny branch of the Roman Catholic Tridentine Mass Church, and had been attending since birth. Most Christian traditions essentially imagine their church or Christian body to be a near perfect body, and to be built by Jesus. Other Christian bodies outside their boundaries are therefore regarded as either corrupted or compromised – a less faithful expression of what Jesus must have intended.

But part of the task of the theologian – or at least those who are engaged in open and interdisciplinary enquiry – is to test truth claims against competing forms of interpretation, in order to arrive at a deeper wisdom. There may be good reasons for eventually accepting or settling upon the explanations provided by the church for its ministry; but such explanations should be tested and probed in order to ascertain their truth and validity. In the section that follows, we sample two mainstream trajectories of enquiry. The first consists of internalized or traditional accounts of ministry that have been generated through a purist ecclesiological approach, and the second consists of a sampling of more revisionist explorations that are sourced through disciplines such as sociology, practical theology and ethnography. These two trajectories are then briefly assessed, before turning to a discussion of evolution as an analogical lens for the study of ministers and ministry.

Studying ministry and ministers – traditional theological accounts

One of the more interesting developments in higher education in recent years has been the rising number of professional doctorates – in education, law, business and, more recently, of ministry. A particular feature of the pedagogical approach underpinning these degree courses has been the stress on academic and applied reflection: on analysing critical incidents; developing a wisdom based on the capital of experience and anecdotes that practitioners typically build up within organizations; and developing a critical stance on the shape, identity and ethos of the profession, that requires some original research. In many cases, the practice of keeping a reflective journal comes to the fore in such courses, since participants are encouraged to discover some-thing of their own distinctiveness and resourcefulness in relation to the profession that they have entered.

The degree of Doctor of Ministry – a long established route to a doctorate in American seminaries – has taken longer to gain a foothold in British higher education, but is now beginning to emerge as a distinctive mode of training and formation. This is to be welcomed, for it is beginning to open up a more critical perspective on some of the givens and assumptions that underpin the patterning of curricula within seminaries and theological colleges, and which to some extent may be reinforced by a somewhat conservative culture in parishes and congregations that values continuity of practice, but rarely pauses to question the desirability of maintaining stability. In such a situation, the reasoning might be that if the tools of mission and pastoral engagement worked fifty years ago, they ought to still work today. The problem is therefore not with the tools, but with the institutions that train their users. In all kinds of informal conversations, one hears congregations muttering about the 'curate who used to visit everyone, all the time' ('those were the days'), or 'when the vicar baptized all-comers' ('the church was full then'). Not only is the past a foreign country; it is also the other side of the fence, where the grass was undoubtedly greener.

Where the emerging study of ministry has become valuable has been in de-bunking some of the myths that often surround the practice of ministry or its status as a profession. It can be liberating, for example, to discover that rates of church attendance in some parts of England were, pro-rata, poorer when compared to the twentieth century. If minds can be freed from the grip of the secularization meta-narrative, clergy and laity alike can discover that patterns of believing and belonging did not collapse with the industrial revolution of the nineteenth century, or with the advent of popular culture and mass consumerism in the second half of the twentieth century. Similarly, discovering that the 'clerical profession' was subject to widespread disrespect and occasional hostility for some periods in most centuries can come as a welcome surprise, since it affirms the experience of alienation as typical and continuous rather than being recent and unpredicted. None of this, of course, is meant to lead to any kind of complacency; on the contrary. What it does mean, however, is that if ministry is studied deeply and properly, then ministers themselves may be freed from some of the more burdensome myths that sometimes imbue the profession, often causing guilt and frustration.

Put another way, one of the tasks of practical theology might be to extricate churches and their ministers from the gripping thrall of 'blueprint ecclesiologies', together with sacralized recipes and formulae. It is, for example, all very well to hold up George Herbert or Parson Woodforde as 'models' of pastoral practice, especially in relation to visiting and parochial engagement. Clearly, there can be no doubt that these clergy were devoted to 'the cure of souls' in their care: they were assiduous visitors. But any models constructed out of their example would have to take proper account of the contextual contingencies of their time; the ease and custom of visiting; the intimate nature of parishes; the proximate housing, and so forth. The seventeenth and eighteenth centuries are not the same as the twenty-first; patterns of believing and belonging may now require a different kind of priestly engagement with a parish. Someone, in short, has to explain the point and value of visiting afresh – to each new generation of clergy.

Yet it remains one of the supreme ironies of the church that in much of its theological reflection on ministry, it lacks any form of critically engaged historiography. Typically, much of the theological work produced by individual denominations amounts to little more than a form of creationism: 'and on the sixth day God created clergy, and saw that it was good'. One does not have to travel very far in Anglican, Roman Catholic or Protestant ecclesiology to find examples of this kind of reasoning. Kenneth Carey's *The Historic Episcopate* (1954) is primarily concerned with proving the problematic but unbroken lineage between Scripture, tradition and episcopate. In common with other books of its type, biblical or early church references are generally seen as full and sufficient warrant for continuity of practice and identity, as though the clergy of the twenty-first century can be traced back to the disciples of the first century, without serious difficulty or interruption. Liturgies frequently align themselves with such theological accounts, affirming the ideology that clerical identities (its roles and tasks) are already given. Indeed, the very etymology of the word 'ordain' confirms this.

The establishment of continuity is something that has coloured and shaped denominational identity and ecumenical relations. Witness, for example, part of the defence of 'valid' (Episcopal) ministry from Kenneth Kirk, a former Bishop of Oxford, writing in 1946:[4]

> If the Church of the New Testament is to continue in being, it must be in interdependence with the ministry of the New Testament – that is to say, as we have seen, the Essential Ministry deriving by succession from the apostles themselves. Neither Church nor ministry can exist without the other; their interrelation is so complete that they cannot even be defined or imagined in separation. Their progress through history is one in which they move together *pari passu*; the sacraments by which they recruit themselves, and incidentally one another, are mutually analogous. What baptism is to the Church, ordination is to the ministry. No doubt the Lord might have appointed some other rite than that of baptism for the initiatory ceremony of His Church; no doubt, too, the primitive Church might have selected a different rite from that of the laying on of hands for admission into the ranks of the ministry. But they did not do so; and we have no alternative but to receive the age-long traditions as they have been handed down to us.[5]

It is that phrase 'handed down to us' that is so telling; unimpaired, unchanged and largely as God has authored it. Here, of course, Kirk is speaking from his own particular context. This is an England that has

---

[4] The quotations from Kirk are lengthy, as readers are unlikely to be familiar with his work.
[5] K.E. Kirk, *The Apostolic Ministry: Essays on the History and the Doctrine of Episcopacy* (London: Hodder & Stoughton, 1946), p. 40.

not yet been shaken by the dawning of a post-colonial era. This is a world in which England and its Church can still make grand claims. This is a church of the state that has yet to be troubled by *Honest to God*. So we can perhaps forgive Kirk for his imperialist assumptions; a world in which the empire of Jesus is duly administered and properly ordered by his most faithful servants, who have self-evidently been chosen and appointed for the task.

Which of course, in turn, accounts for Kirk's less than sensitive ecumenical overtures in the very same essay:

> If then we follow the teaching of Scripture and the tradition of the Church, we are bound to say that a valid ministry is one which, in accordance with primitive ordering, proceeds in due succession from the apostles by laying of hands of the Essential Ministry; and that should such a ministry fail, the apostolic Church, which is the Body of Christ in space and time, would disappear with it (for the two are inextricably bound together), and the whole preaching of the Gospel message to the nations would be in the most urgent jeopardy. These things we do not say of non-episcopal ministries; for judged by scriptural and apostolic test we find them to be invalid. There is much that we can gladly and indeed penitently say of them. In the solemn words already quoted, they have been 'blessed and owned by the Holy Spirit as effective means of grace'; and at times when the valid ministry has been disloyal to its trust, they have nobly borne the burden of the fight. But we cannot say of them, as we say of the espiscopally ordained ministry, that they are integrally and inevitably necessary to the continuance of the apostolic Church; for they do not satisfy the conditions laid down by that Church – the conditions in fact which in the case of the ministry are implied by the word 'validity'. Our overwhelming desire is that they should be brought within the sphere of these conditions; and whatever concession is necessary to this end – provided only that it does not belie or render nugatory the conditions themselves – is a concession we will gladly make.[6]

These sentiments aside, Kirk's skilfully edited collation of essays (including contributions from Dom Gregory Dix and Austin Farrer) was something of a landmark study, even for its time. *The Apostolic Ministry: Essays on the History and Doctrine of Episcopacy* (1946) represents a fine treatment of Anglican polity at a time when there was, perhaps, little need to be circumspect. And yet the essays are, generally speaking, temperate in tone and moderate in their claims, with several of the contributors frowning upon the prospect of establishing a straightforward and deductive theological linkage

---

[6] Kirk, *The Apostolic Ministry*, p. 40.

between the pre-Reformation Catholic Church and the present Church of England. It is not that the link is denied. Rather, the authors prefer to debate the more interesting theological hinterland, where orders are not labelled 'valid' or 'invalid', but 'regular' and 'irregular' – the latter, of course, not being wrong, but merely atypical.

But the weakness of the book – that which renders it an unacceptable approach for today's scholar – is the supposition that church history can never be un-theological. In one sense, of course, that is true; church history would need to be (at least) theologically literate. But the argument advanced in *The Apostolic Ministry* is that histories must be theologically empathetic, to the point where Christian versions of events (i.e., the theological construction of reality) are deemed to be the 'facts'. Thus, there ceases to be a *relationship* between theology and history. In the construction of valid accounts of coherent and consistent patterns of ministry throughout the ages, history and theology have been mystically entwined. Only the true church has the valid account of its origins:

> The first concern of the Christian historian must be the establishing of the Christian historical facts. Yet his safeguard does not lie in any easy determination to exclude theology altogether from his handling of the historical material available. If this were possible to achieve, it would amount scientifically only to the worst possible distortion of the facts. The truly historical interpretation for Church history can never be un-theological. Just because what is under investigation is a complex of facts in the specifically religious history and psychology of a period in the Christian past, the then contemporary Christian theological interpretation of those facts is capitally relevant, from the most coldly scientific point of view. This historian's real difficulty is not the importation of theology into our understanding of Church history, but the fact than none of us, without long study and the most discriminating care, can fully share the then contemporary theological interpretation.[7]

If such approaches were relatively common in the nineteenth and early twentieth century, the post-war era did begin to witness a significant shift in the cadence and timbre of theologies of ministry. This was partly heralded, no doubt, by the impetus generated through the Second Vatican Council, which inspired both caution and confidence in equal measure. Likewise, the burgeoning ecumenical movement, fostered and nourished by the World Council of Churches, ensured that privileged and exclusive claims on origins now needed to be shared, and also expressed with more humility and openness. Some early extracts

---

[7] Kirk, *The Apostolic Ministry*, p. 186.

from the Anglican–Roman Catholic International Commission (ARCIC) set the tone:

> The New Testament shows that ministerial office played an essential part in the life of the Church in the first century, and we believe that the provision of a ministry of this kind is part of God's design for his people. Normative principles governing the purpose and function of the ministry are already present in the New Testament documents (e.g. Mark 10.43-45; Acts 20.28; I Tim. 4.12). The early churches may well have had considerable diversity in the structure of pastoral ministry, though it is clear that some churches were headed by ministers who were called *episcopoi* and *presbytero*. While the first missionary churches were not a loose aggregation of autonomous communities, we have no evidence that 'bishops' and 'presbyters' were appointed everywhere in the primitive period. The terms 'bishop' and 'presbyter' could be applied to the same man or to men with identical or very similar functions. Just as the formation of the canon of the New Testament was a process incomplete until the second half of the second century, so also the full emergence of the threefold ministry of bishop, presbyter, and deacon required a longer period than the apostolic age. Thereafter this threefold structure became universal in the Church.[8]

What is perhaps most intriguing about the early theological method-ology of the ARCIC statements is the premium placed on agreement. That is not surprising, of course, when one considers that the function of ARCIC was to reach consensus in key areas of disagreement, such as ministry, the nature of the church and its sacraments, and more besides (most recently on Marian dogma). But in establishing a theological commission that is centred on achieving agreement, there is also a sense in which closure on more difficult issues is far from assured:

> We are fully aware of the issues raised by the judgment of the Roman Catholic Church on Anglican Orders. The development for the thinking in our two Communions regarding the nature of the Church and of the Ordained Ministry, as represented in our Statement, has, we consider, put these issues in a new context. Agreement on the nature of Ministry is prior to the consideration of the mutual recognition of ministries. What we have to say represents the consensus of the Commission on essential matters where it considers that doctrine admits no divergence. It will be clear that we have not yet broached the wide-ranging problems of authority which may arise in any discussion of Ministry, nor the

---

[8] ARCIC, 'Ministry and Ordination' (London: Church House Publishing, 1973), p. 6.

question of primacy. We are aware that present understanding of such matters remains an obstacle to the reconciliation of our churches in the one Communion we desire, and the Commission is now turning to the examination of the issues involved. Nevertheless we consider that our consensus, on questions where agreement is indispensable for unity, offers a positive contribution to the reconciliation of our churches and of their ministries.[9]

Yet the problem is not merely one of internal politics. It is clear that in these concluding remarks that various issues and questions have, as it were, been put to bed. This is confessional theology that seeks to harmonize divergence and disagreement through historical and theological re-narration. And whilst one might applaud that as a diplomatic goal in the wider interests of establishing consensus, it does not necessarily follow that the truth is ultimately served. The risk, clearly, is that the church ultimately begins to develop one single meta-narrative of how orders came to be, and how ministry has been established, shaped and formed. Put another way, a single authoritative account emerges that is not unlike a form of creationism: all divergent or competitive accounts of origins are swept away by a newly re-united body that has firmly established the correct historical understanding.

If this perhaps sounds a little harsh, it is important to take stock of more recent theological treatments of orders and ministry. James Monroe Barnett's *The Diaconate: A Full and Equal Order* states that in considering deacons:

> It is when we move outside of the New Testament into the sub-apostolic age that we see more clearly the character and function of the various offices within the Church as they underwent a transformation from the apostolic age. This change, however, is not to be considered simply a natural development in a human society. The charisma of the Holy Spirit was fully at work in the Church, guiding its development. Lampe reminds us, 'Though in one aspect, the change was due to the natural pressure of altered circumstances, it did not happen without the guidance and authority of the Holy Spirit.'[10]

If so guided by the Holy Spirit, then all 'histories' of the diaconate can only be read theologically.[11] But this is immediately problematic when one remembers that the office of deacon virtually disappeared in the twelfth and thirteenth centuries. Moreover, and as Urban Holmes

---

[9] ARCIC, 'Ministry and Ordination', p. 9.
[10] James Monroe Barnett, , *The Diaconate: A Full and Equal Order* (Harrisburg, PA: Trinity Press, rev. edn 1995), p. 44.
[11] Cf. Church of England, *For Such a Time as This: A Renewed Diaconate in the Church of England* (London: Church House Publishing, 2003).

noted many years ago, 'ministerial function is related only very loosely to any ontological theories of ministerial order'.[12] Routine rituals and preaching in the church were quickly assigned to the role of the presbyterate (priests), but most other ministerial functions have tended to be quite fluid (as any lay preacher in the Methodist Church, or lay reader in the Church of England will testify). So although the re-emergence of the diaconate may be seen as a welcome revival of a 'lost' ministry or order, it may also be part of a complex and problematic ecclesial economy.

The development of the order of deaconess in the late nineteenth century, initially classified as a lay order (and later, women deacons – an ordained order) in the Church of England, prior to the General Synod vote in 1992 which made provision for women to be ordained as priests, met a cultural and pastoral need. There are undoubtedly many worthy theological treatises on the necessity and value of the diaconate, but a purely theological account would most likely overlook the complex gender-based, cultural and ecclesial arguments that have assuaged the Church of England from the mid 1980s to the present. Women in the diaconate is a history of struggle; a similar one to that of their journey to priesthood. It is an act of sanitization to describe the entire ebb and flow of the debate as 'a work of the Spirit', unless one concedes (as I would) that the Holy Spirit teaches and forms the church through conflict and disagreement as much as it does through consensus.

Likewise, even the most cursory exploration of the diaconate in recent Roman Catholic praxis reveals some simmering tensions. In an ecclesial culture where clerical celibacy for priests and bishops is mandatory, the only ordained pathway open to married men (not yet women) has been the diaconate. But in a number of cases, congregations fail to fathom why their own male deacons cannot be made priests, whilst married men transferring from Anglican churches are to be received into the Roman Catholic Church, and are almost immediately allowed to resume their priestly role, albeit following (re-)ordination. What we have in Barnett's thesis, in other words, like many previous church-sponsored reports and commissions on the diaconate, is an attempt on the one hand to justify the status and role of deacons, affirming their full and vital role; whilst on the other hand, those who are 'kept' in the diaconate often continue to experience this as a form of subjugation, vested in a theological language that focuses on servant-hood.

[12] U.T. Holmes, *The Future Shape of Ministry* (New York: The Seabury Press, 1971).

Studying ministry and ministers – revisionist accounts:

An important key to the problem is, as I have already hinted, arriving at a proper recognition of the context, contingencies and environment that assume a vital role in shaping constructions of ministry and clerical identity, which often occurs *before* the church locates and articulates a theological rationale for why ministries have developed in the way that they have. As Kilian MacDonnell reminds us, 'the formation of the doctrine of ministry was the result of a theological reflection on the pastoral needs'.[13] Some denominations are in fact quite comfortable with the idea that the church learns through experience, and is guided (usually hesitantly, sometimes reluctantly) by an encounter-based type of pedagogical formation. Equally, some denominations resist this, with varying degrees of success or conviction. For example, I vividly recall a conversation with some Romanian Orthodox priests, discussing the issue of clergy who physically abuse their wives. The Romanian clergy were quite clear that priests who did this were not proper clergy, and therefore concluded that there was no issue for the church hierarchy to address, other than that of domestic violence. Their reasoning was that all ministers would naturally live a life of moral probity, and therefore those 'clergy' that did not do this could not really be regarded as 'proper' clergy. I have had similar conversations with House Church leaders (sometimes known as 'Apostles'), who have opined that those pastors who had in some way fallen from grace (i.e., moral lapses, etc.) must have been 'false' all along, because the governance of the true church is ultimately pure and inviolable. External evidence that seems to point to the contrary is therefore dismissed as confirmation that there is a true ministry with true ministers, which God has ordained.

In contrast, however, a number of denominations are more than aware that their decision-making processes are more complex than merely receiving and interpreting direct and unmediated revelation. Anglicans, for example, typically talk of a trilateral – Scripture, tradition and reason – when trying to reach consensus. Moreover, there are aspects of its polity, that even when under intense strain, allow for a period of discernment that is dependent on weighing impressions and experience. Within the wider Anglican Communion, it is this kind of initiative that has enabled the institution of additional 'instruments of unity': symbolic or functional bodies that help to manage potentially damaging diversity. The instruments consist of the office of the Archbishop of Canterbury, the Lambeth Conference, the Anglican Consultative Council and the regular gathering of Primates. Thus, and to return to the Church of England, the debate on women priests allowed for a period of 'reception', in which those who were in favour and against could continue to consider the theological and ecclesiolo-

---

[13] Kilian MacDonnell, 'Ways of Validating Ministry', *Journal of Ecumenical Studie*, 7 (1970), p. 258.

gical issues. A recent study by Ian Jones (2004) has concluded that virtually all those Anglican congregations that were undecided about women priests in the early 1990s have now moved to being affirmative of their ministry. But these congregations have not been persuaded by more or greater theological arguments; rather, they have shifted their position on the basis of their experiences and encounters with women priests, whose numbers continue to rise. In contrast, those Conservative Evangelicals and Anglo-Catholics that have continued to oppose the 'innovation' of women priests have consistently argued that the church cannot be taught or led by experience, since this subverts scripture or tradition.

The difficulty with this type of approach is its refusal to engage with the obviousness of socially constructed reality; what we earlier termed within the realm of ecclesiology as the social construction of revelation, or the theological construction of reality. We simply cannot see the world as St Paul, Aquinas or Martin Luther saw it. God can only be perceived in terms of the world we experience. Each socio-cultural entity constructs its own reality. Urban Holmes' fine study of Episcopalian ministry in the USA, although now a little dated, nonetheless serves to remind us: 'If God is to be perceived in terms of the world we experience, if ministry is both transcendent and immanent, there is only the changing reality within which to work. There is no immutable kernel within the mutable. It is all one, and it is never the same'.[14]

Thus, the church has played host to a variety of theologies of episcopacy down the ages, each needing to be suited to its own particular context. For example, Jerome (circa 340–420) thought that the historic episcopate was essentially a special function of priesthood, the latter being the highest order of calling. The ministry of oversight was, in his mind, a vocation with a primarily functional focus. However, for reasons of governance, polity, the ordering of power and the development of ecclesial praxis, the medieval church saw fit to divide the function of the priest and bishop more precisely. This was achieved through canon law, which affirmed that presbyter (or priest) and bishop held the same order, but differed only in office, power and jurisdiction.

We began this chapter by suggesting that the problem of professionalism has been one of the more vexing issues for clergy during the past two hundred years. Furthermore, the church, by authorizing its own internal historical and theological accounts of ministers and ministry, has essentially refused to address the issues of context and culture which shape identity and practice, and in which the church must (inevitably) develop. However, a number of studies have emerged over the last fifty years, which have paid attention to professional identity and ministry. Broadly speaking, the disciplinary foundations for such

[14] Holmes, *Future Shape of Ministry*, p. 6.

studies can be categorized as sociological, birthed in practical theology, or rooted in organizational studies.

James Glasse's *Profession: Minister*,[15] for example, develops a typography for the minister as a professional: educated in a discrete body of knowledge, possessing skills, institutionally committed, accountable to certain standards and dedicated. Glasse is of the view that the (modern) clergyperson fits the criteria, although his work is clearly in debt to Joseph Fichter's *Religion as an Occupation: A Study in the Sociology of Professions*.[16] More recently, Margaret Harris's *Organizing God's Work*[17] has taken an ethnographic approach, exploring case studies of ministers drawn from different faith traditions (e.g., rabbi, pastor, etc.), and the problems they encounter in relation to the dynamics of ordering congregational life. The detailed study of Stewart Ranson, Alan Bryman and Robert Hinnings (1977) found that clergy were becoming conscious and concerned about the inability of the church to attract young people into the ranks of the clergy, and that amongst Methodist, Anglican and Roman Catholic clergy, all thought that their denominations needed urgent reform. Such studies benefit from being disciplined and external enquiries into the nature of ministry and ministerial formation, and are grounded in the ordinary everyday contingencies that ministers will face, rather than in idealist theological constructions of what ministry is or perhaps ought to be.[18]

At least part of the heart of the dilemma must lie in making a proper distinction between professionals and *professionalism*. Urban Holmes suggests that a convincing if not essential case for the latter within the church can be made. But as for ministers as 'professionals', he is both reticent and critical. In common with a number of pastoral theologians writing on ministry (e.g., Wesley Carr, Christopher Moody, Bruce Reed, etc.), he understands the clergyperson to be 'generalist', a kind of theological and pastoral *bricoleur*. Even when the minister is functioning liturgically (in terms of word and sacrament), this is a role that demands charisma, presence and engagement as much as it may demand a set of skills. The plight of clergy and clerical identity is actually quite acute at this point, since the un-learned and the un-trained may fulfil vital ministerial roles and functions within an ecclesial or pastoral context. Moreover, the church knows this, and has therefore authorized a whole variety of lay ministries that both supplement and erode clerical professional identity. To press the question more sharply, is being a clergyperson a hobby or a profession? The answer, for many denom-

---

[15] James D. Glasse, *Profession: Minister* (Nashville, TN: Abingdon Press, 1968).
[16] Joseph H. Fichter, *Religion as an Occupation: A Study in the Sociology of Professions* (Notre Dame, IN: University of Notre Dame, 1961).
[17] Margaret Harris, *Organizing God's Work: Challenges for Churches and Synagogues* (London: Palgrave Macmillan, 1998).
[18] S. Ranson, A. Bryman and R. Hinnings, *Clergy, Ministers and Priests* (London, Routledge & Kegan Paul, 1977).

inations, has been either or both. Indeed, one might argue that in the case of the Church of England, where livings (or parishes) needed to be purchased in the eighteenth century, ministry was essentially a 'gentlemanly pursuit'.[19]

Holmes suggests that the lack of resolution on clerical identity has led (inevitably) to the current crisis:

> In a conversation I had with a Lutheran churchman about clergy renewal, I was struck by his succinct analysis of the dilemma of the contemporary pastor. Implicit in his remarks was also a possible approach to new ways of thinking of ministry. He made the point that since World War II more and more clergy have been saying, 'Look, I'm just a man like any other man; and I want to be treated this way. I want an adequate salary; I want to pay my way and own my house; and I want to be considered as any other professional man.' The question is asked, 'What is your profession?' The reply is, 'Well, I'm something like a "counselor," but not really. I'm more a "teacher" but not in a formal sense. Maybe you could say I'm interested in change, but not quite like anyone else.' The point is that in pursuit of professional status we have divested ourselves of a different kind of symbolic role, without ever resolving the question as to what precisely our unique professional competence might be. Every time we think we have come up with an answer, someone has been there before us.[20]

For Holmes, this problem can only be resolved by a threefold approach to clergy training, namely a concentration on theological education, professional training and the formation of priestly character. This, argues Holmes, will distinguish clergy as persons with a particular identity, roles and functions, but without collapsing or eliding their distinctiveness into some kind of vacuous professional framework. Ministry is, in other words, both more and less than a profession; it is about being, not just doing. Some of what ministry may entail may have no measurable outcome, or be able to demonstrate any obvious reified success. Indeed pastoral education can be stubbornly 'anti-intellectual', insofar as it requires initiates to enter the realm of feelings and emotional intelligence, and learn to 'read' situations for the way they feel. Thus, for Holmes, there is not one profession of ministry, but a number of professions within ministry (which may include counselling,

---

[19] J.H. Moorman, *Church Life in England in the Thirteenth Century* (Cambridge: Cambridge University Press, 1945), pp. 24–27, gives a detailed account of the office of rector in the thirteenth century, arguing that there were really only two types: (1) devout priests in residence, and (2) individuals who had purchased the living, might be somewhat avaricious, were probably not in residence and might not even be ordained.

[20] Holmes, *Future Shape of Ministry*, p. 245.

teaching, etc.). And the minister, *per se*, is required to be a generalist (quite independent of any specialisms they may have), since it is part of the vocation and calling to be the *person* for the parish. Indeed, the term 'parson' connotes just this.

Holmes' exemplary study of the issues and problems facing episcopalian clergy in the early 1970s has yet to be matched for its grounding in a combination of disciplines: practical theology, history, sociology and anthropology. Indeed, the entire culture of research within US-based denominations is markedly superior to that of Great Britain. Most major denominations in the USA have collected and collated a wide range of statistics on churchgoing trends, congregational life and clergy profiles, and have analysed these deeply, the results of which have often led to transformative developments in mission, outreach and recruitment.

Great Britain, however, has been rather slower to develop deep research into ministry and ministers, although some significant studies have emerged over the past fifty years. Alan Gilbert's *Religion and Society in Industrial England* (1976) presents a sociologically attuned history of changes in chapel attendance and churchgoing, but does not offer significant explicit focus on the shifts in clerical identity experienced by the clergy at the time. Likewise, Edward Wickham's fine *Church and People in an Industrial City* (1957) offered a perceptive 'take' on how the churches were adapting to the burgeoning post-war industrial cities (Sheffield, in this case), although much of his reflection stops short of registering how much these changes mean for clergy and their own adaptation to a new context. Such directives, it seems, are left to pastoral manuals for clergy (Leslie Hunter's *A Parson's Job: Aspects of Work in the English Church*, and published in 1931, comes to mind), which were still being read long after the Second World War. Percy Dearmer's *The Parson's Handbook* (first published in 1932) seems to have an almost charmed list of contents – how to visit the sick, forming processions and notes on seasons are included. Dearmer peppers his manual with advice on such testing matters as how to get wax off altar cloths or candlesticks. This is, to be sure, a manual for professionals. The concerns that were raised in the theses provided by the likes of Gilbert and Wickham were yet to be encountered.

However, the study of ministers and ministry began to take a significant turn for the better in the late 1970s and early 1980s, with the arrival of three fine monographs that began to change the way both the academy and the church understood the changing shape of ministry. David Clark's prescient study of a North East English fishing community (Staithes), exposed the gap between the religion that the church or chapel preached (and supposed that members followed), and the actual realities of religious practice and nascent spirituality in a close-knit community. Clark, working with a primarily sociological and ethnographic framework, was able to show how the minister can appear essentially as an 'actor' within a broader communal drama, performing vital roles (to be sure), but in a tableau that was scripted by the village as much as the church or chapel.[21] Whilst the findings of the book could hardly be said to be revolutionary, there was significant interest in a study that showed ministers, as it were, being used as functionaries for rites and rituals, rather than being pivotal (as they might imagine or hope).

Anthony Russell's study, published in 1980, and although using a less sophisticated methodology than that deployed by Clark, marked a new departure for British theology and ecclesiology, with a clear focus on clerical identity. *The Clerical Profession* argues that the moment of crisis has now arrived for clergy: what is their role in a society that can turn to many other experts and kinds of expertise for help, advice and succour?[22] Russell suggests that in order to gain an adequate sense of the present problems, one needs to understand (historically) how the role of the clergyperson has evolved. In the eighteenth century, the parson (i.e., the person of the parish) was closely allied with the gentry. Clergy would, correspondingly, assume a number of soft civic roles within parishes, such as being a JP (Justice of the Peace), or perhaps engage in academic or cultural pursuits. In terms of dress, the clergy of the eighteenth century dressed as gentlemen did: black knee britches, a type of frock coat, a tight-fitting collar, often with white bands attached. This was the 'uniform' of a gentleman taking a walk or going for a ride in the country. Moreover, with the tithing system being at its most efficient peak (at least in England), many clergy were comparatively well paid, with incomes matching lawyers, doctors and other essential community roles. Although there might have been regrettable aspects of this evolutionary development, Russell carefully notes how the rapid eliding of clerical identity with emerging professionalization in the nineteenth century was even more problematic. Clergy moved quickly from being 'the person of the parish' to being 'a person set apart'. In essence, five key factors determined this move.

First, the rapid changes brought about by industrialization meant that many clergy needed to maintain their visibility in the new and unfamiliar environments in which they found themselves. The pivotal roles that they had undertaken in the country were less easy to develop in the cities, forcing many to retreat into being 'technicians of the sanctuary' or into cultivating 'priestcraft'.[23] Second, the Evangelical and Tractarian movements tended to emphasize a spiritual, social and theological separateness, which underlined clerical identity as being 'set apart', the sediment of which still persists in many constructions of

---

[21] D. Clark, *Between Pulpit and Pew: Folk Religion in a North Yorkshire Fishing Village* (Cambridge: Cambridge University Press, 1982), pp. 116ff.

[22] A. Russell, *The Clerical Profession* (London: SPCK, 1980).

[23] Russell, *The Clerical Profession*, pp. 23ff. See also A. Haig, *The Victorian Clergy* (Kent: Croom Helm, 1984) and M. Sweet, *Inventing the Victorians* (London: Faber & Faber, 2001).

ministerial identity. Third, with the gradual marginalization of religion from mainstream society now beginning to take hold, clergy began to develop and compress their professional identity in order to distinguish themselves and compete with other professions. In terms of clerical dress, the use of continental Roman Catholic 'dog-collars' had become very popular amongst high-church clergy by the 1880s. Clergy also withdrew from London clubs (which they had patronized heavily for several decades), forming their own leagues, associations and the like. This even extended to exclusive clergy hotels and clubs being formed such as the Mentone, where clergy could holiday with professional colleagues. Fourth, the governance of churches began to change, with increasing emphasis on synods, measures and codes of discipline. Gradually, across all denominations, accountability and standards of conduct were introduced. Fifth, distinctive theological colleges began to emerge, often to protect or cultivate particular brands of churchmanship, but also to introduce and develop particular training and education, which, it was deemed, a general theological education at university could no longer provide.

Despite these developments, the emerging professional identity of the clergy did not keep pace with the sweeping changes in education that took root in nineteenth-century Britain. In 1750, it was quite likely that the barrister, doctor and priest would be the most (or only?) educated persons in the parish. But by 1850, the clergy found themselves in parishes in which several others would be at least as well educated, with others perhaps being even more learned. The response to this from churches and chapels was to increase 'religious instruction'. But this initiative merely signals the competitive nature of pedagogical formation that was now beginning to take place in schools, colleges and universities. The values advocated by the church were increasingly found to be at variance with those promoted by teachers and lecturers. Furthermore, social welfare, the provision of which was once dominated by the church, now developed a degree of autonomy, which together with the rise of distinctive personnel and professional standards in this sector, also marginalized clergy. As Russell perceptively notes, 'in an age of professionalism the clergyman became an amateur in all but the charter elements of his role'.[24] Put another way (from the perspective of the Church of England), faced with a choice of clerical roles and identity being either a profession or a hobby, the church predictably opted for the *via media*. Neither one thing nor the other; but then again both; sort of.

Russell concludes his study by suggesting that the professional identity of the clergyperson that the Church of England inherited from the late nineteenth century was still persisting in the late twentieth century, and that there was an urgent need for fresh thinking. Russell

[24] Russell, *The Clerical Profession*, p. 249.

suggests that many of the pivotal pastoral functions of the clergy have been reassigned to the local church, resulting in a deeper crisis of professional identity. If ministry is now something 'for the whole people of God', pastoral work something that can be done by locally deployed teams, and many other aspects of ministry carried out by hired-in specialists provided by the diocese, district or region, then the role of the clergyperson shifts, almost imperceptibly, from being specialist and essential to being general and managerial. Professionalization, in other words, is a double-edged sword for clergy roles and clerical identity. On the one hand it increases the public sense of specialization – the uniqueness of priestcraft – at a time when the general fabric of civic life is being challenged. On the other hand, its subsequent compression lays it open to further marginalization and rationalization. Clergy, in other words, by being apart, can evolve into a profession that stands out as something distinctive within society – which is fine, but only so long as society deigns to take notice.

In many respects, it seems to have been precisely this point that weighed uppermost in the minds of Robert Towler and Anthony Coxon with their *The Fate of the Anglican Clergy: A Sociological Study* (1979). Both authors owe a debt of insight to the Community of the Resurrection (Mirfield) where they both studied for a time. Although published one year before Russell's work, Towler and Coxon's work can, in many ways, be said to pick up the debate where Russell's work signed off. Towler and Coxon base their detailed work on studies undertaken at theological colleges, an analysis of clergy careers (through *Crockford's Clerical Directory*), and questionnaires informed by the work of Eysenck and the Allport–Vernon–Lindsey study of values.[25] The primary focus of the study is the rapid emergence of marginality amongst the clergy in the latter part of the twentieth century, and their articulation of the crisis of identity and function is worth quoting in full:

> Now the clergyman, more than anyone else on the contemporary scene, is a jack of all trades. He occupies a unique position, but the uniqueness of his position has nothing to do with unique skills, or even with unique competence. There is nothing which he does that could not be done equally well by a lawyer or bricklayer in the congregation whom the bishop had ordained to the Auxiliary Pastoral Ministry. He does not have a job at all in any sense which is readily understandable today, and today, more than ever before, a person must have a job in order to fit into society. As a result the clergyman finds himself marginal to society. He is a strange creature who seems not to fit in anywhere. This applies to other people as well, such as the artist or the person of 'private means';

[25] See H. Eysenck, *Manual of the Eysenck Personality Inventory* (London: London University Press, 1954).

and generally they enclose themselves in a little world of their own. A community within the community which is marginal to society but within which the individual does not obtrude. The clergyman, however, is in a position which is marginal to society and at the same time highly visible. He is a public person who, alone in our society, wears a distinctive uniform at all times. When he discards the uniform, as many clergymen do today, he evades the problem posed by his marginality, but he does not solve it.[26]

Towler and Coxon acknowledge that many clergy now try to break out of this mould by re-inventing themselves as generalists. Some leave full-time ministry for work in welfare or teaching; others immerse themselves in voluntary and civic roles, engaging in social or economic regeneration, or working for counselling and support organizations such as the Samaritans. Others go further, and specialize in counselling or psychotherapy, re-offering their ordained life through honing particular forms of pastoral expertise. Towler and Coxon are, however, cautious about the headlong rush towards secular legitimization of the clerical role. They defend the peculiarity and particularity of the calling, and remind their readers that there is a prophetic and priestly role, which although marginalized in an increasingly secular society, is nonetheless something to be held as a judgement and value system over and against contemporary culture.

Another intriguing feature of Towler and Coxon's study is their grasp of the new ecclesial cultural context that has emerged since the end of the Second World War. They suggest that the old order of polarities – Evangelicals and Anglo-Catholics – has given way to new paradigms; a different shuffling of the tectonic plates that underpin the world of the church. Due to the influence of Charismatic renewal, ecumenism and liturgical reformation, the Church of England now divides along conservative/progressive (or radical) lines. In terms of deployment and 'career structure', the fault lines now lie between those who aspire to or defend traditionalist approaches to ministry, and those who are innovative or entrepreneurial. As Towler and Coxon note, the attempts for ministry and ministers to be more adaptive within a climate of marginality bode rather well for the church, although the degree of accommodation and change will need to be carefully watched, if the church is not to lose its distinctive ethos and identity for future generations. Marginality, they gently suggest, may turn out to be somewhat pharmacological: given the right dosage, not necessarily poisonous. And here they believe that 'the future will be with the radicals' – those seeking to be simultaneously adaptive of and faithful to the tradition. In this regard, they defend the radical theological pulses of the 1960s as representing a genuine attempt to 'search for a way in

---

[26] R. Towler and A. Coxon, *The Fate of the Anglican Clergy: A Sociological Study* (London: Macmillan, 1979), p. 54–55.

which the good news proclaimed by Jesus Christ may again be addressed to the whole of God's creation; it is they who seek to address people as they are, rather than as a failing Church that has brainwashed them into being'.[27]

From the literature surveyed so far (albeit briefly), we can see that even those analyses that have been based broadly in the social sciences have, generally, been sympathetic to the crises of identity that have faced ministers in recent times. Most of the studies have engaged empathetically with their subject, and invariably shown a high degree of theological and ecclesiological literacy. To a large extent, contemporary studies of ministers and ministry have continued in the same vein. However, they share a common concern, insofar as they identify the marginalization of status and role, coupled with anxiety about identity, as continuing issues that need to be addressed. Clergy, in short, although called, chosen, trained and formed, have an increasing accretion of difficulties in identifying precisely what it is the 'profession' stands for. Despite valuable theological resources that reassure clergy – theologically and ecclesiologically – on their role and status, many also understand that those same resources lack any public or cultural resonance. Giving an account of a vocation and 'being' is no easy matter in a world that values concrete identifiable professions, measurable results at work, and a world where activity is appraised in a way that ontology cannot be.

Mindful of these difficulties, the recent study from Stephen Louden and Leslie Francis on Roman Catholic priests represents a particularly valuable resource for beginning to understand the gap between formal statements about priesthood and ministry that might issue from a church, and what the ministers *actually* say is occurring. In *The Naked Parish Priest* (2003), Louden and Francis surveyed over 1400 Roman Catholic priests engaged in parochial ministry – the only survey in England and Wales of its kind. The survey probes the views of clergy on priesthood, Catholic teaching, and a range of moral and ecclesial issues: homosexuality, paedophilia, contraception, the ordination of women and the giving of communion to divorced and re-married laity. The results, perhaps unsurprisingly, reveal a clerical caste that is out of step with the official teaching of its own church. The contingencies of pastoral engagement with parishioners tend to lead to more accommodating (some would say liberal) viewpoints. Less than half the clergy, for example, support a total ban on contraception. And on other ecclesial and moral matters, the private views of clergy are far from monochrome. It is clear that there is considerable diversity of opinion.

In concluding this section it is worth recording that for every empirically-based study on the nature or difficulty of ministry, there will be several monographs that either attempt to reaffirm or adapt the

---

[27] Towler and Coxon, *Fate of the Anglican Clery*, p. 205.

existing tradition. A number of these volumes offer deep wisdom, highly developed and nuanced understandings of the complexities of contemporary culture, and an imaginative re-endorsement of the role and identity of clergy. From an Anglican perspective, Kenneth Mason's *Priesthood and Society* (1992/2002) offers a model of priests as 'walking sacraments', acting and living out what they represent, and more concerned with serving the whole of society than merely maintaining or increasing congregational size. Similarly, Christopher Moody's *Eccentric Ministry* (1992) offers an intriguing, anthropologically aware account of the dilemmas facing contemporary clergy. Michael Ramsey's *The Christian Priest Today* (1972) remains a classic, still recommended for ordination candidates. Writers such as Wesley Carr and Paul Avis also continue to make a significant difference to the self-understanding and reflections of Anglican clergy through their teaching and writing.

These bodies of writing show that the clergy are more than aware of the difficulties and dilemmas that now face clergy at the turn of the twenty-first century. The question is: how are issues such as marginalization to be addressed? How are the clergy to respond to the multiple overwhelmings of modernity that appear to threaten not only their identity, but also their very future? In an increasingly rationalized and commodified world, can a distinct body of work, vocation or profession stand out and survive, in such a way that is not only publicly and religiously valid, but also culturally resonant?

Conclusion

We began this chapter by tendentiously suggesting that some aspects of theological reflection on the nature of ministry, and the role and identity of clergy and ministers, could be likened to a form of creationism. That is to say, ideas and models of clerical identity were formed exclusively out of tradition or Scripture, such that ministry might be said to be divinely created and ordered. However, in the chapter that follows, the idea of ministry *evolving* will be pursued and tested more rigorously, with a view to cultivating a new angle on clerical development. It is perhaps important to stress once more that the concept of evolution will be deployed analogically rather than forensically. In so doing, we shall be seeking to demonstrate how theological and ecclesial concepts, ideas and behaviour are as much a condition of adapting to contexts as they are an outworking of tradition. In turn, this has some important implications for understanding the nature of ecclesial structures and functions as they seek to survive and adapt in the twenty-first century.

In developing this type of approach to the study of ministry, some further important considerations need to be borne in mind by the reader. First, the analogical use of evolutionary theory is a kind of intellectual invitation – namely, to consider how Darwinism, neo-

Darwinian syntheses, social Darwinism, socio-biology and evolutionary psychology can be applied to a field that is traditionally tackled through history or a variety of pastoral theologies. Second, and at the same time, this invitation is also suggestive for other areas of consideration in the study of ministry: the application of insights from scientific creationism, intelligent design and theistic evolution also merit consideration. Central to this debate is the question of origins: is the life, composition and identity of ministry something that lives by design or by chance? And is there scope not only for dialogue between these apparently extreme positions, but perhaps some space for a degree of synthesis?[28] In this regard, we are eschewing the atheistically driven evolutionary theorizing of Richard Dawkins, in favour of an interpretative account that keeps both religion and science in play. As Alister McGrath perceptively notes:

> Dawkins suggests that a religious approach to the world misses something out...[but] a Christian reading of the world denies nothing of what the natural sciences tell us, except the naturalist dogma that reality is limited to what may be known through the natural sciences. If anything, a Christian engagement with the world adds a richness which I find quite absent from Dawkins' account of things, offering a new approach to the study of nature.[29]

Third, and furthermore, we might add that 'natural histories' of religious tradition can be highly illuminating. Daniel Hillel's recent work on Hebrew Scripture argues that the eclectic experiences of the Israelites – as they negotiated the contrasting ecological domains of the Near East – had a direct impact on the shaping of their theological outlook. Whereas other societies tended to idolize the disparate and capricious forces of nature, Hillel shows that the Israelites discerned an essential harmony and unity in nature that pointed to a theology that stressed a single omnipresent and omnipotent God. Hillel exposes the interplay between religion and culture, showing how the environment helped to shape the Israelites' view of creation and the creator, leading eventually to ethical monotheism as its theological outworking.[30]

In view of these remarks, readers may wish to hold five questions in their mind as the discussion within this monograph unfolds. First, a question of time. Can theologians who write on ministry and its

---

[28] For an interesting perspective on the emerging convergence in the science/religion debate here, see D. O'Leary, *By Design or By Chance?* (Minneapolis: Augsburg Books, 2004).

[29] A. McGrath, *Dawkins' God: Genes, Memes and the Meaning of Life* (Oxford: Blackwell, 2005), p. 149.

[30] D. Hillel, *The Natural History of the Bible: An Environmental Exploration of the Hebrew Scriptures* (New York: Columbia University Press, 2005).

development take a real account of the religious history that inevitably precedes the arrival of deacons, priests, bishops and other ministers? To what extent do the origins of such identities, roles and tasks lie much further back, in pre-Christian, pre-Jewish and perhaps quite primal human societies? Is the order and function of Zadok the priest anything like that of your average Roman Catholic or Anglican priest?

Second, there is the question of natural selection. Can theology accept that factors such as contingency, randomness and chance actually characterize the process of clerical speciation; that the evolution of clerical functions and identity is not pre-designed, but occurs naturally, and only later, in retrospect, acquires a distinct theological rationale?[31]

Third, there is the question of common descent. Can theology and anthropology account for the differences and similarities across the generations of the species? How close is the ministry of today's apostles (say in house churches) to that of the original twelve? Is there a real ancestry to be traced, and to what extent might there be some shared ancestry (of identity, function, form, etc.) with ministers from other faith traditions? Moreover, are there 'inherited traits' in religious practice (through socialization, rather than biologically), which to some extent determine the behaviour of groups?[32]

Fourth, readers will continually need to consider the question of divine action. If God acts in time – as most Christians would believe and assert – then what kind of action has God performed in the shaping of clerical identity? Has God acted decisively in an *interventionist* way (say through origination, renewal or restoration), as some might believe within a branch of faith such as Anglo-Catholicism? Or has God acted in a *non-interventionist* way, causing ministry to begin with, but equally not abrogating any 'natural laws', such that God's activity can be arguably discerned in synods and other forms of development, but in ways that are influential rather than uncompromisingly interventionist? Or has God acted in a *uniformitarian* manner, causing ministry to exist, but then stepping back, and letting nature (or the church) take its

---

[31] On this see T. Peters and M. Hewlett, *Evolution: From Creation to New Creation* (Nashville, TN: Abingdon Press, 2003), pp. 115–57.

[32] For example, Kate Fox, in her meditation on the English (*Watching the English: The Hidden Rules of English Behaviour* [London: Hodder & Stoughton, 2004], pp. 401ff), discusses 'reflexes...our deeply ingrained impulses. Our automatic, unthinking ways of being/ways of doing things. Our knee-jerk responses. Our "default modes". Cultural equivalents to the laws of gravity...'). She then identifies three basic reflexes that characterize the English: (1) humour, (2) moderation and (3) hypocrisy. She links these to 'outlooks (empiricism, class-consciousness and eeyorishness)' and 'values' (fair play, courtesy and modesty), all of which are designed to combat and address social dis-ease. Fox speculates on the cause of this complex potage that comprises the English character, and suggests that climate, island-identity and history may be factors – but no reductionist or determinist account is ultimately offered.

course – a more Deist view, in which God is akin to the (blind) watchmaker?

Fifth, and finally, there is the theological question of theodicy – what to make of waste, evil and suffering in the shaping of ministry throughout the ages? If creation and the whole of human ecology is somehow subject to God's love and power, then what is one to make of denominations and forms of ministry that essentially die out, or mutate in other ways such that the original becomes extinct or redundant?[33] What do we make of species that eventually perish, such as religious orders or certain functions and offices within the church?[34] Is the teleology of ministry and the church compatible with any kind eschatology?

For any who want to affirm divine action or intelligent design, there needs to be a deep consideration of such questions. It is through turning to such issues that readers will already begin to understand that although the subject of this book is primarily (but also in a way, superficially) concerned with the origins and development of clergy, we are just as interested in the question of divine action. How does God work in the world? And how is what is deemed to be created, actually caused?

[33] Comparisons with the fate of the dodo are inevitable. John Trandescant, who was a naturalist and gardener for Charles II, left a stuffed dodo in his will to the Ashmolean Museum in Oxford in 1659. The last recorded sightings of a dodo were on Mauritius between 1663 and 1681. The birds were, by all accounts, larger than a turkey, but with a rather tougher flesh. The bird was flightless, and had evolved such that it had no natural predators, so were easy prey for visiting Dutch and Portugese explorers, who hunted it to extinction for its meat. The bird's lack of enemies up to this point had made it tame, docile and even friendly towards potential hunters. At the same time, the bird could grow to a metre in height and weigh over 20 kilos. The name 'dodo' comes from the Portugese word *doudo*, meaning simpleton.
[34] A sobering exercise is to stand in some of the great ancient temples of Rome, Egypt or Greece, and reflect on the complete disappearance of the faiths that caused such structures to be built. The worshippers of Diana, Zeus and Ra are all consigned to history. Their temples stand alone, like the excavated fossils of a religion with nowhere to roam; great spiritual dinosaurs that no longer live, but whose outward appearance and behaviour we can now only speculate upon.

Chapter 2

On Origins

The origins of the earth have puzzled people for thousands of years. On one analysis, we have recently celebrated the 6000th birthday of the universe. Sir John Lightfoot (1602–1675), and Vice-Chancellor of Cambridge University, was a contemporary of James Ussher (1581–1656), who was in turn Archbishop of Armagh, Primate of All Ireland, and Vice-Chancellor of Trinity College in Dublin. In 1644, Lightfoot published his calculations relating to the date of the earth. In so doing, he based his work on that of Bede, the eighth-century ecclesiastical historian and chronicler of early English history. Lightfoot published his calculations just a few years before the more famous Ussher completed his own.[1] The prominence of Ussher in relation to the dating of the earth owes itself to the fact that he published his calculations in the Preface to the *Authorized Version of the Bible* in 1701, lending weight to the mathematical calculations that had more than a hint of biblical authority. As Andrew White notes:

> The general conclusion arrived at by an overwhelming majority of the most competent students of the biblical accounts was that the date of creation was, in round numbers, four thousand years before our era; and in the seventeenth century, in his great work, Dr. John Lightfoot, Vice-Chancellor of the University of Cambridge, and one of the most eminent Hebrew scholars of his time, declared, as the result of his most profound and exhaustive study of the Scriptures, that 'heaven and earth, centre and circumference, were created all together, in the same instant, and clouds full of water,' and that 'this work took place and man was created by the Trinity on October 23, 4004 B.C., at nine o'clock in the morning'.[2]

Ussher, building on the insights of Lightfoot, was able to go further, and calculated the dates of other biblical events. He concluded, for example, that Adam and Eve were driven from the Garden of Eden on Monday 10 November 4004 BC, and that Noah's ark touched down on Mount Ararat on 5 May 2348 BC – which was, by the way, a

---

[1] J. Ussher, *The Annals of the World*, vol IV (New York: Master Books, 1658).
[2] A. White, *A History of the Warfare of Science with Theology in Christendom* (London: Appleton and Co., 1897), p. 9.

Wednesday.[3] It is easy to mock such scholars – especially, perhaps, for the apparently pretentious precision of the dates. But it should be borne in mind that Lightfoot, Ussher and others were merely trying to account for the dating and origin of the world with the only authoritative account that they possessed at the time, which came from Christian Scripture. However, one might ask what would prompt such an intellectual enterprise in the seventeenth century?

Part of the answer must lie in the emergence of what we might broadly call 'natural history'. In 1514 Copernicus had challenged Aristotle's claim that the earth was fixed at the centre of the universe. The sixteenth century had also seen the discovery of new worlds, together with the circumnavigation of the globe, which had exposed Europeans to a zoological diversity that they had hitherto not encountered. Discoveries in physics, biology and anatomy also suggested that life might be governed by 'natural laws' (or forces). In the seventeenth century, just as Lightfoot and Ussher were attempting to reassert the primacy and factuality of the biblical accounts of creation, others were developing natural theories of the earth's origins and ordering. Thomas Burnet, in his *The Sacred Theory of the Earth* (1719) suggested that there were seven ages of the earth, which had begun with a chaotic void and would end with a consuming fire. John Woodward advanced the argument in his *An Essay Towards the Natural History of the Earth* (1702) that the earth was primarily a sphere of water, upon which solid crusts settled, but periodically broke up and reformed. William Whiston published *A New Theory of the Earth* in 1696, arguing that the biblical accounts of creation were essentially primitive accounts of historical events; a comet hitting the earth, for example, might have caused Noah's flood (a tsunami).

The eighteenth and early nineteenth centuries continued to speculate on the origins of the earth. Although many Europeans continued to affirm that creation was attributable to divine forces, there was increasing interest in identifying and studying evidence – botanical, biological and geological in particular. Carl Linnaeus (1707–1778), for example, a Swedish Professor of Medicine, produced a small booklet in 1741 called *Systema Naturae*, which argued not only for the diversity but also the 'fixity' of species (i.e., they did not change or evolve).[4] Linnaeus' botany went hand-in-hand with his religious beliefs, and led him to develop a more scientifically based 'natural theology', which together with Deism flourished throughout the eighteenth century, with scholars such as William Paley developing theological schools of this type. (Indeed, Linnaeus' work bore some similarity to that of John Ray – 1627–1705 – who proposed concepts of species and genus to classify animals and plants.) For Linnaeus, because God had created the world,

---

[3] G. Craig and E. Jones, *A Geological Miscellany* (Princeton, NJ: Princeton University Press, 1982).
[4] *Systema Naturae* was later developed into a multi-volume work.

it was possible to understand God's wisdom by studying that same creation. The study of nature would therefore reveal the divine order of God's creation, and it was the naturalist's task to construct a 'natural classification' that would reveal this order in the universe.

Order, however, did not mean 'fixity' for George-Louis Leclerc (Comte de Buffon, 1707–1788). Born to a noble and wealthy French family, Buffon published his *Historie Naturelle* in 1749, arguing that organic change did take place, with species adjusted to new conditions by adapting. In so doing, he began to pave the way for the revolutionary thinking of the nineteenth century, and in particular Darwin's theory of evolution. If Buffon was correct, and species *adapted* to their environment, then questions were necessarily raised about both creation and the creator. Buffon, in his expansive encyclopaedia (running to 44 volumes), also wrestled with the hierarchies of species. Even in an age of Deism, it was still widely thought (theologically) that human beings were the crown of creation – 'made in the image of God', as the book of Genesis proclaims. But Buffon's work is the first to tendentiously note the similarities of humans and apes; he even talked about the possibility of a 'common ancestry' of humanity and primates.

One of Buffon's younger colleagues, Jean-Baptiste Lamarck (1744–1829), was to take these theories slightly further. From 1801, Lamarck began to publish details of his theories of organic change. Where Buffon had merely hinted at the possibility of evolutionary change, Lamarck was more forthright, proposing a more dynamic interplay between organic forms and their environment. In his view, time and favourable conditions were the two principal means which nature employed in giving and sustaining life. 'Lamarckianism', as it subsequently came to be known, was later to draw the admiration and acknowledgement of Charles Darwin. In Lamarck's reasoning, organisms adapt to change in their environment, which in turn caused changes in their behaviour (i.e., acquired traits). Their altered behaviour then led to subsequent superior or slighter use of a given structure or organ. The use would cause the structure to increase in size over several generations, whereas disuse would cause it to shrink, or perhaps even to disappear. Lamarck distilled his thinking into a *Philosophie Zoologique*, published in 1809. His 'First Law' stated that the use or disuse of certain organic structures caused them to increase or contract. His 'Second Law' stated that all such changes could be passed on through subsequent generations of species. The consequence of linking these two 'laws' was to create an early and embryonic evolutionary theory: the continuous, gradual change of all organisms, as they became adapted to their environments.

Confirmation of this kind of theorizing was now beginning to emerge all across Europe, albeit with important modifications. Gregor Mendel (1822–1884), an Augustinian monk who taught natural science, based his work on pea plants, observing and tracing the characteristics of successive generations. Like Carl Linnaeus before him, Mendel's initial attraction to research was based on his love of the natural world. He found that the plants' respective progeny retained the essential traits of the parents, and therefore (against Lamarck) were not necessarily influenced by the environment. Mendel's simple experiments gave birth to the idea of organic inheritance (heredity), which later was also to influence Darwin. In essence, Mendel derived from his studies that there were certain basic laws of organic inheritance: hereditary factors do not combine, but are passed on intact; each member of the parental generation transmits only half of its hereditary factors to each offspring (with certain factors 'dominant' over others); and different progeny of the same parents receive different sets of hereditary factors.

By the mid-nineteenth century, the stage was set for a thorough and radical critique of received Christian theories of origins, and for a new (non-religious) theory that was based on a synthesis of natural history, botany, zoology, geology and palaeontology. Charles Lyell (1797–1875) was typical of many Victorians who combined their academic and philanthropic interests across the disciplinary fields. His *Geological Evidence of the Antiquity of Man* (1863) and *Principles of Geology* (three volumes: 1830–1833) argued for an alternative history of creation; a world which had a 'history' stretching back millions of years, giving time for species to live, die and be fossilized. The Victorian age, in other words, represented a kind of maturing in the genesis of an intellectual culture that had been emerging over several generations, each of which was centred on the question of origins. Broadly speaking, these three trajectories of enquiry were to find their way into the seminal thinking of Darwin: first, the age and origin of the earth; second, the effect of the environment upon species (adaptation); and third, how hereditary trends emerged to be dominant ('survival of the fittest').

It has been necessary to provide some kind of brief introductory historical account of the contested question of origins (before discussing Darwin), in order to illustrate how the debate has evolved over a lengthy period of time. Of course, questions about the origins of the world and in natural history closely resonate with the general groundswell of critiques and doubt that were beginning to emerge in theology in the nineteenth century. Moreover, and analogically, the quest for origins also suggests that there might be awkward issues to face about the original sourcing of authority and power; evolutionary theory not only raises new questions about the ordering and development of the world, but also of institutions. There is a natural sense in which the idea of evolution, whether as a scientific theory or analogical framework for interrogating origins, can be used to probe and query the prevailing theological construction of reality (or the social construction of revelation). Evolution, in short, questions 'givens' and previously privileged accounts of origin and development. Conceptually, the very idea invites enquirers to consider how origins and species are to be accounted for; accepted notions of revelation and theories of natural history can collide at this point. It is to this that we shall turn later: developing the idea of evolution as an analogical lens that can be fruitfully and critically applied to conceptualizations of ministry. But before then, it is necessary to explain Darwin in more depth, in order to prepare the foundation for the remainder of the study.

Creationism, Darwin and evolution: a brief guide

The recent film *March of the Penguins* (2005, and directed by Luc Jacquet) has prompted a fresh debate in the USA on the origins of life and theories of evolution. The film follows the life cycle of the Emperor Penguin (*Aptenodytes forsteri*) on the frozen wastes of Antarctica, focusing on their feeding and breeding habits. Of particular interest is how the birds have evolved: they are mainly monogamous (or so it appears); they huddle together in large groups to keep warm, and take it in turns to form the outer protective 'wall' that shields the rest of the flock from the bitter winds of the region, as they sweep across the ice plains. The male and the female penguin take it in turns to rear the single chick that their union produces, and endure considerably sacrifice and risk to protect this most nuclear of families, yet within the larger context of a collective grouping.

The film charts an extraordinary story of cooperation and endurance, and against seemingly overwhelming forces (nature, predators, the elements, etc.) the penguins seem to not only survive, but flourish. And in a slightly surprising turn of events, the film has been championed by fundamentalists as a kind of 'natural theology' that challenges the theory of evolution. The saga of the penguins – at least in the imagination of creationists drawn from the American religious right – portrays monogamy, selflessness and child-rearing as 'natural': part of the created order. This, the religious advocates of the film argue, provides ample evidence for 'intelligent design'. There is, apparently, no sign of Dawkins' 'selfish gene'; these penguins appear to be committed (even vicariously) to their sociality rather than to an individual instinct for survival. The penguins are now so perfectly adapted to their environment, so creationists argue, that only a creator could endow them with such specious and particular habits to match their habitats. The film, in other words, points two ways. First, it questions 'godless' or liberal assumptions about the identity and purpose of the nuclear family. Second, it points to a creator behind evolution, or even possibly to a creationist theory for the origin of life.[5]

[5] Whether or not the film is read as a parable or analogy, or simply seen as a argument for a kind of fundamentalist natural theology, closer scrutiny of the actual life cycle of the penguin suggests a more complex debate may be required. The Emperor Penguins – in common with more than fifteen similar species of penguin – will change its mate each season. And like other mammals, there appears to be a form of naturally occurring homosexuality in the species, constituting a small but significant percentage of each flock.

The debate that the film has prompted is, in some sense, merely a re-enactment of arguments that have raged over Darwin's theories since they were first published in 1859. The college where I currently work (Ripon College, Cuddesdon, Oxford) was founded in 1854 by Samuel Wilberforce, the very same bishop of Oxford who, goaded by Darwin's theories (when famously debating with Huxley), allegedly asked Huxley whether he was related to the ape on his mother or his father's side.[6] Darwin, of course, had been a student at Christ's College Cambridge – a college where I have also had the privilege of working, and where William Paley (arguably the doyen of natural theology in the eighteenth century) had also been a student.[7] The mention of this coincidence is not in itself important, granted. But the apparently tenuous connection between these institutions again reminds us of how much the debate on the origins of life within Victorian society was fought at such close quarters: between the academy and the church; between colleges and other institutions; between the emerging ascendancy of sciences and the waning grip of theology. This was an age that witnessed a profound cultural turn; away from Scripture and sacred accounts of life, and towards what science could both explain and improve.

Such debates continued well into the Edwardian era, long after the balance of probability had tipped decisively in favour of evolutionist accounts of the earth rather than those propagated by creationists. But the town of Dayton, Tennessee, witnessed one of the last stands made by creationism in the twentieth century, where a high-school biology teacher by the name of John Scopes was charged with illegally teaching the theory of evolution. Tennessee, in common with other southern states within the USA, was inclining to be more culturally resistant towards the new shockwaves of modernity that were rippling across the USA, represented by art forms such as jazz, increased social liberalism, and a new-found economic prosperity that was marginalizing religion. The habitual response to the slightest sign of secularism had been revivalism, and there can be little doubt that the origin of the religious forces unleashed upon the hapless John Scopes gestated in the 'Bible Belt'.

In 1924 the state of Tennessee had enacted a bill making it unlawful 'to teach any theory that denies the story of divine creation as taught by the Bible, and to teach instead that man was descended from a lower order of animals'. But the bill was not without its religious critics, including a modernist Methodist by the name of George Rappalyea, who persuaded Scopes to stand trial for a test case. There is no doubt

---

[6] Although this debate was widely reported at the time, the actual exchanges between Huxley and Wilberforce gained a near mythical status from the moment of the debates' conclusion. Huxley is alleged to have retorted to Wilberforce that if it were a choice between being related to an ape or a bishop, he would opt for the primate.

[7] Darwin had actually lived in the rooms previously occupied by Paley.

that Scopes took the view that biology could not be taught without teaching evolution. Nevertheless, the staged nature of the trial should not be underestimated: two friends of Scopes, who were local attorneys (Herbert and Sue Hicks), agreed to prosecute him. However, the trial quickly developed into something of a circus, with notable local and national legal, political, religious and free-speech advocates joining the prosecution and defence teams. When the trial opened in July 1925, the Anti-Evolution League brought chimpanzees into town, who then competed for the public's attention with the holy rollers and travelling preachers. A test case had become a show trial.

The outcome of the trial was as bizarre as its origins. The trial judge, John T. Raulston, was a conservative Christian, who seemed to be set on denying the defence an adequate hearing. The defence, in turn, closed the proceedings by asking for a guilty verdict to be returned, in order that the trial could be appealed to the Tennessee Supreme Court. Judge Raulston obliged, and Scopes was duly found guilty and fined $100 – a large sum for 1925. But on appeal, the verdict and fine were overturned on a technicality: the jury, not the judge, should have set the fine. The Tennessee Supreme Court then dismissed the case. The impact of all this was a somewhat pyrrhic victory for the Anti-Evolution League; they had won at the County Court, but failed at the State Supreme Court. And of the fifteen states considering legislation restricting the teaching of Darwin's theories, only Arkansas and Mississippi enacted laws.[8]

It is hard to fathom quite what Charles Darwin would have made of the 'Scopes Monkey Trial', as the *Beagle* first weighed anchor in the Galapagos Islands in 1835. But he surely would have agreed with Berra's contention:

For the creationists, the task of explaining the origin of life is dazzlingly easy: it was simply created. For scientists, who look to hard evidence, observable fact and critical thinking for explanations, the task is not so easy – complexities, subtleties, and immensities of time intrude.[9]

Darwin was born at Shrewsbury in 1809, the son of a naturalist and a physician. At sixteen, Darwin left Shrewsbury to study medicine at Edinburgh University. However, he reportedly did not have the stomach for surgery, and left Edinburgh for Cambridge, where he

[8] For a contemporary account of the evolution/creationism debate, see T. Berra, *Evolution and the Myth of Creationism* (Stanford, CA: Stanford University Press, 1990); N. Eldredge, *The Triumph of Evolution and the Failure of Creationism* (New York: W.H. Freeman, 2000); C. Hunter, *Darwin's Proof: The Triumph of Religion over Science* (Grand Rapids, MI: Brazos Press, 2003); T. Woodward, *Doubts About Darwin: A History of Intelligent Design* (Grand Rapids, MI: Baker Books, 2003).
[9] Berra, *Evolution*, p. 70.

attended Christ's College in order to study to become a clergyman. But he was not ordained, and instead chose to attend a five-year scientific expedition to the pacific coast of South America on the HMS *Beagle* from 1831 to 1836, where he worked as an unpaid naturalist. This extraordinary voyage took him to South America, the Galapagos Islands, Mauritius, the Cape Verde Islands (off the cost of Africa), Australia and New Zealand. It afforded Darwin the opportunity to collect fossils and living specimens, explore coral reefs, deserts, tropical rain forests, the pampas, the high Andes and many other habitats. His preliminary observations were published in *Journal of Researches* (*Voyage of the Beagle*) in 1839, which was in turn to prompt his more theoretical and reflective *On the Origin of Species* (published in 1859)[10], and described evolution and natural selection, offering a theoretical explanation for the diversity among living and fossil beings. Darwin's *The Descent of Man*, a more detailed meditation on human origins, existence and survival, was published in 1871.[11]

Darwin's early 'career' as a naturalist should not surprise us. He was able to afford the five-year sabbatical on the *Beagle* because he came from a family of means. Like many clergy of his generation, he was largely free to engage in a variety of pursuits, and as Desmond and Moore note in their biography of Darwin, he 'unselfconsciously assumed the guise of an orthodox clerical-naturalist, a pottering parsonage-living harmless soul'. Like many gentlemen of his generation, Darwin had been weaned on Gilbert White's *The Natural History of Selborne* (1788), which taught its readers to observe the rhythm of the seasons and to record the details of local nature; and he would have also read William Paley's *Natural Theology*, alongside *An Introduction to Entomology*, by William Kirby and William Spence. These writers all had two things in common: a love of nature and being clergy.

It is generally agreed that the most seminal part of Darwin's voyage took place in the five weeks spent at the Galapagos Archipelago. Darwin was mesmerized by the organisms he encountered here – on a group of sixteen islands some six hundred miles to the west of Ecuador. Darwin visited four of the islands, and observed that the finches, tortoises, iguanas and other animals were very similar to ones that had been studied on the South American mainland. However, in the case of the tortoises and the finches, there were distinctive differences. In the absence of predators and other competition, Darwin would later reason that the animals had developed (or mutated) to fit their own ecological niche. Likewise, Darwin knew that there was a species of mockingbird found only in South America, but on three islands of the Galapagos he

---

[10] The full title of the book is, of course, *On the Origin of Species by Means of Natural Selection, or the Preservation of Favoured Races in the Struggle for Life.*
[11] The full enigma of Darwin's life cannot be captured in a slim volume such as this. For a fuller biographical account, readers are referred to the work of Adrian Desmond and James Moore, *Darwin* (Harmondsworth: Penguin, 1991).

found three different types. His conjecture was that a common ancestor had made its way to one of the islands, and through 'branching descent' or the 'radiation of the species', the birds had gradually evolved to be different, whilst retaining very similar characteristics, pointing to an original, common ancestor.[12] In turn, this suggested that species were neither individually created nor immutable; in fact species evolve, to better fit their environment over a period of time. Mulling over the implications of his musings, Darwin wrote:

> When I recollect, the fact that the Spaniards can at once pronounce, from which Island any Tortoise may have been brought. When I see these Islands in sight of each other, & possessed of but a scanty stock of animals, tenanted by these birds, but slightly differing in structure & filling the same place in Nature, I must suspect they are only varieties. If there is the slightest foundation for these remarks the zoology of Archipelagoes will be well worth examining; for such facts would undermine the stability of Species.[13]

From this kind of vantage point, the theory of evolution was now beginning to evolve.

Indeed, and according to Mayr, evolution took more than eighty years to really establish itself as the normative theory for natural biological development. It is now best understood as 'the genetic turnover of the individuals of every population from generation to generation'.[14] Darwin's great insight is, of course, based upon a simple yet profound sequential computation: like begets like, but with some variation (over time and space); all living things produce more offspring than can in turn survive; those organisms that are most fit – or adaptable – to their environment are more likely to survive and flourish; and therefore favourable variations within a species will tend to be preserved, meaning that the species will evolve over time. This process is what Darwin termed 'natural selection', and its logic is entirely consistent and coherent. However, what is observable (as evolution is) is not necessarily explainable, and the contemporary debates between science and religion now tend to concentrate on the mechanisms for change in organisms rather than the actuality of development.

For example, human beings are around 99 per cent similar to chimpanzees, yet clearly nobody would confuse the two. The issue in Darwinian theory today lies not so much in origins as in the mechanisms that control development: what 'switches' genes on and off in certain environments, and why. For the purposes of this book (and using evolution as an analogical lens for analysing the develop-

---

[12] E. Mayr, *What Evolution Is* (New York: Basic Books, 2001).

[13] Desmond and Moore, *Darwin*, p. 186.

[14] Mayr, *What Evolution Is*, p. 76.

ment of ministry and clerical identity), the interest lies in how environments help to determine those facets that flourish, and why others might remain dormant. Such a view creates some distance from 'genetic fundamentalists', who can tend to see genes as utterly determinative. In actual fact, a more nuanced view of Darwin's somewhat hesitant theories contained within *The Origin of Species* allows us to imagine a kind of developmental system, in which reified genes and the environment form a more collaborative partnership to effect the process we describe as evolution.

Because evolutionary theory is being used analogically (for, rather than as, analysis), it is not necessary to delve that much further into the more recent scientific debates it has prompted.[15] However, it is necessary to explain its mechanism in slightly more detail for the purposes of clarity, and in order to underline how it differs from creationism. As we noted earlier, to creationism falls the luxury of promoting a kind of simplicity. Witness how one creationist writer, Carl Wieland, defends the specious environment of the Galapagos Archipelago:

The classic story is that Darwin, a gentleman-naturalist perfectly willing to keep believing in divine creation, stumbled across irrefutable evidence opposed to it in the Galapagos. The 'facts of nature' left him no choice, as it were. The islands' 13 different species of ground finch (called 'Darwin's finches' to this day) play a major role in this legend. He saw that they were obviously from the same ancestral population (something modern creationists would mostly affirm), presumably from the mainland. Yet each was specialized to different environments, food types, etc. And this, we are told, forced him to abandon divine creation.

However, the real story is a bit different. First, his ideas were well on the way to materialism (the belief that there is no supernatural realm) as a young man. His previous theism was more like deism, certainly not based on the Bible's Genesis history. Considering that his grandfather Erasmus published a well-developed theory of evolution, the notion that 'Darwin changed his mind based on the facts' is especially untenable. And, ironically, he did not even know that these birds were finches till well after his return. The idea of divine creation held by many in Darwin's day was more of a caricature of the Bible, in which all animals were created more or less where they are now. Whereas Genesis, of course, tells us that the world was repopulated after being devastated by the Genesis

---

[15] See, for example, S. Jones, *Darwin's Ghost* (New York: Ballantine, 1999); R. Dawkins, *River Out of Eden* (London: Weidenfeld and Nicolson, 1995); S.J. Gould, *Wonderful Life* (New York: Vintage, 1990); W. Baum, *Understanding Behaviourism: Behaviour, Culture, and Evolution* (Oxford: Blackwell, 2005).

Flood. So, naturally the Galapagos creatures were not created on the Galapagos, but migrated to them.[16]

In considering such views, it is important to note that the author is attacking both theology and science. The type of theology that is being opposed is hinted at as being liberal and rationalist, and named as Deism. But behind this is a core and coherent belief system that is committed to an absolutist version not only of creation, but also of revelation. God's action in the world is portrayed as direct and unmediated; the Bible is a fax from heaven; God's word uncompromised by history or human agency. This is simple to believe – but almost impossible to defend.

Wieland's creationist theory – that Darwin's finches are somehow escapees from Noah's flood (rather than fresh creations) – need not detain us for too long. Clearly, the thesis dictates the facts, and no amount of scientific evidence is likely to alter the state of mind that views the book of Genesis as a kind of history that can hold its own in the world of science. But what Wieland's musings do demonstrate is that there is some acknowledgement of adaptation within species, even amongst creationists. Where scientists differ from creationists is in their account of the mechanisms of change, which are ascribed conceptually to the process known as evolution, where the composition and relative abundance of genes in population changes, via mutation, natural selection, migration and random drift.

In this process, mutation is the primary source of genetic variation. Some mutations result in negative traits, but the vast majority will most likely be recessive – passed from one generation to the next, but without being obviously expressed. Many of the random changes that take place in deoxyribonucleic acid (more commonly known as DNA) simply seem to guarantee variability over time, sometimes to the advantage of the species. DNA is, of course, a nucleic acid that contains the essential genetic 'instructions' which specify the biological development of all cellular forms of life. DNA is a kind of molecule (or perhaps vehicle) of inheritance, as it is responsible for the genetic propagation of most inherited traits. During reproduction, DNA is replicated, and then transmitted to the offspring. DNA is the basic building block of life; it contains all the information that living things need to function correctly. In humans, for example, this can cover obvious traits such hair or eye colour, but it can also extend to certain types of ability or disability. DNA is composed of genes inherited from both parents. DNA from both parents ultimately combines to form a new living body through a process of replication and division. As a result, each cell in a living organism contains copies of the DNA from its parents.

---

[16] Carl Wieland, 'Darwin's Eden', *Creation*, 27.3 (June–August, 2005), pp. 12–13.

Natural selection, in turn, is the influence of the environmental factors upon genetic composition that cause a particular species to be more adaptive. As we have noted already, natural selection does not necessarily equate to 'survival of the fittest' (in the sense of 'fit' meaning strength), but refers instead to 'fit' meaning 'most adaptive to environment'. This part of the process of evolution can involve organic, micro and macro changes, with other forms of adaptation such as co-evolution also taking place (i.e., a more imposed form of hybridity occurring). For the purposes of the analogy of evolution being used in relation to religious and clerical identity, one might point here to the formation of the United Reformed Church (URC) in England, which was a union of two distinct but related strains of Protestantism: Congregationalists and Presbyterians. In technical scientific terms, the emergence of URC ministers is both an example of phylogeny (the grouping of organisms based on shared ancestry) and taxonomy (the grouping of organisms based on similarities). The 'species' is, if you like, not unlike a mule – the union of a horse and donkey making for a different but related animal to its parents. So, analogically, we are now in a position to suggest that such occurrences eventually give rise to a species (a population of individual organisms that can reproduce). And that the diversification of species occurs when certain geographic, contextual or climatic changes divide groups, and encourage specialization and adaptation with new environments.

The idea that the process of evolution may somehow serve as an analogical lens for gaining a fresh perspective on religion is by no means unique. Herbert Spencer's notion of 'social Darwinism' was applied to cultural and economic systems in the nineteenth century, and there is a sense in which this book is arguing for a kind of ecclesial Darwinism in his wake. So whilst the breeding that produces each successive generation of priests and ministers is very seldom a biological process, our analogical (or socio-ecclesial) usage of Darwin's theories allows us to suggest that the social and religious processes that produce new clergy would lend themselves to a linguistic or social understanding centred upon a range of concepts, including continuity, development and pedigree. In turn, this opens up the possibility of re-reading religious development, as Steve Jones demonstrates in his updated version of *Origin of Species*:

> The mass is a Christian eternal. As an exchange with God it has its roots in the earliest Church. Wherever he might be, a believer finds himself at home and except for the language differences that emerged with the abandonment of Latin, part of a universal ceremony. Not, however, in Ethiopia. In a minor triumph of comic prose, Evelyn Waugh (who visited the country in 1930) described the responses of an expert to his first experience of a local Mass: 'That was the offertory ... No, I was wrong; it was the consecration... I think it is the secret Gospel...the Epistle... I

have noticed some very curious variations in the Canon of the Mass...particularly with regard to the kiss of peace.': Then the Mass began.

His liturgical confusion has a message for biology. The Ethiopian Church was cut off for a thousand years, safe from the reforms that seized the rest of Christendom. As its rite passed down the generations, the errors grew until whole sections made no sense even to those who celebrated it. They are of interest to theologians as they reveal a history elsewhere swept away by the march of progress. All structures degenerate as soon as their job is done. Once selection ceases, the chaos of nature sets in and evolution loses its way. A relic may hence be better evidence of the past than is the most exquisite adaptation.[17]

The idea that the Ethiopian Coptic Church can be interpreted through evolutionary theory should not strike us as being so strange. The comparison, arguably, likens the Coptic Church to marsupials, a duck-billed platypus, or perhaps to Darwin's first encounter with lizards swimming in the sea of the Galapagos. Cut off from the rest of the world, something odd has evolved in the sphere of religion. In writing like this, Jones has partially aligned himself with the philosopher Mary Midgley (1985), who has the insight to see that Darwin's embryonic evolutionary theory is, in some sense, a 'story'. It so happens that this 'story' is based on Darwin's observation of the natural world, some science and then further reflection. But as a theory, it begins its life first and foremost as story, which gradually develops (properly) into a verifiable scientific theory. Evolution is, in some sense, a kind of 'doctrine of development'; a mode of understanding the composition of complex bodies and societies by paying attention to their origins. And by applying this story to religion, one begins to gain a deeper and broader account of how pivotal theology can become in ecclesiological debates.

David Sloan Wilson's work goes somewhat further than this, and begins to take the radical step of proposing an evolutionary theory of religion. Wilson suggests that the key to this development is to think of society as a complex organism, and of religion and morality as evolved adaptations within such groupings or systems. This allows Wilson to suggest that religion enables groups to function as coherent social units

---

[17] S. Jones, *Darwin's Ghost: The Origin of Species Updated* (New York: Ballantine Books, 1999), p. 302. For a different perspective on evolutionary theory and religion, see David Sloan Wilson, *Darwin's Cathedral: Evolution, Religion, and the Nature of Society* (Chicago: Chicago University Press, 2002); Donald Broom, *The Evolution of Morality and Religion* (Cambridge: Cambridge University Press, 2003); and T. Burge, *Science and the Bible* (Philadelphia: Templeton Foundation Press, 2005).

rather than as a mere collection of individuals. Drawing on a diverse range of examples – from Korean house churches to sixteenth-century Calvinism – Wilson shows how religion succeeds by promoting collective action rather than individualism. Even forgiveness, he suggests, has an evolutionary dimension to it. But just as Wilson's theory is explicit, so is it possible to detect comparable implicit (and more confessionally-based) theories of religion that tilt towards the same goal. Indeed, if one sets aside evolution for the moment, and considers how theologians have debated 'natural' and 'revealed' values, one can begin to see the strength and allure of reading religion from the more general perspective of evolution.

For example, Richard Hooker's *Laws of Ecclesiastical Polity* argues against the purist and elysian ideologies of ministry that were propagated by his Puritan opponents in the seventeenth century. However, Hooker wonders if the 'laws' of Puritanism will be any better than the existing order he seeks to defend. According to C.S. Lewis, the greatest danger from Puritanism is described as 'Barthian reductiveness',[18] echoing Hooker's concern that 'your discipline being...the absolute commandment of almighty God, it must be received although the world by receiving it should be clean turned upside down...' (Pref. 8.5). One could say that Hooker argues for both 'natural' and 'revealed' sources for ecclesial polity. As such, there is one kind of law for Hooker – 'the first law eternal' – which is the law of God's own being or purpose. The second kind of law is what might be loosely termed 'natural': 'that which with himself he hath set down as expedient to be kept by all his creatures' (Book 1.III.1). It is from this second type of law that all others flow, and Hooker then proceeds to categorize them: those which angels obey, those concerning humanity, reason, scriptural law, human law and, finally, laws of commonweal, politic societies and nations.

For Hooker, laws are causal. *The Laws of Ecclesiastical Polity* are really, in one way, a single self-conscious and systematic call for the church to recognize that the operations of God are not confined to those materials that are identified (or elevated) as revelation. Instead, the laws that govern the church are any 'directive or rule unto goodness of operation' (Book 1.VIII.4). Hooker's perspective on law leads him to conclude that all laws, in their goodness, are derived from God. Furthermore, that understanding laws (again in relation to theology) enables us to judge whether they are reasonable, righteous and just. The weighing of laws is a complex task for the church, but also a rewarding one: ultimately, it is an enquiry into the grace of God. And Hooker's task throughout Book 1 is to evolve a broader understanding of law in the face of Puritan attempts to narrow it; for to do so is also to enlarge the vision of God. Thus, Hooker's charge is that the Puritans think that

---

[18] C.S. Lewis, *English Literature in the Sixteenth Century Excluding Drama* (Oxford: Clarendon Press, 1954), p. 453.

'the only law which God hath appointed to men in that behalf is sacred scripture'.

Hooker is, in effect, accusing the Puritans of an early form of creationism or fundamentalism. He meets this with a simple affirmation, that even as we 'breathe, sleep, move, we set forth the glory of God'; and that even 'the law of *reason* doth somewhat direct men how to honour God as their Creator' (Book 1.XVI.5; emphasis mine). In other words, there are more laws than those in the Scriptures, and all individuals and societies are governed by a plethora of beneficent higher powers, which are set down by God 'above every soul'. So Hooker's theology of ministry and his ecclesiology depends on both 'natural' and 'revealed' sources, both of which, he contends, are from God. He rejects the sixteenth-century version of 'ecclesial creationism' (and implicitly its close relative, fundamentalism), but at the same time accepts a theory of revelation. He accepts the 'natural order', but in so doing, is arguing for an early form of 'intelligent design'.

It should by now be apparent that the relationship between religious belief and evolution, although complex, is also generative. Furthermore, that we are 'using' Darwin's theories in the popular sense of their reception and widespread understanding, rather than a more finessed view that would perceive (correctly) that Darwin's own theories evolved over time: he basically held to at least three modified versions of his original account developed from 1859. It is clear, however, and to return to our analogical use of Darwin, that eighteenth-century theories on the origins of life challenged religious belief. In so doing, they began to change the ways in which religious belief was held and developed: evolutionary theory acted as an environment that caused religion to adapt, through which mutations such as 'creationism' and 'liberalism' would be partly formed. At the same time, evolutionary theory also acts as an analogy or story that offers a fresh perspective on the origin and development of religious history and culture,[19] including clerical identity and ecclesial polity. It is therefore to the exercise of establishing a brief 'natural history' of the clergy that we now turn.

Clergy: a brief natural history

Religion has a boundless capacity for diversification and increase. Successive movements within Christianity – renewal (whether Catholic, Charismatic or other), restoration (for house churches, Levellers or other groups wishing to reinstitute the past) and revival (of polity, praxis or order) – have ensured that Christianity in particular has evolved into a highly complex global phenomenon. Certain expressions of the faith are deeply enculturated and linked to their primary habitat;

[19] Burge, *Science and the Bible*, p. 158ff.

other expressions (such as evangelicalism, with its stress on individual piety) appear to be able to take root almost anywhere. The variety of strains, traits and expressions can be identified through the multiplication of denominations, the division of denominations, mergers across denominations, and differences detectable within denominations. John Wesley understood something of the dynamics of (inevitable) denominational diversity when he wrote:

> I do not see how it is possible, in the nature of things, for any revival of true religion to continue for long. For religion must necessarily produce both industry and frugality. And these cannot but produce riches. But as riches increase, so will pride, anger, and love of the world in all its branches.[20]

Although Wesley was writing a century before Darwin, the mention of branches points us towards one of Darwin's more fruitful metaphors for mapping and explaining diversity: branching. In deploying this term, it allows us to link denominations, but also to distinguish them. According to Norman Maclean's acclaimed short story *A River Runs Through*, a Methodist is basically a Baptist that has been taught to read. This definition is attributed by Maclean to a Presbyterian minister. But as any Methodist will tell you, a Presbyterian is someone for whom Methodism is a bit too racy: not unlike the definition of an actuary – someone who finds accountancy a tad too exciting. (Presbyterians, by the way, is an anagram of Britney Spears – although it is not immediately clear how this might benefit either party.)

These waspish caricatures, amusing though they might be, are symptomatic of a bygone era of inter-denominational wars, the kind of which can now only be found in Northern Ireland, Liverpool or Glasgow. For most of the population, religious identity is centred not on the faith of their parents, but on just what happens to be good and local. Ecclesial brand loyalty is a dying phenomenon. Of course, it was not always so. Once upon a time, denominational names (and the pedigree they connoted) mattered a great deal, although their origin is often forgotten. It remains the case that very few denominations chose their own name. 'Anglicanism' is a term that was popularized by James VI of Scotland, and contains a degree of mocking irony. Similarly, 'Anabaptists' had their family name bestowed upon them by their detractors. Equally, 'Methodist' can also be read as a dubious compliment – another mildly derogatory nickname.

But Wesley's argument remains a strong one: religion unites and divides over passionate thoughts and sentiments, and in the midst of intense competing convictions. Moreover, competition can be the engine of increase in the ecclesial world, just as it is in the natural. But

[20] J. Wesley, *The Works of John Wesley*, IX (ed. R. Davies; Nashville, TN: Abingdon Press, 1976), p. 529.

competition also produces the kind of diversity that some religions don't welcome so much: schism. Indeed, and from my own Anglican perspective, the arguments that currently disturb the soul of its polity clearly need to become calmer if anything is to be achieved in the short or medium term. Put another way, only when the intense heat of the arguments that currently bedevil it begin to cool, can Anglicanism recover its poise, and its members start talking and listening to one another rather than shouting. Anglicanism is, arguably, at its best, not unlike the English weather: an essentially temperate affair. It is often cloudy, but with some sunny intervals – and the occasional outburst of rain. But it is seldom born well from a climate of extremes.

In terms of increasing denominational diversity (which threatens the coherence of the identity of a given 'breed' or pedigree of denomination), we might say that if one denomination can learn to live in humility and grace with its profound differences, and not allow itself to be destroyed by pride and anger, then there may be hope for some deeper cross-party denominational rapport to develop. Put another way, controlled diversification may actually enable and strengthen denominational identity. But ultimately, unity cannot be imposed: it has to be discovered and cultivated organically. If the Anglican household of faith can discover a way of keeping itself together with its diversity, it will have made an important contribution to that elusive search for true unity – one that respects the dignity of difference. And in the midst of that, what may also be discovered is that difference is not a sign of weakness, but rather of strength. The diversity within Anglicanism has always been one of its most glorious treasures. It has created the possibility of staying within a faith yet changing, and of moving to and from traditions, yet without abandoning the denomination. Anglicans, like the rest of Christendom, are skilled at adapting the prayer of Jesus (from John 17): 'may we all be one – but thank God we are all different'.

This brief aside on denominational diversity merely serves to introduce the thorny but fascinating issue of clerical diversity. The two are related, of course: clergy are clearly 'creatures' of their denominations. But before exploring the finer (micro) differences in any given denominational clergy species, it is necessary to attend to the macro changes that have seen clerical identity evolve and change over more than two millennia. The move into grounded or natural history is critical, even from the perspective of the church, when one considers how theological discourses on ministry and priesthood continue to be shaped. Although well aware of the history of the functional and symbolic aspects of priesthood, this still does not seem to prevent many modern writers from resorting to the kind of 'creationist' narratives we have previously identified. For example, Ben Gordon-Taylor locates clerical identity in the concept of mystery. Justifying this, he notes:

Mystery is therefore not a convenient theological smokescreen or ecclesiological cop-out, but an expression of the infinite potential of our engagement with God and his with us, most perfectly expressed in the Word made flesh, Jesus Christ. Mystery is not a lifeless theoretical principle: it exists in relation to us, we engage with it, find it within ourselves, and are changed by it. God's self-communication in mystery draws us in and feeds our fascination with him – God moves towards us, and we are enabled to move towards him. In exploring the meaning of priesthood, then, we must allow God to take the initiative. We must allow God to show us how the mystery is disclosed in scripture, in the Church, in priesthood, and in us... Priesthood is rooted in the mysterious and life-giving power of the Holy Spirit... The priest is a disclosure of the paschal mystery of Christ, rooted in his divinity, and yet at the same time is a priest because of his humanity, not in spite of it.[21]

There can be little objection to such sentiments, although one is bound to ask how the theology articulated above can be exclusively linked to priesthood, and made to exclude the laity. But that is not the point. Such theologizing is purposefully shaped to protect the *ultimate* origin and identity of the clerical profession, even though it may at the same time concede all kinds of ground to cultural and social histories that have impacted the culture of ordained ministry. In attempting to answer the question, 'where do clergy come from?', one would naturally expect most theologians to answer 'God', 'Christ', 'the Holy Spirit' or perhaps 'the Trinity'. And in one sense, there can be no quibble with such answers. But part of the burden of this essay is to probe a little deeper into the question of origin, and evaluate (theologically and ecclesiologically) the proper place of social and cultural factors that also play a part in the construction of clerical identity and the shaping of ministry. This is, of course, a pressing issue for theology in its own terms (granted, as a test case or single issue), since it raises questions about the nature of the discipline of theology, and the sources (or evidence) it is prepared to draw upon. And in using the analogy of evolution analytically in relation to clergy (or other aspects of ecclesiology), it allows us to explore the richness of diversity encountered within the species. Expressed in more theological terms, we might say that some openness to evolutionary thought offers the opportunity to develop a kind of natural-incarnational theology to compete on more equal terms with high forms of creationist theology, which tend to privilege themselves in ecclesial and theological arguments for church order and polity.

---

[21] B. Gordon-Taylor, 'The Priest and the Mystery: A Case of Identity' in George Guiver (ed.), *Priests in a People's Church* (London: SPCK, 2001), pp. 11, 13, 18. In a comparable vein, see also E. James (ed.), *Stewards of the Mysteries of God* (London: Darton, Longman & Todd, 1979).

For example, the monastic tradition of Christendom has undoubtedly evolved out of a complex nexus of religious and social traditions, a number of which pre-date Christianity. The etymology of the word 'monk' is rooted in a Greek term meaning 'single' or 'one alone'. In popular parlance it has been used to designate any member of a religious community living vows of poverty, chastity and obedience. But its use beyond the structure of formal religious orders (such as Franciscan, Benedictine, Augustinian, etc.) has extended to hermits and other solitary mystics. The early Celtic tradition of spirituality appears to have been able to support rather looser forms of monasticism, in a rather similar vein to those that could once be encountered in Egypt and other parts of the Near East during the patristic period. Such 'orders' were distinctively ascetic, although less organized than their Western Catholic equivalents.

'Nun', in contrast, is a term that is only correctly used of religious women in an enclosed order; outsiders were rarely allowed in, and members were seldom allowed to leave. However, the post-war period and Vatican II has seen some women's religious orders become much more open. Furthermore, recent and more detailed historical study of women's religious orders has opened up new insights into the power and autonomy that convents may have enjoyed in the past. For example, Caroline Walker Bynum suggests that the evolution of difference between male and female enclosed orders (and their focus upon types of religious experience) may be linked to the gradual deprivation of power that women and their convents experienced.[22] The more women religious (nuns) became marginalized from even minor clerical tasks in the Middle Ages, the more physical union with Christ in the Eucharist became romanticized for women, because it could be symbolized in terms of marriage and sexual consummation, often resulting in ecstatic behaviour. Here, the quasi-eroticism was merely a vehicle for deep spirituality, which no doubt owed some of its power and popularity to its implicit exclusion of the male imagination. As Bynum notes, quasi-erotic Eucharistic spiritual ecstasy was a potential means of reclaiming power for women, and bypassing male authority. It was also a way of embodying religious experience within a proto-feminist construction of reality that was beyond the reach of conventional male-dominated lines of interpretation.

The evolution of orders, in almost any period of history, was often specifically linked to the environmental context in which distinctive spiritualities arose, the need to mark that distinctiveness in a variety of modes, and the necessary reality of facing up to competition – from both inside and outside the religion itself. This partly accounts for Anglican religious orders – a restoration of something 'catholic' to the Church of England (which had been lost in the Reformation), which

---

[22] C.W. Bynum, *Fragmentation and Redemption: Essays on Gender and the Body in Medieval Religion* (New York: Zone Books, 1992), pp. 120ff.

was enabled through the nineteenth-century Anglo-Catholic reformers. In some sense, the restoration of religious orders is the Church of England trying to be catholic again. In so doing, it builds bridges with Roman Catholicism, but at the same time represents threat and competition. Thus, Anglican and Roman Catholic Franciscans, although enjoying fraternal relations, and looking very similar from almost every perspective, are nonetheless found to be quite different. Similarly, 'calced' (i.e., shod) branches of certain Roman Catholic religious orders are distinguished from those that are discalced; the Carmelites wear shoes, but the Teresians don't. Rather like Darwin's finches, one can observe minor but significant differences within the same species, which have been caused by theological mutation, separation and environmental factors over a period of time.

Such evolutionary processes continue today. Some convents and monasteries have reinvented their mission, by re-connecting with society at its neediest junctures. Whilst retaining places of quiet contemplation and relative isolation, houses of hospitality or missions have also sprung up in deprived inner cities, offering help, support and a profound spiritual presence in some very demanding contexts. New 'orders' have also been created, such as the Order of Mission, which is Protestant, Charismatic and Evangelical in ethos, but has developed a system of tertiary association and full members of the Order who are committed to a daily cycle of prayer. Members of the new Order are committed to evangelism, and are helping to establish new cells of the Order across the largely un-Christianized landscape of England's northern cities. The Order of Mission marks a new development in ecclesiological patterning; it constitutes a new self-conscious fusion of charismatic, evangelical, catholic and postmodern spiritualities.

Similarly, the history of clerical ethos and identity is also marked by a remarkable capacity for evolutionary change. The term 'clergy' derives from 'clerk', referring to a (functional) person of learning and duty. The term 'clerk in holy orders' signifies that from a relatively early period in the history of the church, such people were distinguished from minor ecclesiastical offices such as 'lay clerks' or 'bible clerks', functions not requiring ordination. Before the Reformation, the term 'clerk' could be used more broadly to apply to those in 'minor orders', whilst the orders of deacon (and for some centuries, the sub-diaconate), priest and bishop were designated as major, or holy, orders. As we shall see later, the functionality of these offices requires, over time, the building up of distinctive *modus operandi*, clothing and other cultural accruements which enable the species to maintain its identity.

To the casual observer, perhaps from another planet, the diversification of denominations and orders within Christianity presents a dazzling array of colours, practices, behaviour and understanding. The puzzlement over the sheer quantity of species is reminiscent of Gilbert White's musings on what to make of the animals, birds and fauna, which naturalists, explorers and settlers were encountering and writing about in the Americas during the eighteenth century (Letter XXIV, 1769):

> The question that you put with regard to those genera of animals that are peculiar to America, viz. how they came there, and whence? is too puzzling for me to answer; and yet so obvious as often to have struck me with wonder. If one looks into the writers on that subject little satisfaction is to be found. Ingenious men will readily advance plausible arguments to support whatever theory they shall choose to maintain; but then the misfortune is, every one's hypothesis is each as good as another's, since they are all founded on conjecture. The late writers of this sort, in whom may be seen all the arguments of those that have gone before, as I remember, stock America from the western coast of Africa and the south of Europe; and then break down the Isthmus that bridged over the Atlantic. But this is making use of a violent piece of machinery: it is a difficulty worthy of the interposition of a god! '*Incredulus odi.*'[23]

But from where did all this diversity originate? In terms of the clerical species, we can at least trace the macro differences to their medieval origins. Here, parochial clergy were one of the main but distinct groups of clergy, and they were joined by three others: bishops, monks and nuns in their religious houses, and friars. These groupings were often at odds with one another; they operated from different ecclesiastical systems (power bases), and relations were frequently fractious. Friars, for example, often stood out as self-appointed critics of clerisy. Monks and nuns were largely independent of episcopal control. Bishops wielded enormous power and influence, and often presided over vast estates. Parochial clergy (and this has been true throughout most of their history) were at the bottom of the pyramid in terms of wealth and influence. In large measure, this accounts for frequent references in medieval manuscripts to their poverty and comparative lack of learning: 'they were poor, ignorant and corrupt – the dregs of the clergy rather than the clerical norm'.[24] The wealthier and more learned clergy that were not bishops, friars or monks tended to either purchase or procure clerical livings, becoming rectors or vicars – but in so doing, seldom lived in the parishes for which they were responsible. Religious duties were duly assigned to a 'clerk in holy orders', often poorly educated, who would be paid a wage of subsistence. It is perhaps hard to comprehend such a system in today's world, when clergy are generally regarded as educated professionals – at least of a kind. But when one

---

[23] G. White, *The Natural History of Selbourne* (Harmondsworth: Penguin, 1977 [1788]), p. 65.
[24] Towler and Coxon, *Fate of the Anglican Clergy*, p. 5; F.A. Gasquet, *Parish Life in Medieval England* (London: Methuen & Co., 1906).

realizes that the Bishop of Gloucester, in conducting a census in 1551, discovered that more than half his clergy could not recite the Ten Commandments, one begins to appreciate the potential scale of the problem.

Social and political revolutions have a profound effect upon clerical identity. Just as the revolution in France was to marginalize the clergy and challenge its authority, so the Reformation in Britain marked a decisive shift in the balance of power for churches. The asset-stripping and dissolution of the monasteries under Henry VIII in 1539, together with the coercive compliance that was forced upon bishops, meant that bishops and religious orders lost many of their estates and much of their wealth. Power passed from the clergy to laypeople, with the church losing many of its privileges but shedding few of its responsibilities. Whilst the church continued to carry several civic and social burdens – education, welfare, local justice, etc. – the numbers in education for purely secular ends began to rise. Correspondingly, the status of clergy began to decline during the Tudor and Stuart periods. Clergy lacked wealth, making it unlikely the *nouveau riche* gentry created by Henry's favouritism and policies would join their ranks. True, the clerical profession had been 'cleansed' of its small armies of poor and ignorant mass-priests, but gone also was the real means of maintaining a leaner and simpler body of clergy who had some learning.

Yet although the sixteenth and seventeenth centuries could be described as a period of recession for clerical status, this was also something of a golden age for the humble parish priest. Simplicity can give birth to beauty. George Herbert, for example, would be doubtless surprised to see himself commemorated in his own right as a 'founder' of Anglicanism: on 27 February in the Anglican lectionary. A modest man who achieved no preferment in his brief life, he might be puzzled by the fact that he is remembered at all. Born in 1593 (died 1633), he went to Cambridge in 1514, where he became Public Orator. He was then a Member of Parliament before surprising everyone by turning to the priesthood, having spent some time with his friend Nicholas Ferrar at Little Gidding. He went to the parish of Bemerton in 1630 as rector, and it is here that he wrote his hymns and his two books, *The Temple* and *The Country Parson*. His writings come out of an era that gave Anglicanism some of its brightest jewels in spirituality and divinity: Andrewes, Donne, Taylor, Waterland and Hooker, to name but a few. But their common denominator – from the perspective of evolutionary thought – was that their world and means were now much simpler. In the hierarchy of professions and the ordering of society that emerged after the Reformation, clergy were now below the local squire (and far below the nobility), but equally occupied a position in society that assured them of some respect, provided they fulfilled their pastoral duties. From having a secure, privileged and unchallenged status up to the Reformation, clergy had to reinvent themselves as pastorally and civically useful office holders, in order to maintain a position within society.

Paradoxically, it was the profound social and economic shifts in the eighteenth century that were to produce the environmental context for a radical change in fortune for Anglican clergy. The early phases of the industrial revolution ushered in an age of greater agricultural product-ivity, which coupled with land reforms and economic development led to a considerable rise in income for clerical benefices. Glebe lands, and the tithes that issued from them, laid the foundation for a new-found and comparatively comfortable life for many clergy. The gentry now contemplated 'investing' in livings; they could be bought and sold at auction. For clergy, many of whom had diversified in their educational expertise to embrace the emerging sciences of the enlightenment and the fashionable clubs of London that debated the issues of the day, this meant a significant realignment of the clerical profession with the gentry. This was the era of Parson Woodforde, but also of the waspish caricatures and criticism of wealthy clergy to be found amongst novelists such as Jane Austen. Granted, there were still poor clergy, and the new economic conditions that priced parishes according to income gener-ated was to exacerbate the gap between the poor ordinary clergy and those with patronage, incomes and endowments. As Chadwick notes:

> A legend, which at least is *ben trovoto*, tells how a Bishop Ely, receiving a candidate for ordination who came from Cambridge as a senior wrangler and first-class classic, bowed his candidate into the room with 'It would be quite superfluous, Mr. Perry, to examine a gentleman of your well-known acquirements'. When Bishop Blomfield, later the administrative reformer and Bishop of London, was first elevated to a diocesan see, he consented only under pressure to interview his ordinands before their ordination, 'as he did not like to put them to so much trouble'.

But the benefits of the agrarian revolutions of the Hanoverian period were not to last. The industrial revolution – the dominant cultural shaper of the Victorian era – was to wreak a new kind of havoc on clerical identity. The Victorian age began with great promise. As cities grew, new churches were built in new emerging cities such as Sheffield.[25] Clergy engaged vigorously (but not always effectively) with the new challenges that they encountered. But the wealth derived from land and agriculture was now shifting to industry, where the output was seldom tithed, let alone the income. Moreover, the gentry themselves began to lose influence to the new businessmen and the emerging middle-classes. The response of the churches to this radical shift in environmental culture was specialization. The era saw several renewal movements (catholic and evangelical), with clergy jettisoning

---

[25] Cf. W. Odom, *Fifty Years of Sheffield Church Life 1866–1916* (London: Home Words, 1917). See also M. Walton, *A History of the Diocese of Sheffield 1914–1979* (Sheffield: Sheffield Board of Finance, 1981).

the general 'uniform' of a gentleman, and adopting the fashionable dog-collars that were much in evidence on the continent, and the rapid accrual of many other hallmarks of a cultivated and distinctive professional identity. Differentiation soon crept in, with evangelical and low-church clergy adopting different styles of everyday wear to those clergy who were influenced by the Anglo-Catholic revival. By the end of the nineteenth century, and not unlike Darwin's Galapagos, an 'archipelago' of style and content could be clearly identified amongst the clergy. The same species, to be sure; but the variations were noticeable, and the emerging and distinctive ecclesial environments required specialization and adaptation.

In terms of a natural history, it is not unreasonable to say that the fortunes of the clergy, from the Reformation to the turn of the twentieth century, were to some extent shaped by the relationship between affluence and influence. Clergy modelled their own identity (whether consciously or unconsciously) in ways that 'fitted' their changing social contexts, and were also dependent on conducive factors within their environments to effect their influence. However, as we have noted, the adaptive trait should not be underestimated. The relative margin-alization of the clerical profession in the post-Tudor and pre-Hanoverian era, which could be safely characterized as a low ebb for clerical identity, also saw at the same time a deep recovery of trust between parson and people, and the flowering of beautiful (but also accessible) Anglican spirituality, represented in hymns, poetry, prose and architecture. This era began to end when clergy and churches discovered their new-found wealth drew them back towards being identified with a new and powerful elite, the gentry. But this in turn, ironically, created the very conditions for ecclesial competition, with revivalists such as Edwards, Whitfield and the Wesleys able to reach out to a new generation of people who now felt disenfranchised by an elitist parish system, and who craved for the simpler spirituality and pastoral praxis of the seventeenth century.

The profound cultural, industrial and economic revolutions of the Victorian era were also, of course, matched by significant cultural changes, perhaps especially in politics and education.[26] Successive Acts of Parliament paved the way for religious toleration, opening up schools and universities to Roman Catholics and dissenters. In turn, this pressed the Church of England into deeper specialization, which together with a growing secularism in the burgeoning cities, resulted in the formation of several distinctive kinds of theological college for the

---

[26] For some further contextual discussion, see R. Wells (ed.), *Victorian Village: The Diaries of the Reverend John Coker Egerton of Burwash 1857–1888*, (Stroud: Alan Sutton Publishing, 1992); J. Wigley, *The Rise and Fall of the Victorian Sunday* (Manchester: Manchester University Press, 1980); T. Larsen, *Contested Christianity: The Political and Social Contexts of Victorian Theology*, (Waco, TX: Baylor University Press, 2004).

particular training of its clergy (in Oxford alone, Cuddesdon[27] was founded in 1854, St Stephen's House in 1876 and Wycliffe Hall in 1877). These new forms of diversification evolved out of the synergy of ecclesial particularity in relation to perceived social and religious needs. But the resulting mutations were not to everyone's liking. The Archbishop of York complained in 1891 that the clergy that were being produced by the new Colleges were 'all moulded in the same pattern...using party shibboleths and catch-words'. A commission reporting on theological colleges half a century later, in 1942, found that 'they had grown up in haphazard fashion...they tend to encourage points of view representative of the "wings" rather than of the "centre"'.[28]

We will consider the twentieth century in more detail later, but as we pause briefly to conclude this section on natural history, it is important to summarize our findings. The sweeping changes of the Reformation brought about a narrowing of the range of clerical identities, at least in Britain. In other countries affected by the religious revolutions of the sixteenth and seventeenth centuries, the bitter and bloody rivalry between competing strains of Christianity resulted in a more intense form of diversification, which Britain was not to seriously engage with until the Victorian period, by which time it was also joined by industrialization and a growing secularization. Clerical identity – at least for the majority of Anglican clergy, which this section has been mostly focused upon – struggled throughout the nineteenth century to develop a professional accent that competed with other professions, and thereby engaged new recruits. What was developed in place of professional identity was ecclesial particularity, which for many clergy temporarily resolved the conundrum of how to match their increasing specialization with their growing marginalization. Put another way, clergy had moved from dominating their environments in medieval times to being almost entirely shaped by them at the end of the Victorian era.

Thus, the twentieth century was to be, for clergy, a reactive age in which clerical identity had to continually adjust to the faster paces of social change that were dictating ecclesial relevance. The kinds of evolutionary trajectory that can be traced in liturgical renewal (the move from ancient to modern language, from Latin to the vernacular, etc.); in patterns of ministerial experimentation (worker priests, industrial mission, etc.); in doctrinal development (less emphasis on sin and punishment, more on salvation, etc.); and in the structuring of ecclesial governance (the gradual democratization of denominations,

---

[27] See M. Chapman (ed.), *Ambassadors of Christ: Commemorating 150 Years of Theological Education in Cuddesdon, 1854–2004* (Hampshire: Ashgate, 2004) and M. Chapman, *God's Holy Hill: A History of Christianity in Cuddesdon* (Charlbury: Wychwood Press, 2004).
[28] Towler and Coxon, *Fate of the Anglican Clergy*, p. 20.

shifting more power from the clergy to the laity, etc.), simply point to the growing sense of isolation within the church. But in a more positive vein, these developments also point to the inchoate self-understanding of the church; that in order to live and breathe, it needs to continually belong to the public sphere. The clergy, throughout these rapid social and ecclesial changes, have had to adapt their identity at a faster pace than any other period in history, in order to maintain any kind of place as a stakeholder in public life. And it is the maintenance of this position within the public realm that continues to sustain the nutrient and generative environment for clerical identity.

Conclusion: clerical evolution – analogy and theology

Our developing analogical use of evolutionary theory (granted, represented more in its commonly received forms rather than in any of its technical self-articulation) has a threefold aim. First, it points towards how and why ministry and theologies of ministry are shaped by their context or environment. This also, incidentally, explains why many theologies are generally reluctant to admit the role of socio-cultural formation within their realm; by continuing to claim an 'other-worldly' origin (creationist), it is still possible to claim a privileged grasp of revealed rather than natural truth. Second, those ministries that survive and flourish will tend to be the most adaptive in relation to their changing situations. Almost every denomination in every country of the post-Reformation era has had to substantially adapt its practice and public understanding to better 'fit' the culture in which it ministers. Denominations that don't adapt at all, of course, can still be said to be culturally-relative and adaptive, as they express their life in forms of conservatism and cultural resistance. Third, although there is clear continuity in clerical identity that can be traced back through the lineage of ordination and succession, so there is also variation and specialization, as a result of mutation, competition and other factors. Twenty-first-century worker priests and ministers in secular employment (MSE) may link their vocation directly to Paul the tentmaker, but there can be equally no doubt that the conditions which have given birth to new varieties and patterns of ministry are modern rather than ancient.

Lest this sound too reductionist, however, it is clearly important to recognize the place of the transcendent in such deliberations. As many scholars and commentators acknowledge, evolutionary theory can give a lucid account of what is observable, but not necessarily what is explainable. In using evolutionary theory analogically, we are deliberately steering a middle course between meta-theological and atheistically-driven biological accounts of clerical life. The careful sifting of self-serving and privileged theological accounts of ministry is an important task. But being aware of overt reductionism is no less vital.

As one might say of Richard Dawkins's work (and to borrow from George Orwell), his writings display not so much a disbelief in God as a personal dislike of him. But with the cautious use of evolution as an analogical and analytical lens comes the acknowledgement that there is more to ministerial development than what can be seen. Hidden away in each candidate for ordination is a sense of calling, which has come from God, who has created and fanned the embers of vocation. They burst into mystical flame in testing, discernment and service, and become a fire that attracts others by its warmth and brightness. To speak in this way is to begin to utilize the language of love and offering, in which science can have little purchase. And by paying attention to such dynamics, a study of this kind is reminded that 'natural' and 'evolutionary' accounts of ministry are complementary to the world of mystery and revelation.

There is, perhaps, some recognition of this in Darwin's own work. Speculating on the origin of the eye, he writes:

> To suppose that the eye with all its inimitable contrivances for adjusting the focus to different distances, for admitting different amounts of light, and for the correction of spherical and chromatic aberration, could have been formed by natural selection, seems, I freely confess, absurd in the highest degree. Yet reason tells me, that if numerous gradations from a perfect and complex eye to one very imperfect and simple, each grade being useful to its possessor, can be shown to exist; if further, the eye does vary ever so slightly, and the variations be inherited, which is certainly the case; and if any variation or modification in the organ be ever useful to an animal under changing conditions of life, then the difficulty of believing that a perfect and complex eye could be formed by natural selection, though insuperable by our imagination, can hardly be considered real. How a nerve comes to be sensitive to light, hardly concerns us more than how life itself first originated; but I may remark that several facts make me suspect that any sensitive nerve may be rendered sensitive to light, and likewise to those coarser vibrations of the air which produce sound.[29]

Darwin is, in other words, at least open to the possibility of a 'mixed-economy' when it comes to considering creation and evolution. Although he would later revise his opinions more decisively in favour of natural selection, the nuances that are contained within the first editions of *Origin* allow us to offer an analogical lens that makes space for the gestures and initiatives of a Creator within the development of the natural world. This is, of course, a popular and established use (rather than representation) of Darwin's theory, but for our purposes in

---

[29] Charles Darwin, *Origin* (London: Penguin, 1981).

this essay, it presents us with the possibility of acknowledging a wide and varied bundle of sources that come together to develop clerical identity. All those cultural, social, personal, mystical, sensate, rational promptings, together with the downright unexplainable, can combine to offer the call that still draws men and women into ordination and religious orders. Darwin, in his final paragraph of *Origin* (chapter 14), offers the vivid analogy of the hedgerow, which might serve as a cipher for almost how any ordinand might attempt to describe the myriad of forces, impressions and conversations that have begun to shape a vocation:

> It is interesting to contemplate an entangled bank, clothed with many plants of many kinds, with birds singing on the bushes, with various insects flitting about, and with worms crawling through the damp earth, and to reflect that these elaborately constructed forms, so different from each other, and dependent on each other in so complex a manner, have all been produced by laws acting around us. These laws, taken in the largest sense, being Growth with Reproduction; inheritance which is almost implied by reproduction; Variability from the indirect and direct action of the external conditions of life, and from use and disuse; a Ratio of Increase so high as to lead to a Struggle for Life, and as a consequence to Natural Selection, entailing Divergence of Character and the Extinction of less-improved forms. Thus, from the war of nature, from famine and death, the most exalted object which we are capable of conceiving, namely, the production of the higher animals, directly follows. There is grandeur in this view of life, with its several powers, having been originally breathed into a few forms or into one; and that, whilst this planet has gone cycling on according to the fixed law of gravity, from so simple a beginning endless forms most beautiful and most wonderful have been, and are being, evolved.[30]

---

[30] Darwin, *Origin*, p. 470.

Chapter 3

On Development

Description is revelation. It is not
The thing described, nor false facsimile.

It is an artificial thing that exists,
In its own seeming, plainly visible,

Yet not too closely the double of our lives,
Intenser than any actual life could be,

A text should be born that we might read,
More explicit than the experience of sun

And moon, the book of reconciliation,
Book of a concept only possible

In description.[1]

Part of what is at issue in this essay is the status of confessionally-based descriptions in relation to ministry. In attempting to re-cast some of the narratives surrounding the origins of clergy, we are essentially deploying a kind of practical theological method that eschews the exclusivity of fundamentalist or creationist accounts for the origins of the church. At the same time, however, we are not merely substituting one kind of dominant narrative approach for another. Granted, ironic, 'natural', social-scientific and historical readings all have their place; but no one single account can do justice to the multi-faceted dynamics that form ministerial identity. As readers will have detected from the close of the previous chapter, Darwin had a tendency to read 'the book of nature' (note his meditation on the eye, and on the analogy of the hedgerow) as a story, in much the same way that the early nineteenth-century Romantics proposed to read the Bible – as any other book. In so doing, however, a rich irony emerges: '[the] attempt to provide an alternative narrative to Christianity has come to look, in retrospect, fatally, like

---

[1] 'Description Without Place', from *The Collected Poems of Wallace Stevens* (London: Faber & Faber, 1955), pp. 344–45.

trying to take on Christianity on what neither side realized was religion's own home ground: the art of story-telling'.[2]

The question at issue is, therefore, 'what kind of story?' We have already hinted that the Victorian age represents a particular watershed for the clergy story. The great pastoral narratives of the seventeenth and eighteenth centuries (and their critiques, from the likes of Jane Austen) that dominated the English landscape were to be utterly fractured by the upheavals wrought by the industrial revolution. The stories of clerical identity and engagement were successively challenged by the shift of population from agrarian to urban culture, and the consequent marginalization of the church. Culturally, as well as theologically, the Victorian era emerged as an age of development. Descriptions of the church and its ministry will vary considerably; across disciplinary fields, via historical or pragmatic assessments, and weighted differently according to the degree of confessional empathy or critical insight brought to bear upon a given issue. Newman, for example, within the epoch of the Victorian era, now considers Anglicanism (as a convert to Roman Catholicism) to be lacking in self-consciousness, unable to tell its own story:[3]

> As a thing without a soul, it does not contemplate itself, define its intrinsic constitution, or ascertain its position. It has no traditions; it cannot be said to think; it does not know what it holds and what it does not; it is not even conscious of its own existence.[4]

It is probably inconceivable that such writing could have taken root a century before. But the Victorian age was religiously self-conscious, and well aware of the dynamics of spiritual competition. But this is a very different Newman from the one whom had located what we might call the 'real presence' of Anglicanism within the *via media* only two decades earlier; the identity of the Church of England's soul was born of ecclesiological fusion. For Newman, contemplating the origins of the church and their development in *A Grammar of Assent*,[5] there was 'the illative sense' to reckon with: the move from partial theoretical evidence to eventual practical certainty. It was this journey that was to lead him from Anglicanism to Roman Catholicism, but in so doing, to provide yet another example of how scholars of his era were fascinated by origins and development. In Newman's case, what was observable and could be known would only be partial; yet the collective story that

[2] S. Prickett, *Narrative, Religion and Science: Fundamentalism versus Irony, 1700–1999* (Cambridge: Cambridge University Press, 2002), pp 250–55.
[3] Prickett, *Narrative, Religion and Science*, pp. 175.
[4] J.H. Newman, *Lectures on Certain Difficulties Felt by Anglicans in Catholic Teaching Considered*, (London: Longmans, Green & Co., 2nd edn, 1851), p. 7.
[5] J.H. Newman, *A Grammar of Assent* (London: Longmans, Green & Co., 1895). See also *Essay on the Development of Doctrine* (London: Longmans, Green & Co., 1895).

emerged from history, tradition, practice and Scripture could be said to point towards a form of clarity and certainty that offered a completer narrative, that both rivals and echoes some of Darwin's own writings. Thus for Newman, the 'natural history of the church' (or its organic history) points to a higher mind; to a design and to a creator. But in such a theological schema, Anglicanism is ultimately re-narrated: as an un-planned accident – un-created, but all too real.

By speaking in this way, one again becomes aware of the contested nature of description. What is glimpsed, then observed, and finally processed, depends so much on the original vantage point. For Newman, his own emerging clarity about the nature of *true* development afforded him the opportunity to develop an illative theological sense of ecclesial evolution that would eventually lead to his own conversion. In so doing, he would need to renounce his previous convictions. Put another way, the developing theological 'plot' in Newman's works contains a story that properly aligns autobiography with theories. Gillian Beer, in her fascinating study of evolution, notes how the 'reading of *The Origin* is an act which involves [the reader] in a narrative experience':

> The organisation of *The Origin* seems to owe a good deal to the example of one of Darwin's most frequently read authors, Charles Dickens, with its apparently unruly superfluity of material gradually and retrospectively revealing itself as order, its super-fecundity of instance serving as an argument which can reveal itself only through instance and relations.[6]

If evolutionary theory 'can reveal itself only through instance and relations', rather than demonstrate itself absolutely through uncontested experiments and evidence, then there is some merit in likening Darwin's theories to narrative description. That is not to say that evolutionary theory is not to be regarded as 'science'. Rather, it acknowledges that there are a variety of possible stories to tell about the origins of the world, nature or the church, each of which draws on a variety of illative senses of instances and relations.

Some of these observations may appear, at first sight, to elevate creationism or fundamentalism to a level of equity with science and other academic disciplines. But this is neither the case nor the point. In acknowledging the fragmentary nature of evidence (e.g., theories based on 'instances and relations') and the place of narrative in theory, we are merely drawing attention to precisely the opposite of what fundamentalists and creationists would strive for. The debate on the origins of the church, ministry or the world is not about ultimately privileging one grand narrative over another, but rather the recognition that no one

[6] G. Beer, *Darwin's Plots* (London: Routledge & Kegan Paul, 1983), pp. 5, 7–8.

narrative can be wholly complete. It is to resist 'consilience': the idea that there can be a grand narrative that ultimately amounts to a coherent theory of everything.[7]

At the same time, there is no sense in which our musings submit to any kind of vapid relativism, reductionism, or perhaps other traits traditionally identified with postmodernism. The simple purpose of reckoning with a 'natural history' of clergy is to provide a complementary critique to the more usual tradition of theologically driven narratives of ministry, which perhaps inevitably suggest a more coherent lineage of custom than is really the case. Put another way, the debate about origins and development, whether of the natural world or church, needs to be securely located not only in differing narrative streams and in histories drawn from a variety of perspectives, but within historiography itself. It is vital, therefore, to be attentive to the nature of bias, contested 'facts', and whether or not history is an art or science, a form of accurate description or an exercise in narrative persuasion. It is important, in other words, to recognize that history is conceptually disputed, as much as it is materially:

> History is a shifting, problematic discourse, ostensibly about an aspect of the world, the past, that is produced by a group of present-minded workers...who go about their work in mutually recognizable ways that are epistemologically, methodologically, ideologically and practically positioned and whose products, once in circulation, are subject to a series of uses and abuses that are logically infinite but which in actuality generally correspond to a range of power bases that exist at any given moment and which structure and distribute the meanings of histories along a dominant-marginal spectrum.[8]

But why should this matter when considering the development of ministerial practice within the church? The devil, as always, is in the detail. It is the case that in theologically-shaped histories and discourses on ministry, the bias (either to legitimate the present, or to reach for a new vision) invariably results in a distorting of the past; its simplification dressed up as duplication; its overt narration presented as 'fact'. And for theology, just as for history, such accounts of the past are seldom adequate, and can indeed be problematic.

For example, it is not uncommon to find significant groups of clergy

[7] Prickett, *Narrative, Religion and Science*, p. 128. See also E. Wilson, *Consilience: The Unity of Knowledge* (London: Little, Brown & Co., 1998).
[8] K. Jenkins, *Re-Thinking History* (London: Routledge, 1991), p. 26. See also E.H. Carr, *What is History?* (London: Penguin, 1963); G. Elton, *The Practice of History* (London: Fontana, 1969); and A. Marwick, *The Nature of History* (London: Macmillan, 1970). For a recent account of the uses of history within ecclesiology, see R. Williams, *Why Study the Past?* (London: Darton, Longman & Todd, 2005).

who either write about or discuss the history of the church through the construct of 'Christendom'. The narrative that emerges from such constructions is that, until very recently, Britain (or other European countries) were predominantly and self-consciously Christian. In turn, this leads to identifying a moment in time – perhaps the industrial revolution of the nineteenth century, or the popular cultural revolutions of the late twentieth century – that have led to a decline in the practice of churchgoing and adherence to Christianity. Such 'histories', once propagated and accepted, allow marginal and dominant interest groups to develop their power base. Missiological entrepreneurs promoting initiatives such as 'cell church', 'fresh expressions' (of church), 'pioneer' or 'emerging' church as vogue-ish ecclesial models are able to argue that the church was 'successful' or 'growing' in its pre-institutional, pre-denomination or pre-Christendom phase. Therefore, it is argued, in a post-Christendom era, these 'models' are the ones that not only (demonstrably) work, but are also those that are sanctioned by tradition. (In actual fact, neither of these 'facts' is correct: the narratives are merely heavily spun and rather thin interpretations of the past.) Similarly, a more dominant interest group may argue that the advent of a post-Christendom era has been brought about through the churches, capitulation to liberalism, pluralism or other forces attributed to modernity, and that the recovery of ecclesial poise and status in the public sphere requires new initiatives that will re-connect with neglected traditions, emphases or doctrines.

However, a more careful and nuanced reading of church history will normally reveal a considerable diversity of faith and practice behind the construct of Christendom. In saying this, I am not suggesting that Christendom never existed; merely that its strength and meaning were variable, and very far from being fixed and factual. For example, on Easter Day 1800, the registers at St Paul's Cathedral in London record only six communicants. This suggests that at the height of the golden age of clerical identity in the Hanoverian era, there was a marked lack of Christian observance. We have noted previously how clergy in England could hold livings, and yet not be resident. In 1807, it is estimated that nearly two-thirds of English Anglican clergy did not live in their parishes. Such problems were by no means confined to England. As Stephen Prickett notes, 'similar ecclesiastical laxity was widespread throughout Europe'.[9]

If the uniform development of clergy and churches – whether ontological or functional – cannot be proved, then one of the key tasks of the practical theologian is to pay deep and serious attention to the context of ministry, and to the applied discipline of historiography in relation to theological constructions of ministry. We have already hinted that the work of Urban Holmes (1971), amongst others, offers

---

[9] Prickett, *Narrative, Religion and Science*, p. 141.

exemplary insight into the role of context and culture in the fashioning of ministry. He is keenly aware, for example, that its recent development has been linked to its own self-perception of decline. The church, if you like, believes in its own myths of secularization, and then re-narrates itself accordingly. Faced with the bewildering lack of interest in (or, more accurately, adherence to) official religion that has emerged in the post-war era, clergy have often been tempted to compensate for their declining status by aligning themselves with new, emerging professions such as counselling[10] Others have concluded that the strictures and doctrinaire ambience of religion has a deleterious effect upon the image of the church, and have sought either to rescue 'the kingdom of God' from the clutches of the church, or alternatively abandon the church in favour of embracing a more appealing account of spiritual and postmodern Christianity.

In each case, the key to understanding the evolutionary development of the church and its ministers is learning to deconstruct the prevailing myths and histories upon which current perceptions are built. Moreover, in so doing, one invariably encounters biblically-resourced functional or ontological accounts of ministry, which act as authoritative guides to the past, present and future. One of the key tasks of theology, I hold, is to be more honest about the ambiguity of its own sources. It is to this exercise that we now turn, focusing on the development of clerical identity by exploring three key areas: financing and its relation to ministerial praxis (sources of sustenance); the sense of place and parochial identity (the environment); and the development of pastoral ministry in relation to the changes. A final and brief meditation looks at clerical clothing (the evolution of specialist 'plumage'), and the development of distinctive modes of religious (professional) attire.

Sustenance and evolving identity: the funding of ministry

One of the most vexing questions faced in the Church of England today is this: how can it be afforded? The question permeates almost every level of debate on structure, viability and mission. From theological colleges to continuing ministerial education, and from diocese to national headquarters, there is no escaping the financial vagaries and uncertainties that question every appointment, initiative and commitment. An editorial in *The Economist* (US edition) explains the problem plainly:

> The Church of England is suffering from poverty. It has been in a financial fix before, most famously in the 1980s when the Church

[10] Holmes, *Future Shape of Ministry*, p. 139ff.

Commissioners lost money in high-risk commercial property deals. The commissioners, who manage the church's large portfolio of stock exchange and property assets, do better now...[but] the current problem is that the church has underestimated how much it will have to pay in pensions...the income from the Church Commissioners that would normally go to the parishes to support the everyday work of the church now largely has to make good the shortfall...[income handed] over to the parishes has dropped...retired clergy live longer... As a result, the dioceses, which rely for their income largely on gifts from churchgoers, are being asked to provide an extra eleven million pounds a year to keep the church running. Already it is estimated that three-quarters of the dioceses are in the red. The dioceses are urgently exploring ways of preventing the church from going broke.[11]

Yet this analysis only scratches the surface of the problem. As I have recently argued,[12] the Church of England has yet to adapt to the emergent paradigm in which it finds itself; one in which a comprehensive national ministry is now funded by *congregations* rather than its parishes. True, as a 'spiritual public service' to the nation, the Church of England continues to enjoy a high degree of public support at many levels. Occasional offices (e.g., baptisms, weddings, funerals), national religious rites and service (e.g., at times of national grief or celebration, or involvement in politics, education and social situations) and in regional representation (e.g., regeneration initiatives, etc.) all underline the fact that the Church of England continues to serve its people. But all of its people do not fund the church, and in any case have only done so haphazardly throughout its history.

In bygone eras, the tithing of the whole community supported the local parish church – both the building and the clerical stipend. Up until the sixteenth century, non-payment of tithes could mean excommunication; non-attendance could merit a fine. But fines were always difficult to collect and seldom imposed; excommunications were almost unheard of. The practice of tithing was always haphazard, and it waned quickly in direct proportion to the growth of industrialization throughout the eighteenth and nineteenth centuries.[13] Parliamentary reforms in 1836 tried to regularize tithing by replacing the notoriously chaotic 10 per cent levy imposed on all produce (e.g., hay, milk, fish, cheese and any other harvest), with a rental charge imposed on land.

[11] 'Counting the Doomsday Option: Church of England – Another Public Service is in Crisis', *The Economist* (USA edition), 1st September 2001.
[12] Martyn Percy, *Salt of the Earth: Religious Resistance in a Secular Age* (Sheffield: Sheffield Academic Press, 2002), pp. 336–44.
[13] See N.J.G. Pounds, *A History of the English Parish* (Cambridge: Cambridge University Press, 2000), pp. 213ff; Russell, *The Clerical Profession*, p. 128; and Percy, *Salt of the Earth*.

But even this could not last, and in 1864 the law abolished the 'Church Rate' (which had been re-imposed in 1661). As late as 1935 there was a demonstration against tithes in Kent, at which an effigy of the Archbishop of Canterbury was burnt.[14] The practice of paying a tithe on land was finally abolished by the Tithe Act of 1936.[15]

What the Church Rate had tried to do was to put established religion on a more comfortable footing, as it obliged parishioners to financially support their parish church (irrespective of their beliefs). But the cultural and industrial revolutions of the seventeenth and eighteenth centuries questioned this arrangement intensely. Parliament passed the Toleration Act in 1689, enshrining religious freedom in law: and the freedom to worship where you wished inevitably inferred permission to support your own religion in your own way – and to not subsidize the established church. By the last quarter of the nineteenth century, the foundations for the present anomaly were already laid, namely the bifurcation of the economy of the parish with that of the welfare of the parish church. However, parish churches were to be open and available to their respective resident populations, and were to minister to them accordingly. But the cost of that ministry was borne, not by the parish, but by the congregations themselves, and in collaboration with the Ecclesiastical Commissioners.[16] In the twentieth century, further reforms to the financing of the Church of England placed more power in central and diocesan hands. In 1976 the Endowments and Glebe Measure vested all land and its management in the hands of the diocese.

In terms of the viability of churches, there is an increasing historical consciousness amongst the laity that questions the apparently inalienable 'myth' that most communities have always been served by a local parish church. In Sheffield, for example, the nineteenth century opened with there being only three churches.[17] To cope with the increasing population, the Ecclesiastical Commissioners divided the town in 1846 into twenty-five parishes. By 1914 (the year the diocese was created), that number had increased to forty-seven, serving a population of some 450,000. But many of these churches were built by specious 'popular' or 'local' subscription rather than levy, or by private endowment. In other words, the character of many mid-late Victorian foundations for

---

[14] M. Hinton, *The Anglican Parochial Clergy: A Celebration* (London: SCM Press), p. 81.

[15] Victorian Parliaments passed a large number of Acts that related to the financing of the church. The Church Building Act of 1818 encouraged the building of new churches with a £1 million government grant. The Irish Tithe owners were allowed to recover arrears through an Act of 1833. The Established Church Act of 1836 redistributed revenue to poorer churches.

[16] The Church Commissioners were created in 1948, an amalgamation of the Ecclesiastical Commissioners and Queen Anne's Bounty (Russell, *The Clerical Profession*, p. 268).

[17] Odom, *Fifty Years of Sheffield Church Life*, p. 8.

parish churches was primarily *congregational*, even if parochial concerns also motivated the agenda.

The paying of proper attention to congregations and their fiscal narratives is an important theological and ecclesial task. It serves to remind church leaders and dioceses that the primary resourcing of the Church of England is from the local *to* the local. Moreover, the local and the congregational are theologically significant locations where the story of witness and its recollection continues to shape and characterize the ministry of the church. Too often dioceses or central church structures assume that the meta-organization is essential and that the local is small and therefore expendable. In truth, the reverse is true. The Church of England survived more than adequately for many centuries without the substantial national, regional and diocesan resources it presently enjoys. For many parishioners, their primary experience of the Church of England is a local one, occasionally tempered with a visit from the bishop, or an incident in the media in which the Church of England, as 'established' religion, provides occasion for what Wesley Carr terms 'national gossip'.

And as we have already hinted, the evolving identity of parishes and their self-understanding has been accompanied by a similar shift in self-perception for clergy. Even in the nineteenth century, there were wide variations in clergy pay. In 1854 the Archbishop of Canterbury was paid £19,000 a year; but a Curate received only £50 a year. Measures were taken throughout the Victorian era to try and close the gap between excessive wealth and the poverty that the clerical stipends delivered. But there were still some odd anomalies. The twelve canons of Durham cathedral received £3000 a year each, and the Dean of Durham was also the Bishop of St David's.[18] But by 1957 the average clerical income was one fifth of the pay of barristers, doctors, solicitors and dentists – a radical shift from the comparative parity of the mid-nineteenth century. Today, as Russell notes, 'a clerical family with no other income other than a stipend and with two children qualifies for...income supplement...in some parishes both the vicar and assistant priest are dependent on social security for some part of their total income.'[19]

Behind these assertions lurks the deeper question we have touched on previously: what kind of creature is the clergyperson? It is normal for most trained clergy today to assume that they are 'professional', and that in being ordained, they join, in effect, a profession. But this understanding of the clergy is comparatively recent, and a brief understanding of their financial history is essential if we are to move forward with the parallel financial questions. In Anthony Russell's ground-breaking *The Clerical Profession* (1980), we are introduced to the idea that the clergy only became 'professionalized' in the late nineteenth century, as they gradually lost their stake-holdings as landowners,

---

[18] Towler and Coxon, *Fate of the Anglican Clergy*, pp. 16–17.
[19] Russell, *The Clerical Profession*, p. 269.

gentlemen, magistrates, almoners, arbitrators, essayists, political figures and generators of improvement in health, education and overall social well-being. The rapid industrialization of society squeezed clergy out of many 'soft' mainstream public roles or diffuse role obligations, and created the pressure for a new intensification of identity, or what we call 'professionalization':

> As a result of these processes, the clergy of the mid-nineteenth century were disposed to accord greater significance to that central and irreducible religious function of the priestly role, the leadership of public worship. In this element of his role at least the clergyman had a monopoly of legitimate function. In an age which came to accord high status those who possessed socially useful technical knowledge, the clergy, by their emphasis on liturgical studies, attempted to become technologists of the sanctuary.[20]

The Oxford Movement helped this process along, with its emphasis on frequent celebration of Holy Communion, and a fondness for inventing rubrics, customs and protocol. Clergy now wore albs, amices, cinctures and stoles. The communion cup was now augmented with a Pall, Priest's wafer, Paten, Purificator and Corporal, together with a Ciborium, Lavabo bowl and jugs, and cruets. (The putting of these together, in the right order, can resemble the kinds of instructions one sometimes sees for self-assembly furniture.) Less than fifty years earlier, most English people had only been used to receiving the sacrament once a year – and it was a much simpler affair.

The Evangelical revival also encouraged the intensification of professional identity, with an emphasis on discipline, systematic visiting, and schools for preaching and catechizing. As we noted earlier, within a very short space of time, English clergy began to dress differently from other 'gentlemanly professions' in everyday wear by sporting dog-collars, something they had not done previously.[21] Furthermore, clergy were now being 'trained' at special theological colleges rather than taught divinity at university (another new development),[22] which also enhanced the emerging professional identity.

This rapid development in professionalization would normally be something that is welcomed in the vocational or occupational spheres of work. But in ministry, its status as a 'profession' has never been something that could be easily agreed upon. Neither, for that matter,

---

[20] Russell, *The Clerical Profession*, p. 40. See also J. Robins, 'Doing God's work, but denied rights as employees', *The Observer*, 11 September 2005, p. 203.
[21] G. Parsons, *Religion in Victorian Britain*, vol. IV (Manchester: Manchester University Press, 1988), p. 25.
[22] For an American perspective on the nineteenth century, see D. Scott, *From Office to Profession: The New England Ministry 1750–1850* (Pennsylvania: University of Pennsylvania Press, 1978).

has it ever been something the Church of England could easily afford. As Russell notes, the number of paid clergy dropped steadily throughout the twentieth century: there were 25,000 in 1901, and less than half that number one hundred years later.[23] The number of residential theological colleges in the same period has dropped from forty to eleven. Yet in the midst of this, clergy have shown a marked reluctance to be reformed in line with other professions, even as their social and cultural 'capital' has steadily declined. The Paul Report of 1964 (*The Deployment and Payment of Clergy*) recommended the abolition of freehold, but aligned it with better proposals for pay and working conditions. The Report and its recommendations were defeated by the Church Assembly, the precursor to the General Synod. The Morley Report (1967: *Partners in Ministry*) made similar suggestions on the security and status of clergy, but it too was defeated by the clergy, who feared for the loss of their freehold. The attitude of the clergy towards too much professionalization is summed up neatly in a letter to *The Times*, written by a clergyman in 1957:

> The parochial clergy of the Church of England are becoming transformed into the salaried members of a diocesan staff, living in houses provided and maintained for them on incomes fixed and guaranteed by diocesan stipend funds'.[24]

The disdain towards equality and uniformity expressed in this letter may seem paradoxical to some. After all, do the clergy not want to be treated like professionals, in which their rights, privileges and salaries are guaranteed? The answer is both 'yes' and 'no'. 'Yes', in the sense that they want to be regarded as specialist purveyors of knowledge, rites and techniques – 'technologists of the sanctuary'. But 'no' in the sense that they do not want to be rationalized or organized into a properly hierarchical or accountable body, in which their right to freedom and dissent is jeopardized.

Perhaps inevitably, various categories of minister have sprung up in the gap created by the smaller numbers of paid priests in the Church of England, and also to reflect the ambivalent attitude that prevails in relation to ministerial provision. As Russell candidly notes, 'proposals have been placed before the Church in almost every decade in the last 120 years'. Schemes have ranged from a voluntary diaconate (first proposed in the mid-nineteenth century, but regularly resurrected as an idea) to Auxiliary Pastoral Ministry (APM), which was later to become known as Non-Stipendiary Ministry (NSM). Many dioceses now have Ordained Local Ministers (OLM). In addition to these categories, the number of 'sector ministers' – chaplains in hospitals, the armed services, prisons and education – has risen significantly. The blurring of

---

[23] Russell, *The Clerical Profession*, p. 263.
[24] Russell, *The Clerical Profession*, p. 271.

the boundaries between full-time and part-time ministry, and the emergence of 'house-for-duty' clergy, has also meant that there are difficulties in specifying what constitutes 'professional' ministry in the Church of England; it no longer means 'paid', if it ever once did.

Having a very basic understanding of the convoluted evolution of 'professional' ministry is important if we are to return to the question of financing the ministry of the Church of England in the near future. We have already noted that nationally, resources are stretched. At the level of the local congregation, much of the narrativity about funding is conditioned by anxiety and pressure. Clearly, the impasse will eventually have to be broken. One answer may be to have more and more OLM and NSM clergy, but this might undermine the value of those who are in paid full-time ministry. There is also some ambivalence about providing greater numbers of 'cheaper' clergy, which, hitherto, few in the Church of England have been willing to face.

Eventually, the Church of England will have to face the complex evolution of its sustenance, and in so doing begin to face its future in a realistic rather than an idealistic way. At what point does the 'supplement' become a major part of the staple diet? Other solutions will undoubtedly include reducing the number of churches in cities, towns and villages; in effect reversing the avaricious tendencies of the Victorians, who built too many churches.[25] But the closure and merger of parishes creates resentment, and of course whilst saving some money, may also lead to the further loss of income: a parish church that no longer exists ceases to contribute funds to its diocese. Another solution may be to slim down diocesan staffing to skeletal levels, sharing out the work across regions (trans-diocesan) or amongst ministers. But each of these options is fraught with difficulties, and will not make a decisive difference to the endemic financial crisis the ministry of the Church of England faces:

> When great institutions decline they do not suddenly fall over a precipice; they simply slide down the slope, a little further each year, in a genteel way, making do in their reduced circumstances, like a spinster in an Edwardian novel.[26]

The purpose of this brief sketch has been to illustrate how much the status and identity of clergy has depended on fiscal sustenance – an area that is generally neglected within theological reflection. However, close attention to the history of monetary support for ministry allows us to

---

[25] In consulting Odom's history of Anglican churches in Sheffield, it is interesting to note that some of those churches built in the mid and late nineteenth century did not even survive to be counted amongst the congregations of the city when the diocese was inaugurated in 1914 (Odom, *Fifty Years of Sheffield Church Life*, p. 31).
[26] Lord (Kenneth) Baker, from a speech in the House of Lords, and quoted in *The Economist*, 16 November 2002, p. 11.

make three distinct observations within the context of evolutionary development. First, and perhaps obviously, wealth creates the basis for independence. In both the pre-Reformation and Hanoverian age, when religious orders or parish clergy were economically prosperous, 'religious professionals' enjoyed power and status, and were comparatively free to define their role within society. Second, despite enjoying considerable power and status in society, there was widespread resentment directed at religious prosperity, which may have alienated large sections of the public. Third, when the wealth of the church began to disappear, clergy were inevitably pressed into deeper collusive alliances with their congregations and dioceses, who were quickly becoming responsible for providing their funding. This led, inevitably, to a gradual loss of independence for parochial clergy, which in turn led to the profession becoming less desirable amongst the middle and upper classes from which clergy had traditionally been recruited.

Yet, as John Dolan notes, the relationship between clergy, congregations and money has affected all other denominations, including those that sought to minister within a working-class culture:

The people are groaning under the pecuniary burdens which are imposed upon them from time to time. One collection follows another in rapid succession, and they never know where the misery will end. There are more than seventy collections every year, either public or private – was this always the case? We answer, It was not; a time was, when Methodist preachers had little more than fifty pounds per annum; their wants then were few, they laboured for souls, and success in their labours was to them a sufficient recompense. Superfine coats, water-proof hats, silk stockings and gold watches were never the object of their pursuits. Surely, Sir, this cannot be said for the present race of Methodist Preachers.[27]

To put this in slightly starker terms, the independence and diversity of clergy can be linked to the sources of its sustenance. The fewer the victuals, the more likely it is that clerical identity will be both thinned and compressed. That may mean parish clergy developing a more concrete professional identity, in order to counter-act the loss of independence to local (congregational) power and increasing centralization. At the same time, this also accounts for the comparatively recent proliferation of specialist ministries (e.g., chaplaincies), which offer clergy the opportunity to flex their muscles in a more independent way within environments that tend to have less specific demands in terms of role and function. Whilst the fiscal rewards within these new environs may vary, it is important to see that part of what the attraction of chaplaincy now represents for many clergy is the recovery of a sense

[27] J. Dolan, *The Independent Methodists: A History* (Cambridge: James Clarke & Co., 2005), p. 48.

of freedom in ministry that it is rare to find in parochial ministry today, but which was relatively common in the eighteenth century.

Spatial awareness: evolving clergy and their environments

If the evolution of clerical identity can be linked to its forms of sustenance, it follows that the environment in which it operates will also figure as a key aspect of its development. Like any other living organism, the church and its clergy belong to a context. No matter what functional or ontological statements may be made about the timelessness or otherness of the church, it is also a place in the here and now that has to co-exist with other forms of life and sociality. As an institution, it is in competition for the time, resources, desires and interests of people. The wider space which it in inhabits is contested, both in purpose and meaning. Even in its own space, which it may determine to be 'sacred' in a particular way, it will discover that the meanings prescribed can be interpreted in other ways.

That said, the English parish church is part and parcel of the cultural furniture of the nation. To some it is 'more than a place of denominational worship. It is the stage on which the pageant of the community has been played out for a millennium'.[28] For others it is the natural focus of the community, 'markers and anchors. . .repositories of all embracing meanings pointing beyond the immediate to the ultimate. . .[the] only institutions that deal in tears and concern themselves with the breaking points of human existence'.[29] Still for others, the parish church is a place of Christian witness within a defined community. It is the *ekklesia* of the *parochia*;[30] the means of spiritual sustenance, ethical endeavour and social shaping within a given community that becomes 'the social skin of the world. . .always laid out in particular ways, *ordered* in such a way as to be suitable for its place'.[31]

To be sure, these idealist descriptions of the parish church all have their merit. But what does it mean to talk about a parish church today? The question is a timely one when one considers the various subtle and inimical forces that appear to have eroded the identity of a parish church. Religious pluralism has been a feature of the landscape of English religion since the Reformation; a parish church is no longer the sole focus for the religious rituals of its people, nor for their spiritual aspirations. Changes in population and churchgoing habits have also left their mark. Robin Gill has remarked on the Victorian inclination to

---

[28] S. Jenkins, *England's One Thousand Best Churches* (London: Allen Lane, 1999), p. 3.
[29] G. Davie, *Religion in Britain Since 1945* (Oxford: Blackwell, 1994), p. 189.
[30] Pounds, *History of the English Parish*, pp. 37–40.
[31] D. Hardy, *God's Ways with the World* (Edinburgh: T&T Clark, 1996), p. 27.

build greater numbers of churches and of larger sizes, even in areas where substantial depopulation was occurring.[32]

And yet there have been many other periods when the apparent over-provision of church buildings effectively threatened parochial sustainability and viability. For example, Winchester could once claim to be 'the most over-churched city in England',[33] with, in the twelfth century, a cathedral, two monasteries and at least 57 churches for a population serving no more than 8,000 people; that is, one parish church for every 130 people. (Similar figures are cited by Pounds for Worcester, York, Norwich and other medieval towns and cities.) But what did 8,000 people *do* with 57 churches and a cathedral? It would appear that these churches, although mostly proper parish churches insofar as the *parochia* supported the *ekklesia*, were made up of congregations serving relatively small communities. It was economically viable then, but only just. By 1535, the number of parish churches in Winchester had fallen to just 13 – a quarter of the number for the twelfth century.

The idea of a parish church can be said, to some extent, to be a bit of an evolutionary accident, even as it may be theologically defensible and desirable. As Pounds points out, the Saxon age is the first phase in the development of the concept. The *parochia* was a partly secular and partly sacred arrangement. Minster churches – hundreds were dotted around England – devolved spiritual responsibility to smaller *parochia* that were charged with the task of ministering to local communities. Minster churches themselves owed their very existence to royal estates or other dimensions of the feudal system granting rights, privileges and land to the church. A parish was, primarily, a governable and economically viable agrarian or urban community that could not only pay its secular taxes, but could also afford its spiritual duties. In Saxon England, as today, it cost money to be buried in a churchyard. Even then a system of tithing existed to support the ministry and fabric of the church, which was to survive well into the nineteenth century. In short, the viability of a church was deeply connected to the viability of a community; church and parish lived in a relation of intra-dependence. Payment of fees to the church meant that the poor were cared for, sacramental ministry provided, the dead buried honourably, and the moral welfare of the community was generally catered for – although the secular authorities were mainly responsible for enforcing the law. The church needed a parish; and the parish needed its church.

As we noted earlier in this chapter, one of the great paradoxes of late modernity is that churches believe in the steady decrease of public faith almost more than any other group. During the last half of the twentieth century, it has been popular to believe in a new credo: secularization. Promoted by a few busy sociologists in league with disenchanted voices in the media, the faith is simple enough. The more advanced or modern

---

[32] Robin Gill, *The Myth of the Empty Church* (London: SCM Press, 1992).
[33] Pounds, *History of the English Parish*, p. 123.

society becomes, the less it looks to the spiritual and the religious. Ergo, church attendance declines, and the once golden age of Christendom, at least in the West, is coming to its end. The thesis appears to be supported by statistics; less people go to church than, say, a hundred years ago, so the long-term prognosis seems to be correct. Correspondingly, the churches suffer from what might be termed a 'collective low-grade (but not clinical) depression', believing themselves to be in the grip of a neuralgic pathology, and increasingly inclined towards panaceas that deal with symptoms, but seldom causes.

As with most things, the truth is not nearly so simple. We now know enough about churchgoing habits to make a more sober, less bleak judgement about the parish church. It doesn't take a mathematical genius to figure out that churchgoers who once went 52 times a year (and on high days and holy days), but now only go 47 times a year (allowing for vacations) leads to a 10 per cent drop in attendance. But there are not 10 per cent fewer people attending church; what has changed is the performance of the worshippers. It may be the case that more people come to church less frequently, and that *regular* church-going is in decline, but the appetite for occasional church attendance seems undiminished. Granted, fewer people belong, formally, to a Christian denomination when compared to the inter-war or Victorian periods. But almost all forms of voluntary association have declined steeply since those days. As Robert Putnam perceptively points out,[34] associational disconnection is an endemic feature of modern life; but, ironically, churches are holding up far better than many of their secular voluntary and associational counterparts.

But surely there is some truth in the idea that fewer people are turning to official or mainstream religion? To a large extent, the answer will depend on what periods in history are being compared to the present. For example, the Victorian period saw a revival of religion and religious attendance that lasted for about forty years. Yet the beginning of the eighteenth and nineteenth centuries were eras that were very much the opposite of this: church attendance was, on the whole, derisory. Even though a system of fines for non-attendance persisted late into the Middle Ages, the penalties were notoriously difficult to enforce; and anyway, only the head of the household was required to attend church – children, wives, servants and those who were ill were always excused.

In a rather different vein, James Woodforde's *Diary of a Country Parson* provides an invaluable window into the life of the clergy and the state of English Christianity in the eighteenth century. Woodforde clearly thinks it is reasonably good to have 'two rails' (or around thirty communicants) at Christmas or Easter, from 360 parishioners. Such figures would be low by today's standards in some rural communities.

---

[34] Robert Putnam, *Bowling Alone: The Collapse and Revival of American Community* (London and New York: Simon & Schuster, 2000).

Woodforde tells us that the only time his church is ever full is when a member of the Royal family is ill, or when there is a war on. Generally, the context of his ministry is one where he baptizes (in the parlour of his home, the church being 'too cold'), marries and buries the people of his parish, but the week-by-week Sunday attendance is not something that would force many ministers of today into a frenzy of excitement. But Woodforde is not bothered by this – not because he is especially lazy – but because the *totality* of his contact with his parish constitutes his ministry. He is *with* his people in all their trials and tribulations, not just his congregation. He is their man for all seasons; an incarnate presence in the midst of a community that waxes and wanes in its religious affections.[35]

More could be said about the apparent indifference of the English towards their parish church, but space does not permit. What needs to be stressed in this short section is that the parish church and the ministry that issued from it was, generally speaking, greatly valued by the parish. However, that valuing did not necessarily translate into frequent and intense church attendance on the part of the masses. Mostly, it seems that the English have tended to *relate* to their parish churches in a variety of ways; it partly reflects a relationship of affection (sometimes grudging), of vicarious religion (of having others to believe in those things that one can't quite be so certain of – 'say one for me, padre', etc.), and of 'believing without belonging', to borrow the oft-quoted maxim of Grace Davie. Certainly, it can be asserted that statistical surveys continually support the thesis that England is a place where the vast majority of the population continues to affirm their belief in God, but then proceed to do little about it. So although church attendance figures remain stubbornly low, it does not follow that this is a modern malaise. It is, rather, a fairly typical feature of many western societies down the ages. Granted, there have been periods of revival when church attendance has peaked. But the basic and innate disposition of the English is typical of Western Europe – one of believing without belonging. Of relating to the church, and valuing its presence and beliefs – yet without necessarily sharing them. Or, as the ageless witticism expresses it: 'I cannot consider myself to be a pillar of the church, for I never go. But I am a buttress – insofar as I support it from the outside.'

With these brief reflections in mind, we now turn to the ambiguity of the parish church in contemporary English culture. The idea of a 'parish' may seem to be obvious to many: still part of the cultural furniture, and sufficiently resonant to command attention and respect. For many established churches worldwide, the parish is the fundamental unit of organization, the 'place' where the church is located. It is

---

[35] J. Beresford, *James Woodforde: The Diary of a Country Parson* (Norwich: Canterbury Press, 1999), p. vii. For further discussion, see A. Russell, *The Country Parson* (London: SPCK, 1993).

odd, then, that so little attention has been focused upon identifying what a parish is and means, particularly in relation to theology, ministry and ecclesiology.

As many ministers of religion already know, the shape and content of parish ministry has altered radically over the last century. An increasingly professionalized clergy, coupled with an uneasy mutation in public perceptions of parochial identity, have led to some profound and subtle shifts. Whilst clergy are still all curates – with the 'cure of souls' for the whole parish – it is becoming less and less clear in a mobile, transient, globalized and compressed world what might be meant by terms such as 'community', 'local' and 'place', let alone 'parish'. 'Parish visiting' used to be a standard feature of many parochial ministries, but its tenure as a staple part of the average clergy timetable has been all too brief. Whilst Woodforde and his parsonic predecessors (e.g., George Herbert) were often wont to call upon their parishioners for a mixture of social, secular and sacred reasons, it was the Victorians who developed what was a pastoral habit into a systematic discipline – but with mixed results. Wickham's study of religion in industrial cities confirms that, typically, out of one street of hundreds of residents, 'you perhaps see a solitary instance where a whole household of several persons are regular attenders'.[36] Gerald Parson's study of Victorian Christianity clearly shows that, in spite of the clergy cultivating a professionalism (including, as we noted earlier, the sporting of 'dog-collars' from about 1860, the first time clergy had really begun to dress differently to mark them out in day-to-day wear from other gentlemanly professions), the vast majority of the population remained unmoved, and didn't take 'serious Christianity' that seriously.[37]

Whilst it is true that rates of churchgoing were buoyant during the Victorian era, the peaks and troughs of church-attendance figures have nearly always depended as much upon cultural factors (e.g., the shifting population from agrarian to industrial contexts, or in the case of the Billy Graham evangelistic campaigns of the post-war era, the shift from cities to a new suburbia) as they have on the intensity of engagement between a church and its parish. Thus, the 'serious Christianity' of the Victorian era engaged in intense parochial ministry for a mixture of reasons: baptism visiting was especially encouraged, but the development of Sunday Schools and Adult Bible Classes, which flourished between 1875 and the late Edwardian period, owed as much to the desire to encourage education and self-improvement as it did to anything else.

So far as one can tell, the impact of all this expended effort was somewhat limited. Parish churches and their ministers throughout the nineteenth century were, in effect, being forced to re-invent their connectedness to the parish. The obligation of tithing was withering, if

---

[36] Wickham, *Church and People*, p. 14.
[37] Parsons, *Religion in Victorian Britain*, p. 25.

not altogether defunct, which meant that the parish now had no necessary economic relationship with its church. As we have already noted, tithing was a mixed blessing for the parish church. In general, it was not resented by most parishes; people understood that this was their due to God, and the church was merely the collector. But many did resent the manner of collection, and to what ends the monies were used for. Some complained that they were taxed several times over: once for the grass, then for the hay, then for the milk, and then for the cheese – and finally for the cow too. This led to some disgruntled protests, such as pouring a tenth of the milk yield all over the chancel steps. Even as late as the eighteenth century there was a riot in the Cornish fishing village of Madron when the rector attempted to collect the tithe of fish. The fisherman argued that parish boundaries did not extend into the Atlantic Ocean; the clergyman replied that they were landed on the soil of his parish, and he was entitled to his due.[38]

It was only a question of time before the literal payment in kind of a tenth of all yields was ended; what worked haphazardly for agrarian economies would never translate into the emerging industries of the late eighteenth century. The Tithe Commutation Act duly came into force in 1836. (However, it would be another century before tithing was finally phased out, as rents and glebe land persisted well into the twentieth century.) But consider, for example, this description of Charles Darwin's father, and his hope for Charles' career in the church:

> Dr Darwin, a confirmed freethinker, was sensible and shrewd. He had only to look around him, recall the vicarages he had visited, and ponder the country parsons he entertained at home. One did not have to be a believer to see that an aimless son with a penchant for field sports would fit in nicely. Was the Church not a haven for dullards and dawdlers, the last resort of spendthrifts? What calling but the highest for those whose sense of calling was nil? And in what other profession were the risks of failure so low and the rewards so high? The Anglican Church, fat, complacent, and corrupt, lived luxuriously on its tithes and endowments, as it had for a century. Desirable parishes were routinely auctioned off to the highest bidder. A fine rural 'living' with a commodious rectory, a few acres to rent or farm, and perhaps a tithe barn to hold the local levy worth hundreds of pounds a year could easily be bought as an investment by a gentleman.[39]

But fundamentally, parish churches and their ministers were gradually becoming disconnected from the local economy. The 'church-rate' that levied a tax on local people for the upkeep of the parish church was abolished by law in 1864, leading to the present anomalous situation,

---

[38] Pounds, *History of the English Parish*, p. 213.
[39] Desmond and Moore, *Darwin*, p. 47.

whereby the whole parish has access to the parish church for baptisms, weddings, funerals and other rites, but only the congregation are obliged to pay for the upkeep of the building. In short, the experience of Victorian parochial ministry was one of more intense engagement as the parish and the church underwent rapid bifurcation, with the parish – as a space – ceasing to be defined in ecclesiastical or spiritual terms, and collapsing back into its secular shape, only this time it was ordered by boroughs and civic authorities. Or, to put it another way, the increasing loss of the parish as a recognized 'space' that began in Victorian England – a product of industrialization, capitalism and early globalization – led to the parish church becoming a more intense *spiritual* place, and to the clergy being more obviously differentiated as a professional class, replete with their own separate colleges for training and formation (not something that had existed in previous centuries).

But where do these reflections on spatial awareness now take us? In her book *Space, Place and Gender*,[40] Doreen Massey, a geographer with interests in cultural theory, feminist theory, philosophy and sociology, makes a number of pertinent and illuminating points in relation to our discussion of the *ekklesia* and the *parochia*. First, places are only defined in relation to or over and against other places. Second, places have many identities – they are not flat or static. Third, place and community do not necessarily correlate. Whilst there may be a longing for such coherence, it is important to grasp that communities are often at odds with their environments. (In distinguishing between 'place' and 'space', I adopt fairly simple definitions based on the etymology of the terms. 'Space' refers to a defined area, whereas 'place' stipulates the additional value, identity and definition attributed to *something* in that space. Or, put more simply, 'place' tends to be a more socially constructed idea than 'space', although even the idea of 'space' requires some social definition.)

In order to explore these ambiguities further, let us briefly return to Millhouses for a moment, where we began this essay. It is the former parish of Oliver Tomkins, being a small suburb nestling in the city of Sheffield. The place name comes from a ruined Abbey a few miles down the road, which was built in 1178 by a penitent knight who was implicated in the assassination of Thomas à Becket. So Millhouses owes its origins to a Frenchman, who built the Abbey on the farthest extent of the Arch-Episcopal province of Canterbury. Over the centuries, Millhouses moved away from (very modest) agrarian dependency to water-powered mills making metals and machines. The area prospered. Today the area mostly comprises post-Edwardian housing, whose residents are either retired or youngish-middle-aged people who are working in professions or middle-management – the 'posher' parishes

---

[40] Doreen Massey, *Space, Place and Gender* (Cambridge: Polity Press, 1994).

lie on its borders. Today, the parish numbers 4,000, but with over a third of the area still covered in protected woodland.

Yet that is only one way of describing Millhouses. In terms of education, the infant and junior schools are amongst the most sought after in the city, which has pushed up the house prices; education by postcode. The parish also falls in the right catchment area for the best secondary schools. Yet in the parish itself, there is a struggling secondary modern school, which draws all its pupils from the poorer parts of the city, including those from the ethnically diverse neighbouring parish. So, every day, there are bus loads of children of every ethnic colour and hue coming to school at the bottom of Millhouses Lane, whilst there are (four-wheeled drive) car loads of children, mostly caucasian, who leave the top of Millhouses Lane for other schools. In other words, even in a largely unselfconscious parish such as Millhouses, the phenomenon of what David Sibley calls 'geographies of exclusion' have to be faced.[41] Millhouses is a place where feelings and images of difference can surface, where borders are ambiguous (e.g., educational, class, work-related, residential?), and exclusion and inclusion are no longer confined to physical boundaries.

So for whom is Millhouses local? The answer is clearly 'many more than its 4,000 residents', but they are all experiencing the same shared space very differently. Commercially, the ethnic shops just outside the parish depend on custom from within the parish. But those shops face stiff competition from three large supermarkets, which are fairly 'upmarket'. So for many, either as a shop owner or shop worker, Millhouses is a place of work, and perhaps of economic struggle. Then there are the pubs competing for more than local business, and the restaurants that depend more on passing trade than residents.

Clearly, to minister in such a community would require one's attention being constantly drawn out of the parish, because the identity of the parish can never itself be settled. It is an arbitrary 'space' that is experienced in many different ways by several different types of community; yet it is also a 'place'. Whatever Millhouses is, it is not static; it is a contested place, an ambivalent locality. The 'cure of souls' for the parish necessarily and inevitably extends across the simple frontiers of residency.

But let us briefly return to the relationship between the *ekklesia* and the *parochia*. We have already noted that their identities had begun to undergo a process of bifurcation that can be dated from the Reformation, and in all probability well before that. For example, even from the early Middle Ages, it became increasingly difficult to order and police growing populations through the auspices of the local church. Courts of law, the rise of civic authorities and guilds, the need for better transport infrastructures and the like meant that many people

---

[41] David Sibley, *Geographies of Exclusion* (London: Routledge, 1995).

looked beyond their immediate parochial boundaries for their liveli-
hood. As we observed earlier, in small cities such as Winchester, what
passed for 'parochial worship' was essentially congregational in character – a parish church may just have consisted of a few extended
families worshipping together, and whatever sacramental ministry they
could afford. In turn, this dynamic emerged afresh in the wake of the
Reformation, when religious services could easily be said at home,
presided over by the head of the house, and gathered around the word
and not sacramental worship. Furthermore, the economic ties that
bound parishes to their parish churches were beginning to break down
as commerce became increasingly cosmopolitan. Increasingly, the local
mattered less and less as people became more mobile. These trends,
present long before the Renaissance, never mind the Reformation, were
only to increase during the industrial revolution. It is possible to identify
many points of interaction between the *ekklesia* and the *parochia* where
the process of bifurcation began to take root, but two are singled out for
further discussion here: birth and death.

The evolution of pastoral offices: baptism and funerals

Minster churches had once monopolized the rite of baptism; it was a
sacrament undertaken by patronal churches, and the origin of the
phrase 'mother church' partly lies in this sequential control. Under the
Saxon Minster system, there were chapels and places of worship that
were the *parochiae* of the Minster, but these places rarely had fonts of
their own. The fight to acquire the status of parish church was thus
often about local autonomy and prestige, and against the interests of the
Minster – and perhaps even about finance. Although there was no fee
levied for the sacrament of baptism, there was inevitably some financial
benefit that accrued to the Minster by controlling who was admitted to
the sacred fold (and, by implication, who was excluded, as non-
payment of tithes normally led to formal excommunication – although
the exclusion could always be overcome upon the payment of fines). To
be a parish church meant owning a font, and this in turn enabled the
local *ekklesia* to be truly a part of the *parochia* in its own right. Parish
churches symbolized not only the presence of God in the midst of a
community; they also made a powerful economic and social statement:
this is a viable, living community that can support itself and support its
God. A chapel said something different: we are dependent on another
area for our welfare.

To return to Millhouses for a moment, we can see that the history of
the local churches follows these contours neatly. All Saints Ecclesall is a
large church that sits atop a hill that would have once partially
overlooked the site of Beauchief Abbey. The original church was built
in the thirteenth century for a local dignitary who tired of the journey up
and down the hill to hear Mass at the Abbey. His solution was to give

lands to the Abbey for agriculture and milling at the bottom of the valley (Millhouses), and in return he built a chantry chapel next to his manor, and a priest from the Abbey came to him each day to say Mass. In the late nineteenth century the Millhouses area acquired its own 'chapel of ease' to accommodate the burgeoning population, and in the twentieth century it became a parish church, symbolizing the area's new-found identity.

Yet baptism is only one half of the equation that allowed medieval chapels to make the uneasy transition to parish church. The other space that was required was a graveyard. Again, economic factors may have played a part in the development of parish churches. Burials were a source of income for the priest, sexton (who dug the grave) and the church, and also allowed the community to 'own' their place of worship in a very particular way. In other words, the identity of a community could be entirely tied-up with the location of the dead, and how the living memorialized them. The right to bury the dead signified that this 'place' was not transitory, but established. Not only was it a viable economic community, it was also a place that had a history and a right to a future.

I make these observations about parish churches in Saxon and medieval times because they were clearly important in maintaining a sense of place and in creating a kind of local identity, which was secular, sacred, religious, civic, communitarian and catholic. Yet many parish churches today struggle to 'connect' with their locations in ways that are similar. In the case of births, baptismal rates have dropped steadily in England since the turn of the twentieth century, the trend accelerating with noticeable speed from the 1960s. The response of the churches, interestingly, to this loss of *extensive* connection, has been to reify baptismal rites into a more *intensive* form of religious experience. Gone are the accommodating cultural customs of bygone eras in which the clergy baptized large numbers of children at times that were mainly convenient to families (i.e., Sunday afternoons). Baptism, as a negotiated point of entry into the life of the church (and who can say where the church begins and ends?), has lost its communitarian and ambiguous feel as a social rite of passage – even the term 'Christening' is discouraged – and has been replaced by something more definitive. Namely a more demanding series of liturgies that requires the parents to say more (the 1662 *Book of Common Prayer* did not expect or demand this), with the baptismal service now more usually being situated within a normal Sunday morning service such as Matins or a Eucharist.

The effect of this is hard to measure, but it would not be unfair to say that the parish church, in its loss of extensive connectedness with its own locality, has attempted to re-engage its disparate community by becoming more intense in its religious expression and by sharpening up its actual identity. Observers may say that this is inevitable: the allegedly invasive forces of modernity such as pluralism and consumerism require commodities in every competitive environment – including the spiritual marketplace – to be clearer about their identity in order to be noticed (or differentiated) in order that they may be purchased. Yet we can also say that such a trend, if it exists, points to the lack of importance we now attach to places as spaces that provide us with our identity. We are more defined by where we can go; not by where we are.

Similar problems can be seen in relation to death. For most of the twentieth century, new churches that were built did not provide graveyards; gardens of rest for interred remains are a relatively late innovation. Death has moved, sociologically and culturally, from a commonplace event that was central to the life of all small communities and localities, to becoming something that is removed from the mainstream of society, and placed on its margins. Most deaths occur in hospitals, hospices or residential and nursing homes. The vast majority of funerals are conducted in anonymous crematoriums that form no spatial, spiritual or social attachment with the bereaved. The memorialization of the dead – once the main point and function of a parish church – has been speedily eroded by the contemporary utilitarian forces that have tidied death up (in the name of clinical cleanliness) and swept it into the corners of modern life. Death is not seen; it is not heard; it does not speak.[42] Even those graveyards that remain open and accessible are more often than not closed for burial.

Predictably, the responses of the English parish churches to this have been pragmatic and pastoral. Remembrance Sunday refuses to die, long after its veterans have all been mourned. The festival of All Souls has undergone a renaissance in recent years, as churches have sought to restore the memorialization of death and the reality of bereavement, as well as speaking of resurrection, into a relationship with the communities they serve. The spaces and places for death may no longer exist in the way they once did, but there is always the compensation of calendrical ritual. And, as many churches discovered after 11 September 2001, or after the death of Diana, Princess of Wales, an open church, in which to light a candle or say a prayer and sign a condolence book, is still the first port of call for many people, and still more usually preferred to posting a message on the web.

Our reflections so far have suggested that the gradual bifurcation of the *ekklesia* from the *parochia* was a process that began prior to the Reformation, and has been as much about economic realities as it has about anything we might call secularization. We might also add that the gradual atomization of public space – a feature of modernity stretching back to the industrial revolution – has forced the parish church to reconsider its own sense of place. It is not that long ago that parish churches were the only places within a community that could house debates, discussions and social gatherings. But their monopoly has been broken by the endemic pluralization of public space: taverns, cinemas,

---

[42] Martyn Percy, *Salt of the Earth*, pp. 315–18.

community halls, as well as competing denominations and a host of other arenas. Of course, such places have always been a feature of the English townscape, but there can be no question that public space has now become more ambiguous; there are now many centres for any one community; its focal point is seldom obvious. Arguably, the media – in its most general capacity as the purveyor of information, recording and memory – is the new public space. It would appear, then, that parish churches are beginning to lose their point. A parish, as a place, is no longer defined by its capacity to support a church or its clergy. Modern communities are unsettled and mobile, something recently conceded by the Church of England in its proposals on marriage reform. In future, banns will perhaps no longer need to be published (but they may still be said, and so remain as a 'custom'), and there will be greater freedom in choosing venues for matrimony; one need no longer be tied by the constraints of residency.

But it would be extremely premature to sound the death knell for the parish church. True, few couples who apply to be married at their local church (or the one they liked the look of, near the reception venue) appear to know which parish they belong to; it is not just the church that is lost in the complex public space of urbanity – the parish has also lost its point and identity for many people. Yet my narration of the parish church in English cultural history clearly suggests that its identity has always been evolving, so there is arguably little cause for alarm. Every generation of churchwardens has had to face an apparently insuperable set of problems ranging from apathy to poverty through to clerical negligence and absence. Indeed, all that we may say here is that the parish church is losing its identity because the concept and feel of parishes has been lost first. The next line of defence, then, is for the recognition of *local* churches, and that is arguably the key mutation of modernity for the parish church: its identity is shifting from the parochial to the local. And of course, the local church – from the Latin word *localis* – is still located and known.

Having said that, with parish churches no longer linked to the *local* economy and what that space generates in terms of wealth and income, parish churches have to re-invent themselves as places of worship that are less extrinsically linked to their communities. In that sense, it is right and proper to speak of a kind of *institutional* secularization, provided it is understood that this is not taken to mean that people are less spiritual or religious in late modernity. So where does this take us? The parish church has always been a complex pottage of competing convictions and interests, brought together in the focus of a building and a ministry, the ownership of which has always been open to interpretation. But the *ekklesia* is, after all, 'the assembly' of aspirations, hopes, memories, celebration and sacramental life, and where possible, it continues to embody the life of the *parochia*. So what the parish church needs now, arguably, is to continually rediscover this most public of ministries; one that engages with contemporary culture in interrogative, empathetic and critical-friendly ways. If it can be the place for people within a space, then the rumours of its imminent funeral are greatly exaggerated.

Conclusion: on clerical plumage

The purpose of this chapter has been to offer some observations on how the changing shape of parochial ministry, together with its funding, has impacted the environment and evolution of clerical identity. As we have noted in Chapters 1 and 2, the clerical response to the compression of their role and status has been one of increasing specialization and professionalization. This can be read as a mode of praxis that simultaneously attempts to resist culture as well as engage with it. Perhaps unsurprisingly, the expression of this dynamic finds its way into ever more distinctive and discrete understandings of ministry. The less public and the more private religion becomes, the more religious professionals acquire a specialist language and culture that sets them apart from the competition; but at the same time, there is a continual need to engage the public through distinctive modes of engagement.

As we have noted, the relatively recent history of the clerical dog-collar can be understood in this way. Because the clerical profession is no longer identified with the gentry, and the gentry, insofar as they exist, no longer have a standard way of dressing, clergy, in order to be publicly visible on a day-to-day basis, have needed to acquire a mode of dress that makes them identifiable. Moreover, and rather like the Galapagos Archipelago, we can observe some rapid evolutionary changes that reflect the nuances of specific environments. One type of collar might reflect a high churchmanship or Catholicism; another might indicate low churchmanship. Whilst these subtle differences may be lost on the public, they are noted by churchgoers, and make for easy identification. But such differentiation was not to everyone's taste, even in the Victorian age. Bishop Samuel Wilberforce, founder of Cuddesdon College, sometimes complained of his ordinands:

> I consider it a heavy affliction that they should wear neckcloths of peculiar construction, coats of peculiar cut, whiskers of peculiar dimensions – that they should walk with a peculiar step, carry their heads at a peculiar angle to the body, and read in a peculiar tone.[43]

In the year that the College was founded, the first Vicar of Wheatley had noted how the Cuddesdon students skated at nearby Shotover, 'smoking clay pipes and wearing Fez's with their cassocks'. But distinct

[43] D. Newsome, *Godliness and God Learning: Four Studies of a Victorian Ideal* (London: John Murray, 1961), p. 208. See also J.S. Reed, *Glorious Battle: The Cultural Politics of Victorian Anglo-Catholicism* (Nashville, TN: Vanderbilt University Press, 1996), pp. 75ff.

modes of dress are hardly confined to Anglo-Catholicism. Similarly, one can still find the vestiges of gentry codes of dress for clergy within discrete strains of contemporary evangelicalism. For some conservative evangelicals, brogue shoes, corduroy trousers and a sports or tweed jacket (mimicking a certain upper-class affected 'Sloane' style) will still operate as an informal uniform for some clergy in their ministry amongst the more well-heeled congregations of major cities.

Of course, the appropriation of secular dress for clerical uses is by no means new. We have no evidence that the first disciples wore anything distinctive to mark their status as apostles. But as early as the reign of Charlemagne, we find charges directed to clergy to wear sombre colours to reflect their renunciation of worldly things. This, combined with a distinctive styling of the hair (shaved partially or completely, the style varying across Eastern, Latin and Celtic regions) was all that marked belonging to Holy Orders. Indeed, as Holmes points out, the actual style of dress adopted in the first few centuries was the simple attire of the medieval peasant. As secular and sacred modes of dress evolved, the accent shifted from eliding clerical identity with poverty to that of seriousness.[44] The early medieval period saw clergy adopting long coats (later to be cassocks) – essentially the same uniform for doctors and lawyers. However, around 1300 this changed with the advent of the Renaissance, where the fashion for short coats and clothes returned. It is at this point that there was a kind of shift in the tectonic plates of clerical fashion culture. The land mass of the church broke away decisively from the public continent, and clergy continued to wear long clothes to symbolize their difference and their resistance to fashion.

However, the evolution of everyday clerical wear was by no means complete. The early version of the cassock (a long, dark 'coat' with tight sleeves) was rejected by the Reformers, who for theological reasons preferred to wear academic gowns: dark, loose and open at the front. It is important to mention, however, that the cassock had an entirely secular purpose in its day, being a coat used for horse riding, as well as the basis of the uniform for cavalry. Whilst this was worn by many clergy on the continent, Church of England clergy simply adopted the gentleman's dress of the period. In the eighteenth century, this was black knee britches, gaiters, a frock coat and white bands attached to the cravat or collar. From 1700 a tight-fitting collar (stock) was worn, to which a black silk shirt could be attached. Some clergy still wear this today, although most have adopted its evolved form: the clerical shirt, with a white plastic 'dog-collar'.

Of course, these evolutionary shifts do not take account of the development of liturgical dress, which has a rather different history. The biography of the stole, cope, chasuble and mitre: all have their own story. However, even here, one cannot escape the complexity of

---

[44] As Holmes points out, the Lateran Council of 1215 ruled against clergy wearing bright colours (*Future Shape of Ministry*, pp. 291–92).

evolution in terms of clerical attire. The wearing of maniples – once a senatorial badge of office in the Roman Empire – became translated into ecclesiastical use. But its virtual disappearance from medieval times is perhaps not as surprising as its revival under Anglo-Catholicism. This, in turn, raises a question: what is the apparent restoration of neglected clergy attire intended to achieve? For those who wear such things, I suspect the answer lies in doctrine rather than presentation; but the reverse is probably true. It is the presentational that expresses the difference, marks the culture out as discrete, and makes the ecclesiology distinctive. The emergence of the celebration of colour and dress in Anglo-Catholicism is a subconscious if deliberate evolutionary trait that separates it from its dourer Protestant relations.[45] It reflects the fact that Anglo-Catholicism was born out of a bourgeois 'Oxbridge' reactionary reflex, which essentially embraced ritualism and performance before it found any kind of theology. Revelling in the mystical, it was also bound to be anti-rational. Equally, the refusal to wear clerical clothing can also symbolize a form of ecclesial partisanship. In 1842 a dozen evangelical clergy refused to obey the Bishop of London and wear a surplice, objecting not to the garment, but what it had come to mean. Even today, some (albeit very few) Evangelical clergy will still refuse to wear a stole or alb.

However, just as the evangelical and catholic wings of the church – whether as expressions of Anglicanism, or more generally – led to expressions of presentation that to some extent reflected their theological outlook for a century or more, we should also note the arrival of some mutation in the post-war era. Charismatic renewal, for example, although primarily born and cultured within Evangelicalism and Pentecostalism, has rapidly embraced varieties of presentation that are more influenced by Catholicism. Within the Church of England, this leads to some interesting anomalies. Evangelical clergy may still wear preaching scarves rather than coloured stoles for theological and liturgical reasons. But then for other theological reasons (largely personal), they have adopted brightly coloured preaching scarves, highly decorated with symbols and motifs, rather than the more usual sober black or blue. The colour in vestments, moreover, is now matched with splashes of colour in the church building itself. There may not be altar hangings, but there are brightly coloured banners festooning the pillars and the walls. Gone are the plain whitewashed walls and a solitary table; colourful symbols surround the worshipper.[46]

In conclusion, we can point to the diversity of clerical wear as analogical expressions of differentiation and competition between the

---

[45] For a deeper discussion, see Reed, *Glorious Battle*.

[46] Similarly, African and Asian churches that have been shaped by strains of Evangelicalism that once stressed simplicity, can now be found to be revelling in colourful robes and exotic ceremony, more accurately reflecting enculturated Christianity in a post-colonial era.

species. Because competition is the engine of increase, it is natural that rivalry between different branches of the church would start to be expressed in fashion and colour, just as it is in nature. However, it is also important to remember that the emergence of distinctive clerical everyday wear from the late nineteenth century has two common environmental causes: namely, the relatively sudden realization that clergy needed to be identified apart from whatever was left of the gentry (very little from the late 1860s); and that to survive as a species, the clergy needed to become a profession in terms that the world would begin to recognize. But in Darwinian terms, this has allowed the evolution of clerical wear to develop its own separate ecosystem, unchecked by either the fashions or the attentions of the world. The results of this can be as amusing as they are unsurprising. Today, some clerical outfitters not only sell clergy shirts and other professional attire; they also offer nightwear, underwear, coats, suits, shoes and other clothes. In the separated islands of the archipelago, every environment must be utterly self-sufficient. It is precisely under these conditions that specialization begins to evolve. Darwin was able to find more than a dozen sub-species of the same giant tortoise in the handful of Galapagos Islands he visited; each had evolved according to whether they lived on high escarpment or low ground, and what kind of vegetation was available within their specific domains. As with tortoises, so it is with the clergy. It is the case that without the challenges of connectedness and competition, such contexts allow those who have become marginal and solitary to still imagine that they are dominant within their domain. And to some extent they will always be right; but their world is a small, small place.

Chapter 4

On Praxis

If the natural history of the clergy can be related to a formational environment, then it follows that certain ecclesial behavioural patterns can be traced not simply to a hermetically-sealed tradition that might be located in the past, but also to the demands and opportunities of the present. Expressed in a slightly different way, we might say that, invariably, the church forms its distinctive praxis through a relation with a quadrilateral consisting of revelation, tradition, culture and reason. Churches will differ in the weight that they give to the corner (or angle) of the quadrilateral, and it is also possible that some churches will be less than honest with themselves about the attention paid to certain quarters. But even if the quadrilateral is not seen as a kind of theological processing grid for addressing contentious and pressing issues (a crude kind of foundation for a methodology, if you like), the quadrilateral nonetheless functions (at the very least) as a reliable descriptor that indicates how ecclesial communities attempt to practise their beliefs within a wider culture. In saying this, we are merely recognizing that the prompts and cues that prod churches into reflection, action and eventual adaptation do not necessarily come from tradition or revelation, but rather occur because of environmental factors (i.e., culture), which persuade the church of the need to reconfigure its life and renegotiate its role and function within contemporary society. Traditionally, this is the ground on which pastoral and contextual theology stands, but it is also material in considering the evolution of clerical identity and ministerial praxis.

To take perhaps an obvious example, one seldom hears of many clergy boasting about the number of older people they have in church, Sunday by Sunday. It would a rare thing to meet a priest who, sitting comfortably at a Chapter Meeting with their fellow clergy, sat back and waxed lyrically about the rising number of pensioners that were now attending his or her church. Such bragging, were it to take place at all, would be read by most as a trope of some sort, or perhaps interpreted as a kind of wistful sardonic irony that was trying to make some other point. This may immediately strike one as being rather odd when one considers that many churches are actually (but quietly) rather good at attracting the older person. Older people give time, money and expertise to churches. They tend to be the church's most loyal and constant supporters. But typically, the discussion about the future of church attendance is shaped around anxieties relating to the young:

Young people are important members of the Church today, and they also hold the future in its hands. This future is by no means certain. To quote just one statistic, churches lost 155,000 teenagers between 15 and 19, from 1979 to 1989, a loss far greater than the decline of 15 to 19 year olds in the general population.[1]

There are good reasons for these types of anxieties being expressed, to be sure. Concerns about young people and the church are perfectly legitimate missiological issues that need to be addressed. But having said that, one might note that the work of the church with the young has a curiously brief history. True, in the 'golden age' of pastoral ministry (from the Reformation through to the beginning of the industrial revolution), many parish priests catechized the young as part of their priestly duties, although there was no particular or specialized outreach to young people worthy of note. George Herbert (1593–1633), for example, advises that children be admitted to Holy Communion as soon as they can distinguish between ordinary bread and consecrated bread, and when they can recite the Lord's Prayer: he estimates the age at which these things come together to be at around seven. Similarly, Parson Woodforde (1740–1803), whilst clearly showing an awareness of young people in his parish, has nothing remarkable to offer them in his ministry.

But lest this sound too complacent, the advent of the industrial revolution caused many parents to begin to dread Sundays. As the only day that was free of the toil of the factories (in which the children also worked a six-day week), church services became increasingly rowdy. With traditional village and rural ties broken, the 'new generations' of children were also less likely to be inducted into any kind of religious instruction or church custom, and there was general concern about the lapse of the young into crime and delinquency. The relatively rapid change in culture prompted an equally swift evolution of the churches and their ministry. In Gloucester, England, Robert Raikes (1735–1811), the owner and printer of the *Gloucester Journal*, decided to establish a 'Sunday School' for the children of chimney sweeps, housed in Sooty Alley, opposite the city gaol. The School began in 1780, and was an immediate success, offering general and religious education to children from the working classes. The idea of the schools spread with astonishing rapidity. By 1785 a national Sunday School Organization had been established, and many thousands of children were attending in most major cities.[2] In 1788 John Wesley wrote that: 'verily I think

[1] Sylvia Collins, 'Spirituality and Youth', in M Percy, *Calling Time: Religion and Change at the Turn of the Millennium* (Sheffield: Sheffield Academic Press, 2000), p. 221 (quoting P. Brierley, *Act on the Facts* [London: Marc Europe, 1992], p. 214).
[2] T. Kelly, *A History of Adult Education in Liverpool*, (Liverpool: Liverpool University Press, 1970), pp. 74–76.

these Sunday Schools are one of the noblest specimens of charity which have been set on foot in England since William the Conqueror'.[3]

Sunday Schools continued to spread and develop throughout the nineteenth century, with their aims and objectives altering in the course of their evolution. By 1851, three-quarters of working-class children were in attendance, and many adults too.[4] In Raike's original scheme, social action and evangelization had been the primary motivation in the formation of the schools. Yet by the mid-1800s, some scholars assert that the primary focus of the Sunday School had become a means of expressing emergent working-class values (e.g., thrift, communalism, self-discipline, industry, etc.). In other words, the Sunday Schools had become a means of providing some generational continuity and identity. Moreover, the 'associational' character of the Sunday Schools also provided a significant social environment in which young and old, male and female, could meet and interact. Thus, Joseph Lawson, writing in the 1890s, notes:

Chapels are now more inviting – have better music – service of song – which cannot help being attractive to the young as well as beneficial to all. They have sewing classes, bazaars, concerts, and the drama; cricket and football clubs, and harriers; societies for mutual improvement and excursions to the seaside.[5]

Lawson's observations from over a century ago are illuminating because they draw our attention to the fecund associational nature of Victorian religion. Indeed, this lasted, in all probability, well into the twentieth century, with religious bodies providing significant social capital, the means whereby malevolent and anti-social forces were overcome by the purposeful encouragement of 'mutual support, cooperation, trust, institutional effectiveness'.[6] Religion, in its many and varied associational forms and offshoots, provided social capital that was both bridging (inclusive across different social groups, trans-generational, gender-encompassing, etc.) and bonding (exclusive – clubs and societies for particular groups, boys clubs, girls clubs, etc.), and was therefore part of that new social culture which now obviated the generational gaps that had first awoken the reformers of the early nineteenth century. But the mid-twentieth century was to mark further changes for the churches. As Putnam notes of North America, in the 1950s roughly one in every four Americans reported membership with a

---

[3] John Wesley, *The Journals of John Wesley* (Chicago: Moody Press, 1951), p. 216. This quotation is dated from 1784.
[4] T. Laqueuer, *Religion and Respectability: Sunday Schools and Working Class Culture*, (New Haven: Yale University Press, 1976), p. 44.
[5] H. Cunningham, *Leisure in the Industrial Revolution*, (Beckingham, UK: Croom Helm, 1980), P. 181.
[6] Putnum, *Bowling Alone*, p. 22.

church-related group, but by the 1990s that figure was cut in half to one in eight. Americans now devote two-thirds less of their time to religion than they did in the 1960s.[7]

What has led to this evolutionary change? There are a variety of theories that offer 'generational change' in religious affiliation as a way of framing the causes and trajectories, and the insights, although of a fairly general nature, are useful. Putnam, for example, states that:

> The decline in religious participation, like many of the changes in political and community life, is attributable largely to generational differences. Any given cohort of Americans seems not to have reduced religious observance over the years, but more recent generations are less observant than their parents. The slow but inexorable replacement of one generation by the next has gradually but inevitably lowered our national involvement in religious activities.[8]

For Wade Clark Roof and William McKinney, the transition is marked by movement from formal religious observance and membership to 'surfing' from congregation to congregation, not belonging strongly to any one particular body of believers, and an increased appetite for spirituality:

> Large numbers of young, well-educated middle-class youth[s]... defected from the churches in the late sixties and seventies... Some joined new religious movements, others sought personal enlightenment through various spiritual therapies and disciplines, but most simply 'dropped out' of organized religion altogether...[there was a] tendency toward highly individualised [religion]...greater personal fulfilment and the quest for the ideal self...religion [became] 'privatised' or more anchored to the personal realms.[9]

We might add to these observations a remark from Margaret Mead, that 'the young cannot learn in the old ways' and that 'the old are outmoded rapidly' in the speedily advancing and saturated world of media, science, questing and consumerist cultures.[10] The idea that large-scale disaffection with organized religion is primarily a post-war phenomenon in both Britain and America has proved to be attractive to many within the church, who are looking for something that explains the mixed fortunes that churches encounter when trying to engage with

---

[7] Ibid., p. 72.

[8] Ibid., p. 72.

[9] W.C. Roof and W. McKinney, *American Mainline Religion: Its Changing Shape and Form* (New Jersey: Rutgers University Press, 1987), pp. 7–8, 18–19, 32–33.

[10] M. Mead *Culture and Commitment: The New Relationships Between the Generations in the 1970s* (New York: Doubleday, 1978), p. 78.

the young. Besides secularization, the fluctuating fortunes are probably also due to broader cultural streams that the churches have no direct control over. Such cultural changes might include the rise of the 'post-associational' society, consumerism, individualism, an accentuation of generational identity and familial atomization. However, it is important not to allow such descriptions to become the only frames of reference for determining the rocky evolutionary road to our present reality. To this end, some problems with traditionally understood historical accounts of the churches' dealings with youth are worth pointing out.

First, it needs to be remembered that our ways of talking about generations – especially childhood – do not have fixed points of meaning. Historians of childhood often quip that a child over the age of seven in medieval times did not exist. The term 'teenager' and the very idea of adolescence are comparatively recent 'discoveries'. The mergence of a 'buffer zone' of development between childhood and adulthood is something that is mostly attributable to economic and social conditions that can afford such space for maturity and advancement. The cultivation of such a zone as an arena for further specific forms of consumerism only serves to concretize and consecrate such identities. (Today, in many developing countries, a 'child' of ten can be the main 'breadwinner'.) Before the onset of the industrial revolution in Western Europe, it should be recalled that the churches could not claim to be doing any special work with children. As Heywood points out, prior to 1800, there was 'an absence of an established sequence for starting work, leaving home and setting up an independent household'.[11] Indeed, it is only the child labour laws and schooling that provide 'age-graded' structures for social ordering at this level, and such provisions are less than two hundred years old. Often, the work of churches went hand in hand with educationalists, and a newly perceived need to provide 'nurseries of Christian character' at every 'stage' of childhood, from infancy through to the age of twenty, in order to advance civilization and good social ordering.[12]

Second, generational change in religious adherence does not necessarily mean the rise of secularization. Callum Brown, for example, cites 1963 as the beginning of the end for the churches.[13] So how long would it be before Britain becomes truly and wholly secular? Brown does not say, but the teasing question draws our attention to the underlying assumption that seems to govern his thesis; namely that popular culture and modernity have irrevocably ended religious

---

[11] C. Heywood, *A History of Childhood: Children and Childhood in the West from Medieval to Modern Times* (Cambridge: Polity, 2001), p. 171. See also F.K. Goldscheider and C. Goldscheider, *Leaving Home Before Marriage: Ethnicity, Familism and Generational Relationships* (Wisconsin: University of Wisconsin, 1993).
[12] J. Kett, *Rites of Passage: Adolescence in America, 1790 to the Present* (New York: Basic Books, 1977).
[13] C. Brown, *The Death of Christian Britain: Understanding Secularisation 1800–2000* (London: Routledge, 2000).

affiliation. Whilst it may be true that the sixties, with its revolutions of popular culture, social liberalism and political upheaval did more to question and shake the foundations of institutions than in previous generations, it would appear that Brown is also guilty of shaping his facts around his thesis. Whilst it is clearly helpful to assess religious adherence down the ages through the lens of generational change, it simply does not follow that if the present generation are uninterested in religion or spirituality, then the next will be even less so. Moreover, is it not the case that many religious movements began in the 1960s? Ecumenism, Charismatic renewal, the New Age movement and a variety of sects, cults and new religious movements were part and parcel of the culture of experimentation that dominated the 1960s. Would it not be fairer to say that, far from turning off religion, people were rather turned on by it, and tuned into it in new ways (e.g., spirituality) that simply reflected the emerging post-institutional and post-associational patterns of post-war Britain?

Third, far from seeing generational change as a threat to the churches, the cultural forces that shape debates should be seen in the wider context of general social change. In a capitalist and consumerist culture, it is probably reasonable to go along with Putnam's hypothesis that the late twentieth century has seen a dramatic collapse in many forms of civic association, and a corresponding rise in individualism. However, churches have tended to hold up rather well under this pressure when compared to their non-religious counterparts. That said, changes in the way people spend 'free' time does appear to have had a deleterious effect on associational forms, and in all probability no agent of change has been more influential than the television. Initially, the creation of the 'electronic hearth' was a family-bonding and generation-bridging experience. But as consumerism and individualism have steadily increased, this phenomenon has changed. In the USA, the average adult now watches almost four hours of TV per day. As the number of television sets per household multiplies, watching programmes together has become more rare. Television has evolved into an example of 'negative social capital'; it is the new public space through which the world speaks to us, but it means that we no longer talk to one another. Putnam points out that 'husbands and wives spend three or four times as much time watching television as they spend talking'.[14] Similarly, Putnam points out that 'unlike those who rely on newspapers, radio and television for news...Americans who rely *primarily* on the internet for news are actually *less* likely than their fellow citizens to be civically involved'.[15] But of course, this does not mean that technology spells the end for civic life, associations and religious adherence. Rather, it suggests a new mutation of social and religious values.

[14] Putnum, *Bowling Alone*, p. 242. My italics.
[15] Ibid., p. 221.

Because every generation that has ever lived has done so within its own modernity, each new generation that faces its past, present and future does so with a sense of being on the cusp of time. Continuity between generations may be valued, but it is also evaluated as it is appreciated, and then perhaps subjected to alteration. But how true is it that the cultural and social forces being addressed at the present are more problematic than those faced in the past? Can it really be said that the transformations of the late twentieth century are more disruptive than those experienced in the industrial revolution, or in the wake of the economic and social re-ordering that followed the Black Death in medieval England? It seems unlikely when one considers the ample evidence of continuity, despite evolution and rapid changes within the environment.

In general, it would be imprudent to argue (historically) that one generation has struggled more than another, and that the forces shaping religion and society are now more or less inimical than another period. It is important that in any sociological and cultural analysis, proper attention is paid to (proper) history, before engaging in any kind of speculative futurology. There is a well-known aphorism that needs heeding by every would-be cultural commentator: 'sociology is history, but with the hard work taken out'. To avoid the endemic sociological habit of generalizing, it is important that any discussion of the generations is rooted in a sound grasp of historical enquiry, and, where possible, married to data, ethnography and other forms of intellectual garnering that are rooted in methodological rigour.

Sylvia Collins bases her assessment about the future shape of spirituality and youth on just such foundations. Her research is not motivated by confessional or denominational anxiety, but is rather located in the quest to discover how young people are changing in their attitudes to belief. Contrasting 'baby boomers' (those born between 1945 and 1960) and 'baby busters' (those born after 1960), Collins skilfully notes and narrates the changes between the generations. On balance, 'boomers' tended towards radicalizing religious traditions in the wake of post-war settlement. This was to include an emphasis on liberation, justice and political involvement, but was also coupled to an increasing tendency to experiment with religion (e.g., innovative 'sects', New Religious Movements, Communitarianism, etc.). Thus:

> [The] baby boomer generation...saw spirituality among young people move in line with social change from its location in one main tradition associated with the old established order, through to a new spirituality that sought to break the bonds of establishment and set the self free to reach its new potential. Even more widespread, however, was a growing apathy and indifference

towards the spiritual realm altogether in favour of materialistic self-orientation in terms of hedonistic consumption.[16]

Collins argues that 'baby busters' followed up and extended these changes. She notes, in common with other sociologists such as Hervieu-Leger (2000), Walker (1996), Francis and Kay (1995), that the late twentieth century has seen 'a thorough-going fragmentation in lineage of Christian memory', that 'gospel amnesia' has set in, as society has come to observe the fragmentation of belief and decontextualization of spirituality. But lest this sound too pessimistic already, Collins points out that religion has merely mutated rather than disappeared:

> Spirituality...has moved from the self-spirituality of the boomer generation to a more aesthetic spirituality, a spirituality which is focused on pleasure and experience in and of itself... Successful churches, it seems, offer an atmosphere and intimate experience of God over and above doctrine...the spirituality of intimacy of the millennial generation will be deeply bound up with the consumerism that has increasingly concerned youth throughout the post-war period.[17]

Collins's analysis is persuasive on many levels; her descriptive arguments appear to be a good 'fit' for young people and spirituality at the dawn of a third millennium. However, one important caveat should be mentioned, namely that of change. Interest in, or even a passion for 'an intimate experience of God over and above doctrine' is not necessarily sustainable over a period of time. It does not follow that those things that are valued and cherished in teenage years or one's early twenties will even be regarded in one's thirties or forties. For example, many young people are enchanted by the discipline, fellowship and spiritual atmosphere of a Christian Union (UCCF) whilst at college or university. But large numbers of students will quietly forsake this type of commitment for a different *attitude* to belief in later years: something altogether more mellow, temperate, open, ambiguous – a faith that can live with doubt.

This transition from the early twenties into 'young adulthood' raises some intriguing issues for the consideration of generations. Wade Clark Roof notes that 'in times of social upheaval and cultural discontinuity especially, generations tend to become more sharply set off from one another'.[18] The added power of consumerism in late modernity reinforces this sense: niche marketing to almost every age group for every stage of life is not only prevalent, but also highly successful. And

---

[16] Collins, 'Spirituality and Youth', p. 229.
[17] Collins, 'Spirituality and Youth', p. 233–35.
[18] W.C. Roof, *A Generation of Seekers: The Spitirual Journeys of the Baby Boom Generation* (San Francisco: Harper Collins, 1993), p. 3.

in the early years of adulthood, the desires appear to be less clustered around fulfilment and more around authenticity. As Parks notes, there is a 'hunger for authenticity, for correspondence between one's outer and inner lives...a desire to break through into a more spacious and nourishing conception of the common life we all share'.[19] Parks, work is one of the few treatments of faith and belief in the 'twenty-something' age group, and her work is a prescient consideration of how generational change evolves within itself, even to the point of questioning the contemporary bewitchments of consumerism and self-fulfilment.

The idea that changes take place *within* generations, and not simply between them, is an important one to grasp in the consideration of the future of religion, spirituality and the churches. Personal and communal beliefs have to be sufficiently robust to cope with all stages of life (if they are to last), and they also need the capacity to be able to negotiate the standard ruptures in mundane reality that raise questions about meaning and value. Such occurrences are typically located in the traditional turning-points moments of life such as birth, death and marriage.[20] And of course, as we have been inferring throughout this essay, cultures themselves can undergo rapid changes that make adaptation essential, particularly for institutions, with which we are also concerned.

The idea of churches adapting to culture is as old as the hills. There is no expression of ecclesiology that is not, in some rich and variegated sense, a reaction against, response towards or the attempted redemption of its contextual environment. Churches may choose to regard themselves as being primarily for or against culture (following Niebuhr), but as I have recently argued,[21] what mainly characterizes ecclesial responses to culture is their *resilience*, either in the form of resistance or accommodation, but, more usually, by combining both in the church's strategic survival and mission within late modernity. This observation is important here, for it reminds us that religion is both deeply a part of and also totally apart from culture. Its sheer alterity is what gives it its power, as much as it is wholly incarnated within space, time and sociality. In other words, religion is that material which generations will attempt to fashion and shape around their needs and desires. But the power of religion will also fashion and shape its 'users', causing them to question, reflect and wonder. Religion evokes awe; the numinous inspires; the spiritual invites a quest of ceaseless wondering.

That said, many theological, ministerial and ecclesial responses to the rapid cultural changes of late modernity, coupled with the apparently

---

[19] S. Parks, *Big Questions, Worthy Dreams: Mentoring Young Adults in Their Search for Meaning, Purpose and Faith* (San Francisco: Jossey Bass, 2000), pp. 9–16.
[20] Goldscheider and Goldscheider, *Leaving Home Before Marriage*, and Kett, *Rites of Passage*.
[21] Percy, *Salt of the Earth*.

dynamic differentiation between generations, have caused the spilling of much ink. Christian bookshops are awash with literature on how to reach the young, how to engage with secular culture, and how to reach those who are 'spiritual but not religious'. Typically, the character of these works is conditioned by a general sense of panic and fear, with churches engaging in ever-more neuralgic responses to the perceived crisis: flight, fright and fight would not be too wide of the mark. This is especially true in the arena of 'popular culture', where, ironically, spiritual motifs, symbols and ideas are plentiful: one trips over such 'cultural furniture' all the time in the somewhat haphazard assemblage of late modern life. There are, of course, more sophisticated attempts to read 'the signs of the times', and come up with compelling and thoughtful responses to the apparent 'generation gap'.

Paul Albrecht (1961), for example, offers a serious theological and ecclesiological programme for the churches that was pregnant with prescience for its time – the crucible of the early 1960s. More tangentially, Milton Rokeach (1979) provides a way of understanding how human values are translated and learnt from one generation to the next, and from groups to group within institutions. Indeed, there is now an abundance of works that could be at the service of the churches, helping them to read cultural and generational change.[22] But on the whole most theologians ignore such tasks, leaving the arena free for smaller confessional voices to shout and narrower tribal interests to be developed.

So far, I have deliberately avoided mentioning postmodernity – the 'name' for the 'condition' that many of the present generation are supposed to be labouring under. I have chosen this path because I do not think it is especially useful to add further characterization to the present debate. Of course, I am prepared to concede that there are aspects to postmodern reflection that are appropriate and analytically descriptive for our purposes here. For example, I find that Lyotard's quip that postmodernity is essentially 'incredulity at metanarratives' to be an apt encapsulation of our political, social and civic times. It is true that attitudes to truth have shifted too, but this does not appear to mean that Western civilization is about to collapse, or that my grandparent's generation will have proved to be more truthful than that of my children's. It is also true that many belief systems – for individuals and institutions – more often than not resemble a new assemblage and collage than any strict continuity with tradition. But at the same time, no one can convincingly prove that this situation for society is new, namely a morass of competing convictions, and that pluralism is

---

[22] See, for example, J. Hall and M. Neitz, *Culture: Sociological Perspectives* (New Jersey: Prentice Hall); D. Strinati, *Popular Culture: An Introduction to Theories* (New York: Routledge, 1995); E. Thompson (ed.), *Cultural Theory* (Boulder: Westview Press, 1990); G. Zoltman, *Processes and Phenomena of Social Change* (New York: Wiley, 1973), etc.

particular to late modernity. It isn't. From earliest times, Christians have carved out their faith in a pluralist world, settled churches in alien cultures, and adopted their practices and customs that have eventually become 'tradition'.

I suspect that the litmus test for assessing the extent of generational change and its implications for mission can probably be best understood by speculating about death and memorialization in the future. If our cultural commentators – who speak of 'gospel amnesia' and 'a thorough-going fragmentation in lineage of Christian memory' – are right, then what will a 'Christian' funeral visit look like in fifty years' time? At present, many ministers conducting funerals can be confident that, unless otherwise requested, there will be Christian hymns and prayers at the ceremony. The Lord's Prayer may be said, and is still mumbled by many in traditional language. Some hymns – a number of which were learned at school – can be sung, and it is just possible that certain passages of Scripture and collects will be familiar to a number of the mourners. But despite this, the funerals of today already show signs of change, with mourners now requesting more popular music (e.g., 'Wind Beneath my Wings', 'Stairway to Heaven', etc.), as well as poetry or prose from non-religious sources. So what of the future, where prayers, collects and hymns are not likely to have been part of the schooling for the vast majority of mourners? What types of religious sentiment will be uttered by the generation that is, in all probability, non-conversant in the language of formal religion, but fluent in the many dialects of spirituality?

To partly answer my own question, I turn to an analogy drawn from the world of art history. Restorers of paintings sometimes talk about the 'pentimento', the original sketch that is underneath an oil painting beginning to show through as the painting ages. The pentimento is a kind of skeletal plan (the first lines drawn on canvas): where paint falls or peels off, the earliest ideas for the picture are sometimes revealed. The analogy allows us to pose a question: what will the spiritual pentimento of millennial children look like when it comes to their funeral? It will, I suspect, at least at a church funeral, be primarily Christian, provided we understand the term 'Christian' broadly. It will be a kind of vernacular, operant (rather than formal), folk Christianity, not that dissimilar from what many ministers already encounter. But it will also be a more spirituality open and evocative affair, with perhaps readings from other traditions. It will also be more therapeutic, centred less on grief and more on celebration. In all likelihood, the funeral of the future will be able to tell us just how much change there has been between the generations. There will be gaps, to be sure, but they are unlikely to be unbridgeable. Evolution guarantees change; but also continuity. Previous generations have always found a way through to the next; there is no reason to suppose that this generation will lack the wisdom and the tenacity to do likewise.

Gender and change: an evolving church

If youth and generational continuity can be said to pose an adaptive problem for the church, then it follows that other cultural shifts will also have a bearing upon the shaping of the church, its clergy and ministry. It is of course recognized that it is, strictly speaking, quite improper to neatly divide religion from culture, or theology from spirituality. The doctrine of the incarnation has consistently been suggestive in this respect: God works through and with time and culture – there are no agencies of grace that exist in modes that are outside natural, human or cultural development. God speaks through words, signs, actions and other spheres that are in one sense ordinary, whether that is fire and cloud, or wine and bread.

Of course, the same applies to popular culture. A public under-standing of clerical identity and ministry, has, in the past, been developed through the novels of Geoffrey Chaucer, Anthony Trollope and Jane Austen, to name but a few.[23] Such caricatures act as a kind of barometer, reflecting the affections and tastes of the public in relation to their clergy. On television, one can encounter a number of examples of clergy being portrayed as innocent, other-worldly, naïve, gangly, fussy and slightly eccentric – *All Gas and Gaiters* and the vicar from *Dad's Army* particularly come to mind. But more recently, two television programmes have reflected a significant shift in the cultural attitude towards the portrayal of clergy. *Father Ted* has come to prominence as a 'sit-com' that follows the ministerial escapades of Fathers Dougal, Ted and Jack in their clergy house, on a remote island off the coast of Ireland. Whilst making Roman Catholic clergy the subject of humour is hardy new (one thinks of Dave Allen), the significance of *Father Ted* is that the viewer is invited into a satirical world which actually highlights insoluble pastoral situations and the ambivalence of the clerical role.[24]

---

[23] For further discussion see R. Chapman, *Godly and Righteous, Peevish and Perverse: Clergy and Religious in Literature and Letters: An Anthology* (Norwich: Canterbury Press, 2002); A.N. Wilson, *Church and Clergy* (London: Faber & Faber, 1992); Hinton, *The Anglican Parochial Clergy*; T. Beeson, *The Bishops* (London: SCM Press, 2002); Hinde, *Field Guide to the English Country Parson*.

[24] A detailed discussion of comedy actors playing clergy on stage and in film merits a more serious study than is possible here. Suffice to say, the prominence of clergy in comedy is suggestive of both an affection for and a distancing of religious figures in public life. Rowan Atkinson's foppish cleric (*Four Weddings and a Funeral*), Alan Bennett in *Beyond the Fringe* ('. . . life is like a tin of sardines . . .') particularly come to mind. In literary portrayals, Henry Fielding's *Joseph Andrews* (Parson Adams), Laurence Sterne's *Tristam Shandy* (Parson Yorick), Jane Austen's *Emma* (Mr Elton) and *Pride and Prejudice* (Mr Collins) retain a strong cultural resonance, as do Anthony Trollope's Revd Obadiah Slope (in *Barchester Towers*) and Oscar Wilde's Canon Chasuble (in *The Importance of Being Earnest*). In more recent times, the British magazine *Private Eye* continues the tradition of clerical satire with figures such as the Revd J.C. Flannel, and the Vicar's Newsletter (attributed to the Revd A. Blair).

Similarly, *The Vicar of Dibley* invites the viewer to see the funnier side of ministry, although it differs from *Father Ted* insofar as the main subject is a Church of England clergywoman (played by Dawn French), where gender continually features as a lighthearted issue. Another difference between these two recent offerings from television is that *Father Ted*, representing the dominant tradition of portrayal, still invites audiences to (gently) mock and laugh at the clergy. Whereas in *The Vicar of Dibley*, the female lead is a catalyst for orchestrating humour that is directed more towards the bizarre and eccentric parishioners of Dibley; we mostly laugh with and through Dawn French at what she has to contend with.

A further aspect of *The Vicar of Dibley* is that it has made a significant contribution to the normalization of female clergy in public life and contemporary culture, something understood by Ian Jones in his recent research on women priests (2004). The role of the media in shaping understandings of clerical identity should not be underestimated; such presentations offer portraiture of how the church is perceived by the wider world, which is then reflected back to the church. Thus, the headline in *The Sun* ('Church Votes for Vicars with Knickers') which appeared on 12 November 1992, the day after the General Synod had approved the Measure to ordain women to the priesthood, captures something of the quirky affection with which the church is held. In one sense, the continual interest in the clergy that is evident in the popular media provides us with further evidence of the role of the environment in shaping ecclesial praxis. To a large extent, this role has grown progressively since the enlightenment. More or less across Europe and prior to the enlightenment, the crown (or state) and church acted as censors of material available in the public sphere, thereby ensuring that the crown or the church were seldom subject to wider scrutiny. But the enlightenment – which both enabled and substantially extended the size and scope of the educated 'middle class', and also created new environments for debate, dissemination and the exchange of ideas – necessarily placed the church and crown within an enlarged public sphere, in which they quickly moved to becoming subjects for discussion rather than indisputable objects of reverence. This is an important aspect of the evolution of the environment to grasp, since it partly explains why some churches are resistant to public pressure and accountability, often at quite subconscious levels. Roman Catholicism, whilst obviously grappling with post-enlightenment theology, still functions with an ecclesiology that struggles to comprehend why and how 'secular' authorities might intervene in its affairs on matters such as employment, clergy discipline or even child protection. Similarly, some new churches, in trying to reclaim the apostolic period, expect and anticipate that their affairs can be ordered according to higher principles (i.e., theological) that override any current environmental pressure in respect of transparency, accountability and good practice.

Whilst some caution would need to be exercised in determining precisely how cultural change affects the inner workings of the church, there is no question that most ecclesial communities in late modernity are beginning to discover afresh that they are increasingly reacting to and evolving with the environments in which they find themselves, rather than shaping them from some position of inherited privilege. This is particularly true when one considers an issue such as gender, and the myriad of ways in which cultural change has begun to shape the polity and praxis of churches. Whether one is looking at the established churches of the Baltic states, or considering the embryonic reform-minded movements of Roman Catholicism, the evidence of pressure for change is abundantly apparent.

Similarly, there is never a shortage of priorities in the Church of England. So when it comes to considering the question of women bishops, issues of faith, order, culture, communion and charity, all can claim some precedence. For example, it seems important that any move to consecrate women as bishops does not lead to the 'un-churching' of those who oppose such an initiative; nobody wishes to see schism. No less important is the desire of the Church as a whole to see women in positions of authority and leadership: according to a recent *Church Times* survey of almost 5,000 persons, 80 per cent have welcomed women priests, and 66 per cent would welcome women bishops. True, the Church of England is not a democratic body in which the will of the majority always prevails. But neither is it theocracy, governed by self-appointed guardians of the faith. The Church of England is a *via media*, part Catholic, part Reformed, part Episcopal and part Synodical. The will of the majority is important, but not necessarily decisive. And yet who is to say that God does speak through a democratic process; that God's will is not achieved through the mechanisms of a synod?

The Church of England is also a public body, and the interests of its many supporters (e.g., 35 million people visited an English cathedral in 2000) as distinct from its 'members' should not be lightly dismissed. I suspect that I am not alone in surmising that one of the main reasons the vote to ordain women to the priesthood went through in 1992 was related to the issue of public credibility. Like many people who stood outside Church House on 11 November 1992, I went to a nearby pub to celebrate after the voting was announced. I have never quite got over the fact that hundreds of people in the pub – none of them, as far as one can tell, churchgoers – were genuinely pleased for the church. There were pats on the back, cries of 'welcome to the twentieth century!', and even a few drinks bought. I cannot imagine what it would have been like trying to be part of the public face of the Church of England had the vote gone the other way. No matter what theological arguments there are against women priests or women bishops (and there are very few that work well in Anglican theology), the Church of England is obliged to be a publicly credible body as much as it is mysterious.

The argument for or against women bishops can never just be about convincing stalwart church members; the arguments have to convince a nation. To my mind, most of the arguments against women bishops that appear to function, do so either as almost entirely internalized theological debates (e.g., issues of order and authority construed through 'private' ecclesial rhetoric), or on some sort of ecumenical premise (e.g., relations with Roman Catholics). But I have yet to encounter an argument against women priests or bishops that might function as an example of 'public theology' that will engage the English people in the twenty-first century. This takes us to the very core of the dilemma for those who are charged with coming to a common mind about women bishops. As members of the Church of England intuitively know, the identity of the church is disputed, and the methodologies and authorities that it uses to clarify its life and define its identity are invariably incomplete and contestable. There can be no appeal to an absolute authority to decide a theological question. Theological questions can only be settled by ongoing theological work, and by a process that tests itself through scripture, tradition and reason.

My point about Anglican identity – and granted, much more could be said about this – may perhaps serve to remind us that the Church of England does not own, and perhaps never has, the clear and settled ecclesiology that might be enjoyed by other denominations. It is a creature of its environment, and whilst it has become populous overseas, it remains a curiously English animal. Thus, within the Church of England there has always been room for the tradition of 'loyal dissent', and this now extends, arguably, to the Anglican Communion as a whole. Thus, Anglicans in the Diocese of Sydney can argue for (male) lay presidency at the Eucharist, and can trace their theological rationale not only in Scripture, but also in tradition, by appealing to the seventeenth-century Puritan strain of Anglicanism that was once so influential. Thus, an apparently simple dispute about faith and order is not easily settled, since there is no one tradition that makes up Anglicanism. As a church it is inherently plural; a pottage of competing convictions held together by liturgical, familial, doctrinal, cultural, theological and other ties. It knows that compromise is a virtue, not a vice; for it needs the complementarity of several distinctive traditions that on their own would be deficient.

Arguably, the question of women bishops is not one of those issues that can be settled definitively either way. The Anglican Communion is in a constant state of open process; it recognizes that its state of being evolves. That does not mean that it stands for nothing; nor does it mean that everything it tries and does is temporal or experimental. Rather, I choose the term 'open process' to remind us that Anglicanism has never been afraid of factoring praxis into its theological formulations and ecclesiological outcomes. It may be the case the women priests are, for some, within a period of reception. But the same is true for Provincial Episcopal Visitors (also known as 'flying bishops') and the Act of Synod (which protects the sensitivities of those opposed to women priests and women bishops); proponents of women priests do not expect such things to endure either. The middle way – so beloved of Anglicanism – is to speak of integrities, and to try to get along in spite of difference (and perhaps because of it).

Such issues are timely for the Church of England, as it continues to ponder the question of women bishops. The Church of England is necessarily and continually sifting and weighing the various contributions that are offering perspectives on the issue. But what weight to give to such contributions? Is a plea for a moratorium on the issue worth the same as a plea for progress? Is tradition something to be preserved, or part of the organic life of the church that is always changing? The uses of tradition are a curious feature of such debates. My attention has recently been drawn to a new book that insists on the revealed 'maleness' of Jesus. In Robert Pesarchick's book *The Trinitarian Foundation of Human Sexuality as Revealed by Christ According to Urs von Balthasar: The Revelatory Significance of the Male Christ and the Male Ministerial Priesthood* (The Vatican: Editrice Pontificia Universita Gregoriana, 2000), the author argues that priests must be men, because they represent Christ's maleness, which is part of God's self-disclosure. It is a curious book in many regards, not least because it assumes that the partiality of analogy must nevertheless reveal the fullness of reality, besides assuming (with Aristotle, and wrongly, of course) that men are creative (i.e., life-giving of their seed) and women more passive (i.e., nurturing and receptive of the seed).

But as we have noted in the first two chapters, the question of the origin and development of clergy cannot be settled solely by eclectic appeals to revelation or tradition; there must be an account of 'natural' development too, which may be no less spiritual. Thus, the issue of women bishops in the Church of England cannot simply be settled by previously established meta-theological arguments at the expense of new insights, and neither can the debate be settled by epic or idealized accounts of the church. Anglicanism is committed to a matrix of Scripture, tradition and reason, and the innovative approach that Nicholas Healy takes to his ecclesiology – Anglican in character – reminds us that attention to context is no less vital than to theological authority[25]. Perhaps the Holy Spirit is already ahead of the church, speaking to it through culture, and calling it to a more faithful embodiment of its discipleship through the culture of equality and complementarity? It is not easy to discern, but the matter cannot be easily dismissed. For not everything that the Church of England has done in relation to women priests has a clear theological rationale. The decision to ordain women to the priesthood was made on unambiguous theological grounds (for Anglicans), approved by Synod and

[25] Nicholas Healy, *Church, World and Christian Life: Practical Prophetic Ecclesiology* (Cambridge: Cambridge University Press, 2000).

Parliament, and affirmed by the vast majority of the nation; any process of reception is ongoing, but shows no sign of reversing. But the theological rationale for the Act of Synod and PEVs (Provincial Episcopal Visitors or 'flying bishops') is less clear; Anglicans accept, in a semi-fractured communion, that such measures are more pastoral and pragmatic. Of course, such measures are intrinsically Anglican, since cherishing 'loyal dissent' is part of the glory of the Communion. Nevertheless, the issue of women bishops – perhaps like that of lay (male) presidency at the Eucharist (as proposed by the Diocese of Sydney) – is seen as a bridge too far for some. So what is to be done? How can the church adapt? Three brief comments on praxis seem appropriate at this point.

First, I rather doubt that women bishops in the Church of England pose quite the threat to unity that some suppose. There are already some Anglican provinces that have women bishops, and the Church of England is in full communion with those provinces. Although some English diocesan bishops would wish to conditionally re-ordain priests who relocated from, say, the USA to England (presumably as deacons and then again as priests), there can be no escaping the fact that for the vast majority of Anglicans, globally and in England, the orders and ministry of such priests are already valid. It should really be accepted that women priests are already a welcome development that most people in the church support, and in the wider cultural sphere. And in time, women bishops will be demanded – as much from the nation the Church of England serves as from its own 'members'. It may be an astute and prudent form of public theology that anticipates this public (and spiritual) demand, and then goes on to show the church in a more progressive than retrograde light.

Second, the sensitivities of those who oppose women priests must continue to be protected. If the Church of England accepts the ministry of women bishops, it will be important to affirm the place of those who engage in 'loyal dissent'. This is not meant to be patronizing; it is a genuine confirmation of the Church of England's mixed pedigree in regard to ecclesial polity. It will be important that those Anglo-Catholics and Evangelicals who cannot accept the mind of most of the church are truly supported by the church as a whole. True, communion may be impaired by the decision to move forward; but doing nothing or delaying will not heal or address the frustrations of many, and the deficiencies of a male-only episcopate.

Third, the debate about women bishops highlights the strengths and weaknesses of the Anglican Church, and its attempts to reach theological consensus on almost any matter. In a church where compromise has often had to form the basis for communion, and where competing convictions have sometimes threatened to tear the church apart, the debate offers a genuine opportunity to recover the charity that Anglicans need to live together as faithful disciples, yet also as those who do not agree on certain matters of faith and order. A fuller appreciation of the richness and variety of traditions that make up the Anglican Communion – including those who espouse loyal dissent – will help the church come to a deeper understanding of its precious (if sometimes precarious) polity. Moving towards gaining women as bishops is, I believe, a necessary and important step for an established church that wants and needs to be taken seriously as a public and inclusive body.

But to conclude this brief section, we might reflect on how those parts of the church that are implacably opposed to the ordination or consecration of women are meant to adjust to a changing church and culture. For those people within the wings of the church for whom this is a step too far, there is a struggle to comprehend the difference between remembering a past in which they felt validated, and recalling that past. To re-member is a Eucharistic act that involves forgiveness and reconfiguration: to put back together again, but in ways that speak of hope and resurrection. In other words, to take the 'dis-membered', and rediscover its proper shape and identity. To re-member, then, is to engage in an activity that reconstitutes. By recollecting and recalling, we make and pledge ourselves anew to each other, and to God. So remembering is not a dry duty. It is a vital and hopeful form of recall that re-shapes us for the better. So, remembering the past is really all about facing the task of living anew. It is about hope, and about recommitment.

However, there is a world of difference between *reminding* people of the past and *remembering* it. Reminders can simply recall, and all too easily lead, if one is not careful, to the perpetual contemplation of pain (and the anger that evokes). The wounds never heal; they are left open, and are prodded and poked on a regular basis, so that others may participate in the pain afresh. But remembrance is different. It is a faithful and engaged act of recollection, which is both constructive for the present and hopeful for the future. Both reminding and remembering need history – but they do different things with time and memory. One will not let go of the past; the other is committed to learning from it, living by it, but not being bound to it. Arguably, the future for those parts of the church that feel disenfranchised by the ordination or consecration of women lies not in recovering the past, but in re-membering it in ways that are flecked with forgiveness and hope. Such a call echoes the words of Jesus, who asked his disciples on the night before his torture and death to 'do this in remembrance of him'. The church is not asked to continually recollect the taste of bitter herbs; it is asked to re-member its body, and then to live in the reconciling light of Easter.

Ecclesial power and authority: competition in the environment

Waspish comments on the shortcomings of the clergy and church abound in literature. The comedian Lenny Bruce once quipped that 'every day people are straying away from the church and going back to God'. Benjamin Jowett advised that 'you must believe in God, in spite of what the clergy tell you'. J.B. Priestly once opined that 'it is hard to tell where the MCC ends and the Church of England begins'. Henri de Montherlant described religion as 'the venereal disease of mankind'. And for Karl Marx, religion was the 'opium of the people'. Penetrating critiques of religion are a reminder that the formation and evolution of religious organizations take place within an environment that is both compliant and hostile. Whilst plenty of religious traditions struggle with their own interiority as they seek to adapt to their life and tradition, it remains the case that what is exterior to the faith also poses questions. As we have already seen in this chapter, the absorption of the church with youth work is an attempt to adapt to the equivalent of a significant cultural climate change. Likewise, the considerable cultural shifts in relation to gender over the past one hundred years have led many denominations to adapt their praxis. Failure to do so, arguably, would lead to a de-contextualization of the church (which would be welcomed, of course, by some groups), followed by the removal of a public body into the private sphere, resulting in a kind of self-imposed environmental exile.

As if we needed reminding, the heart of the matter lies in understanding how God works in the world, with ecclesial communities beginning to honestly recognize and resolve how their traditions have evolved. For some groups, theology only arises because it has been revealed – faxed from heaven, as it were – which is akin to a kind of creationism. But for other groups, the view of inspiration and authority is more subtle, seeing God's activity primarily through the lens of the incarnation. So for a theologian like Don Browning, theology is always rooted in praxis:

> All [theology] is essentially practical. The social and intellectual context in which theology is brought into conversation with the vision is implicit in pastoral practice itself, and with the normative interpretations of the faith handed down in the traditions of the church. Theology thus arises from practice, moves into theory, and is then put into practice again.[26]

---

[26] D. Browning, *A Fundamental Practical Theology* (Philadelphia: Westminster, 1991), p. 3; cf. Stephen Pattison and James Woodward (eds), *A Reader in Practical Theology* (Oxford: Blackwell, 2000), p. 6.

The recognition of theology as something that arises out of practice has some particular ramifications for understanding the evolution of power and authority within ecclesial communities. Max Weber suggests that there are three basic types of authority that operate within organizations. First, there is 'legal' or 'bureaucratic', where obedience is owed to rules and systems of governance rather than to people, although individuals may be charged with (or elected for) the maintenance and discharge of this type of authority. Second, there is 'traditional' authority, which rests on the sacredness of the social order, and is therefore rooted in the past. Third, there is 'charismatic' authority, which depends on the giftedness of an individual, such as a prophet, healer, preacher or charismatically endowed leader. Whilst this type of authority is the rarest in religion, it is also highly prized. However, it is also the type of authority most prone to 'routinization', which eventually returns the authority-type to legalism and bureaucracy (type one), especially after the death or departure of a founder. A number of 'house churches' have experienced this trajectory within recent times, and in less than a generation (see Chapter 5).[27]

Granted, Weber's typology can only serve as a basic guide for our study here. Clearly, many ecclesial communities will be dependent upon all three types of authority, to some degree. New (house) churches will need their leaders to be more charismatic than bureaucratic. Established churches require leaders who have a sense of what traditional authority constitutes. At a local level, it is not uncommon for churches to choose (riskier) charismatic leaders when they sense their identity and membership is in need of energizing. Or, equally, a congregation may opt to choose a more traditional authority-type who will consolidate growth and identity after a period of rapid expansion. But in understanding such dynamics, we inevitably begin to be drawn in to the paradoxes of clerical identity. They might regard themselves as professionals, or as priests. But their essential operation (together with the distinct cultivation of their identity) is something that *also* lies in the hands of congregations – the environment in which their ministry is received. No matter what authority-type a clergyperson thinks they represent, and no matter how much that is based upon their own reading of a tradition, the very nature of equitable power relations in social and ecological environs will stipulate that ministry and clerical identity must adapt to the temporal conditions in which it finds itself. Malcolm Torry, noting these difficulties, writes:

---

[27] For example, the Ichthus network run by Roger and Faith Forster, which began as an entrepreneurial collation of house churches in the 1970s, is currently struggling to clarify its identity as the leadership ages. Similar problems are faced by other networks of 'house churches' where the founding (charismatic) leader is either unable or unwilling to hand on responsibility for governance to a fresh generation.

We thus find a complex picture. Clergy are intimately bound up with their congregations, but their distinctive position within a variety of faith, authority and compliance structures gives them distinctive roles and imposes on them distinctive pressures. Amongst those pressures is being accountable to a *very* broad range of individuals and institutions: the denomination, a particular theological tradition, normative texts, hierarchical authority-structures, congregational office-holders, congregational members, civic leaders, civil institutions, local residents – and God.[28]

We are once again drawn to clerical identity and roles, and their deep complexity. And on the basis of what we have deduced in preceding chapters, we can now see that their environment only permits priests or clergy, as a caste, to be *partially* professionalized.[29] Moreover, this professionalization is also diverse; the increasing numbers of non-stipendiary clergy are both a symptom and a cause of the reduced social status of clergy. Granted, clergy could, in one sense, be seen as the very first professionals: there was a time when they were the only people of learning in a given community. But as science, education and society have advanced, and as secularization has increased, clergy have found themselves increasingly forced into more compressed roles.

The specialization that begins to emerge under such conditions has a peculiar pharmacological quality. On the one hand, clergy become distinctive purveyors of skills, rituals and knowledge. When gathering together as an exclusive group, for example, clergy often find that the subject quickly turns to funerals, or to other pastoral situations that have been acutely intense and demanding. Such conversations confirm the validity of the role in a way that a conversation about preaching, administration or visiting may not – because others can do these things. The tasks are not reserved to the clerical office. At the same time, however, such specialization needs congregational support, and this requires payment, accountability, rationalization and relationships, which erode the autonomy of the minister, and increase the power of the laity. Clergy, therefore, find that the evolution of their praxis now begins to emerge out of a complex matrix of power relations, together with a myriad of assumptions about the nature of power itself.

Power in religious institutions can be as inevitable and ubiquitous as anywhere else. It can be the power of virtue or vice. Equally, it can be a power that drives a morally ambiguous potency, or the naked assertion of a particular fecundity. Power can be seen gorgeously vested; splendidly arrayed in ritual, material and organization. But it can also

---

[28] M. Torry, *Managing God's Business: Religious and Faith-Based Organizations and their Management* (London: Ashgate, 2005), p. 139. See also M. Harris, *Organizing God's Work: Challenges for Churches and Synagogues* (London: Macmillan, 1998).
[29] Torry, *Managing God's Business*, p. 143.

be disguised in the apparently ordinary and insignificant, only erupting as problematic when a synergy of events causes the hidden face of power to be revealed.

An understanding of power, then, is a crucial hermeneutical key for arriving at an understanding of clerical identity of the local church, and in specific relation to congregations. To understand the nature of power in churches, it is not necessary to be engaged in a reductive sociological or psychological task. It is, rather, to recognize that any social body (and this includes churches) can benefit from a form of 'deep literacy' (to borrow a phrase of Paulo Freire) that readily faces up to the myriad of ways in which power is present, distributed, wielded and transformative. Furthermore, and perhaps inevitably, attention to the phenomenon of power as a primary motif within congregations can provide a degree of illumination that leads to transformative self-critical praxis within a congregation. In seeking to understand clerical roles and identity, attention to the dynamics of power can go some considerable way to providing some causal explanations related to organization, mission and congregations.

Because the nature of power is essentially contested – either within any one individual discipline, or in dialogue between the disciplines – there is no common analytic or explanatory language that uniquely commends itself to the study of congregations or the local church. Theologically, it is commonplace to speak of the power of God. In turn, most denominations will have a conceptualization of how that power typically is expressed or reified (i.e., materially manifested) in the midst of a congregation. Put another way, the 'pure' power of God is known through particular and given 'agents' which (or who) are deemed to most faithfully express that power, and the nature of the giver (God). Thus, for some denominations, the power of God is made known in the celebration of the Mass; or in a particular individual; or in the exposition of an inerrant Bible; or in the faithful gathering that witnesses miracles, signs and wonders; or in debate and dialogue, where fresh vistas of perception are reached through new patterns of communion.

What is interesting about 'mapping' theological conceptualizations of power in this way, is noting how conflated the giver and the gift become. Critics of the traditions mentioned above will often remark upon how the Mass is raised to a level of apotheosis; or how the Bible is almost worshipped; or comment upon the exalted status given to ministers who are gifted in thaumaturgy; or on how democracy can sometimes be paraded as the eleventh commandment. These prelim-inary critiques are all linked, insofar as they have identified one of the most pressing problems in expressions of theological and ecclesiological power: the problem of conflation. In other words, the inability to distinguish between the power of God, and then again, on the other hand, the power of the agencies or channels through which such power is deemed to flow.

Typically, attention to power in clerical formation focuses on abuse and the problematic. High-profile cases are often reported in the media: clergy who sexually abuse adults or minors; arguments over money and trust; disputes about promises made, and then broken. But it is a pity to become fixated on the pitfalls of power and to overly problematize it, since a deeper appreciation of the dynamics of power can reveal the hidden governance, resources and untapped potential in a congregation. Too often, it is the fear of power and its potential for harm that prevents many congregations from coming to a more assured appreciation of how they (as a body) might symbolize that power to the wider community. Understanding power is essential for mission, organization and transformation; its dynamics need ownership, not shunning.

In paying attention to the reality of power in the local church (as an environment within which clergy function), it is virtually inevitable that a whole set of social and material relations will become subject to scrutiny. In turn, some of the theological rationales that support those relations will also need to be assessed. For example, the defence of a particular tradition or custom is not 'simply' a group of people protecting what they know to be the truth. It is also a statement about a way of being; a preference for one type of tradition over another; a formula that affirms one pattern of behaviour, but at the same time resists others. Power, therefore, is not one 'thing' to be discovered and studied. It is, rather, a more general term that covers a range of ideas and behaviour that constitute the fundamental life of the local church.

To help us think a little more about the nature and relation of power to clerical identity, it can be helpful to begin by focusing on different types of leadership, which in turn tend to embody different views of power. Consider, for example, three different caricatures of how Church of England bishops might operate within a diocese. One may see their role and task as primarily *executive*: being a hands-on manager, making key strategic decisions on a day-to-day basis. Such a view of pastoral power thrusts the bishop into the contentious realm of management, efficiency and rationalization, where they operate as a kind of chief executive officer in a large organization. This is a form of *rationalized* authority, and it will typically empathize with reviews, strategies and appraisals.

Another may take a different approach, and see their power in primarily *monarchical* terms. There are two faces to monarchical power. One is to rule by divine right: like a monarch, the bishop's word is law. But the second and more common manifestation of monarchical law is manifested in aloofness. Like most monarchs, bishops seldom intervene in any dispute decisively, and choose to remain 'neutral' and 'above' any divisive opinions or decisions. This is not an abrogation of power. Rather, the adoption of the second type of monarchical model proceeds from an understanding that others ('subjects') invest mystique and meaning in the power of the ruler, which in turn leads many monarchs and bishops to be 'officially silent' on most issues that have any immediacy, or are potentially divisive. Their symbolic power is maintained through mystique, and ultimately reticence. This is a form of *traditional* authority, where the power is primarily constituted in the office rather than in the individual charisms of the person holding it.

Another model is more *distributive*, and is concerned with facilitation and amplification. In this vision for embodying power in any office, the bishop becomes an enabler, helping to generate various kinds of powers (i.e., independent, related, etc.) within an organization. He or she will simply see to it that the growth of power is directed towards common goals, and is ultimately for the common good. But in this case, power is valued for its enabling capacities and its generative reticulation (i.e., the energy derived from and through networking, making connections, etc.); it is primarily verified through its connecting and non-directional capacities. To a point, such leadership requires a degree of *charismatic* authority, since the organization constantly requires a form of leadership that is connectional and innovative.

To be sure, most bishops will move between these models of power (and their associated types of authority), according to each case, and with each situation dictating which mode of power is deployed. But most bishops will naturally favour one kind of model over another, but perhaps without realizing it. The advantage of looking at power through models of leadership, though, is that it illuminates other issues. For example, how is power 'conceptualized' in this situation or place? Who is said to have any ownership of power? How is power shared or dispersed in a congregation or denomination?

These issues are important when one considers the perpetual puzzling that often persists in relation to the status of charismatic leaders. For power is at its most obvious when it is at its most concentrated, and is intensely experienced. For this reason, an understanding of the complexities of power in relation to the local church is an essential element within the study of congregations. And there are at last three ways of 'mapping' the power as it is encountered.

In one sense, power can be understood as *dispositional*. This refers to the habits and worldview of a congregation, and will closely correspond to their normative 'grammar of assent'. Appeals to an almighty God and Lord will have direct social consequences in terms of the expectations set upon obedience and compliance. On the other hand, *facilitative* power describes the agents or points of access through which such power is accessed. Here, the status of those agencies will normally match the power that they are connected to. Then again, *episodic* power, however, refers to those events or moments in the life of a congregation that produce surges of energy, challenge or opportunity.

Putting this together – with a charismatic congregation serving as an example – one could say that the worship is dispositional, the leaders are facilitative, and the invocation of the Holy Spirit a cue for episodic manifestations of power that are unleashed. This sequence, of course, quickly becomes a dynamic cycle: the episodic confirms the validity of the facilitative and dispositional, and in so doing, creates further expectations of episodic manifestations of power, and the strengthening of other kinds. There is a real sense in which the local church is a 'circuit of power', replete with connections, adaptors, converters and charges of energy. The local church evolves into a complex ecology of power, where energy of various types can flow in different ways, be subject to increase and decrease, and be converted and adapted for a variety of purposes.

Closely related to power is the question of authority. All Christian denominations evolve over time, and their patterning of power and arrangements for agreeing on normative sources of authority are also subject to change. Again, given proper scrutiny, excavating models of authority and power can reveal much about the structure of a church or congregation. Following Paula Nesbitt's sociological observations,[30] we might note that in the first evolutionary phase of denominationalism, or in specific congregational evolution (which can currently be seen in the early history of new house churches), institutional relations usually can be governed through obedience, and, if necessary, punishment. We might describe this as the exercise of *traditional* authority, where power over another can be nakedly asserted.

However, in the second phase, interpersonal contracts emerge between congregations, regions and individuals. Here 'ecclesial citizenship' is born, and law and order develop into agreed rather than imposed rule. We might call this *rational* authority: it has to be argued for and defended in the face of disputes and questioning. Again, a number of new churches are now at the point where their power and authority needs explaining in relation to their context and other relations. In the third phase (postmodern, etc.), more complex social contracts emerge between parties, which require a deeper articulation of a shared ethos and an agreement about the nature of a shared moral community. To retain unity and cohesive power, authority must be *negotiated*. It is here that the denomination effectively crosses the bridge from childhood to adulthood. Congregations learn to live with the differences between themselves.

Finally, there is *symbolic* authority. This states that authority and power are constituted in ways of being or dogma that are not easily apprehensible. Networks of congregations may choose a particular office ('chief pastor') or event ('synod') or artefact of tradition ('Bible') and position it as having supreme governance. However, the weakness of symbolic authority is often comparable to the dilemma faced by those who prefer monarchical power. By positing power in an office that seldom intervenes in a decisive way, symbolic authority normally has to justify its substance. If it can't, it loses its power and authority.

---

[30] Paula Nesbitt, *Religion and Social Policy* (Lanham, MD: Alta Mira Press, 2001), pp. 161ff.

Conclusion

Whilst it is commonplace to pay attention to abuses or collapses of power in churches, the purpose of this last section has been to show that there are deeper reasons why a focus on power is important for the study of the evolution of clerical identity within the environment of the local church. First, the contested nature of power means that its study is essential if one is to clarify the situation of clergy in relation to the culture, theology or anatomy of the local church. Second, there are conventional understandings of power that can illuminate ecclesiological analysis; clergy are both producers of and produced by their environments. Third, there are often hidden ways of understanding the identity and location of power which also merit attention. To simply study 'official' authority in the church is to only undertake half the task, since there are hundreds of subtle and unofficial forms of authority that are no less significant. Ultimately, it is only by immersing oneself in the study of the nuances of clerical behaviour and the local church that one can begin to understand the complex range of power forms that make and shape ecclesial environments. And in the act of immersion, the scholar needs to develop a deep literacy that is attentive to the multifarious dynamics of power.

To illustrate this, I offer a fictional case study. In a local congregation, a new minister is sought to lead the church forward. The brief from the leading laity in the church is very particular. The church is conscious that its membership is ageing, and it seeks a dynamic minister who will attract young families, energize the youth work, and establish a programme of outreach that will lead to numerical growth. At the same time, the congregation cherish their customary ways of worship, and seek someone who will not alter the existing pattern of services, or change the ethos and tradition of the congregation.

A new minister is duly hired, and sets about a vigorous programme of evangelism, visiting and youth work. However, the new recruits to the church do not find the existing patterns of worship to be welcoming or conducive. Despite the best efforts of the minister, new recruits tend to drift off and find other churches. The minister calls the lay leadership of the church to a meeting, and demands that there are changes in the patterns and forms of worship to accommodate new members. But the lay leadership of the church are unwilling to abandon the existing traditions and ethos of the worship. There is stalemate.

After some months, the minister begins to lose heart, and the energetic programme of visiting, youth work and outreach begins to peter out. However, the minister decides that the problem lies with the lay leadership of the church, and sets about challenging their authority. Changes are made to worship. Channels of consultation start to fail, and very quickly the worship services become a 'battleground' of competing convictions that reflect very different visions about the future of the church. This spills over into some acrimonious meetings, in which the new minister attempts to assert his authority, and strong elements in the congregation seek to re-establish their sense of ownership – of the building, worship and character of the church. Both aggrieved parties eventually appeal to the parent denomination in an attempt to resolve the dispute. The denomination responds by relocating the minister. The congregation is offered the opportunity to recruit a new minister. But the underlying causes of the dispute are not addressed by the denomination. The dispute is eventually characterized by the denomination as being 'an unfortunate clash of personalities'.

By taking the issue of authority as an example, it should be fairly obvious that a minister will be able to exercise some power simply by virtue of their office. However, one might begin asking 'power over what?' This might be power in the formal governance of the church, control of the actual make-up of the worship week-by-week, and perhaps in other spheres. But the power may be limited elsewhere. Individual members of the church may not explicitly reject the power of the minister to operate in matters of 'formal' belief. Congregations may implicitly signal their disquiet relating to a minister by attaching more significance to their 'operant' religion, or placing a greater stress on their own spirituality rather than the teaching of the church. Equally, there are other aspects to studying power in the church that need factoring in to any kind of local, contextual or congregational study. Buildings, and the meaning and symbolism vested in them, can hamper the most energetic and charismatic clergy with change on their agenda. Vested interests in maintaining traditions in liturgy, ritual and other practices can also complicate the study of power relations in churches. The environment of the minister, in other words, is a place of formation as much as it is to be formed.

So, just as cultural factors such as youth and gender have a bearing upon the shaping of ministry, so does the contested nature of power and authority within the Christian tradition. One way forward, therefore, in studying the evolution of clerical identity and roles, is to 'plot' or 'map' the different kinds of power relations. Who or what has 'power'? What kinds of power are there in a congregation? Are there situations or issues in which power interests necessarily come into conflict? How does power 'flow' in a church? Does it simply flow 'top down', or is the model more complicated, whereby power flows in a variety of ways? What kinds of social or civic powers shape ministry and ecclesiology? It is through addressing such issues that one can begin to gain some sense of how ministry functions and fits within its wider environs; how it adapts, and how it might survive, and ultimately flourish. And it is to the question of survival that we now turn.

Chapter 5

On Survival

One of the more pressing puzzles that face evolutionists and conservationists lies in providing a coherent account of why a species might become extinct. However, leaving aside the speculation surrounding dinosaurs (global warming? an ice age? a giant meteor?), it is possible to trace a clear relationship between habitat and survival. The Galapagos Islands, with their unique marine iguanas and varieties of tortoise, which evolved in isolation, have only recently become accustomed to goats, rats and cats, which have been introduced during the last fifty years. Their arrival has disturbed the balance of nature: the rats attack the seabird colonies, the cats eat the iguanas and the goats graze on almost all the vegetation, threatening the habitat of the tortoise. Similarly, the Iberian Lynx, once found throughout Spain and Portugal, is now reduced to a handful of tiny remnant populations, perhaps numbering less than 250. Moreover, the populations cannot link up, and the threat of extinction within the next twenty-five years is very real. The decline in numbers is largely due to the demise of its main prey, the rabbit, whose own numbers were decimated by myxomatosis.

Likewise, the fate of the clergy is inextricably linked to the health of the denomination in which they serve. If the environment in which clergy function is adversely disturbed by internal or external forces, their numbers are likely to decline. Of course, no one can rule out revival, renewal and the activity of God within such equations, in which the predicted trends and outcomes are altered, rather against the (reductionist) run of play. However, the role of environmental factors within denominational identity, which in turn has an impact on the evolution and survival of the clergy themselves, cannot be discounted. A popular rhyme from the nineteenth century contrasts the fortunes of the declining (established) Presbyterian Church of Scotland, and the then newly established Free Church of Scotland (from 1843), which enjoyed a considerable following:

The Free Kirk, the wee Kirk,
The Kirk without the steeple.
The auld Kirk, the cauld Kirk
The Kirk without the people.

The rich irony of the rhyme is, of course, that the Free Church has declined significantly in the last fifty years, whilst the established

Church of Scotland has managed to hold its place. In a number of cases, former Free Church chapels have been absorbed back into the mainline Presbyterian fold, becoming church rooms or other facilities. But before testing our hypothesis on development further – Methodism and independent Charismatic churches are the main case studies – we can begin to illustrate the impact that cultural change has upon denominational and clerical identity, with a short excursion into a distinctive world within the vast archipelago of Anglicanism, namely the islets of Anglo-Catholicism.

Strictly speaking, Anglo-Catholicism began as a movement on the defensive. The cultural context is crucial to understanding the trajectory of the movement. Throughout the eighteenth century, government legislation had essentially privileged the Church of England over and against Roman Catholicism and Nonconformity. But the political reforms of the early Victorian era challenged the power of the established church on two fronts. First, by extending the vote and engaging in electoral reform, parliamentary democracy began to develop and evolve without the same kind of patronage that tradition-ally supported the church. Second, the 1828 Test and Corporation Act was repealed, which paved the way for dissenters and Roman Catholics to hold public office, including within parliament. The combined effect of these moves was to deliver a parliament which now comprised dissenters, Roman Catholics and others who were outside the sphere of influence of the Church of England, but who could nonetheless legislate on its internal affairs. This parliament duly did, by proposing (very reasonably, it has to be said) the amalgamation of some Irish bishoprics, as some dioceses actually had very few Anglicans within them.

It is the defensive reaction to this political initiation that Anglo-Catholicism owes its status as a subspecies. Tracing its origins to John Keble's sermon before the judges of the Oxford assizes (1833) at the University Church, he argued that as the state no longer defended the church, so must the church defend itself. The movement quickly evolved, energetically producing tracts (hence the name 'Tractarian'), acquiring a distinctive theological and aesthetic temperament. It began to distance itself from the Reformation, which it re-narrated as the source of compromising alliances with the state and, therefore, with political and social liberalism. Inevitably, and partly through its own roots in Romanticism, this drew the movement towards Catholicism, which was perceived to be purer, separated and, therefore, able to administer its own world. The instinctive move towards the 'real' church of the apostles and away from the compromised church of the state was rapidly reified in the adoption of 'catholic' spiritual, aesthetic and ecclesial tastes. The distinctiveness of the movement began to express itself in architecture and art, but also in a wide variety of somewhat idiosyncratic and eccentric plumage – something that not even the departure of John Henry Newman for the Roman Catholic Church in 1845 failed to prevent.

As with Evangelicalism, Anglo-Catholicism flourished as a 'party' within the Church of England for a considerable period. The movement had a pronounced effect upon liturgy, ritual and the shaping of ministry. The more dominant (or perhaps widespread) legacy that the movement has produced is to be found in a broad expression of catholicity with Anglicanism, a subspecies that we might refer to as 'Liberal', 'Open' or even 'English' Catholics.[1] In the mid-twentieth century, writers such as Percy Dearmer might be said to best exemplify the movement. And in the late evening of the twentieth century, it is this brand of Anglican catholicity that deemed to be most transferable, highly adaptable, engagingly popular, and also capable of self-renewal. Recently, one English Anglican theological college, which has an Evangelical foundation, was able to claim more members of 'Affirming Catholicism' than any other college, pro rata.[2] In contrast, a much narrower and more distinctive brand of Anglo-Catholicism has also grown up alongside its more accommodating close relative. This 'exotic and aesthetic counter-cultural extremism' (as Mark Chapman describes it), has struggled to maintain its size, influence and identity in the post-war years:

In the contemporary Church of England, partisan Anglo-Catholicism looks like a movement that has lost its direction. *New Directions*, the publication of Forward in Faith, the group organised for those opposed to the ordination of women, is a bitter, sad and defensive magazine of rant. Such negativity has not proved popular: no more than a couple of hundred parishes have opted for 'extended Episcopal oversight'. Where Evangelicalism flourishes in parishes and attracts increasing numbers, Anglo-Catholicism is declining...the future for Anglo-Catholicism does not look rosy.[3]

Romantically inclined Anglo-Catholics who identify themselves with the species may argue that their particular brand of ecclesiology is facing ecological annihilation. There is some truth in this, although it must be remembered that the movement was always more congregational and sectarian than many of the inhabitants of the islets ever suppose. But with the alleged persecution over women priests, and an increasing external intolerance of the ambivalent homo-eroticism that can still feature very heavily within the movement, apologists for sectarian Anglo-Catholicism argue that like the Blue Whale or the Javan

[1] On this, see N. Yates, *Anglican Ritualism in Victorian Britain: 1830–1910* (Oxford: Oxford University Press, 1991).

[2] Affirming Catholicism was founded in the wake of the Church of England's decision to ordain women to the priesthood in 1992. It affirms this decision, but also stands for a less reactionary and moderate form of catholicity within Anglicanism, in contrast to groups such as Forward in Faith.

[3] M. Chapman, *Anglicanism: A Very Brief Introduction* (Oxford: Oxford University Press, 2006), p. 48.

Rhino, they are being hunted to extinction. They therefore continually plead for protected status, so that their numbers can recover. In reality, the call for a Third Province in which Anglo-Catholics can administer their own affairs is akin to a plea to be released into a protected game reserve. But in truth (and to faintly echo Coleridge's *Ancient Mariner*), the decline in Anglo-Catholicism is more akin to the ecological (rather than the proverbial) curse of the albatross. It is the success of the 'industrial scale fishing' of Evangelicalism and other cultural factors that have deprived Anglo-Catholicism of its feeding and breeding grounds. In short, the gin, lace and biretta brigade have not adapted well to modernity; many try to resist it at every turn, scowling at innovation and progress, hoping wantonly for a return to a mythic past, a golden age of Catholic Christendom festooned with Gothic and Baroque motifs.

Granted, this is a caricature. But when one begins to compare Anglo-Catholicism to movements of renewal within the broader church, the scale of the problem comes sharply into focus. On a recent trip to Taize – an ecumenical centre designed for young people, prayer, peace and reconciliation, and founded by a Lutheran, Brother Roger – one is immediately struck by its broad appeal. The altar is simple, and surrounded by clay drainpipes with flickering candles. The backcloth is made of yacht sails, which flutter gently in the breeze, suggestive of the Spirit. The music is engaging yet plain, and the liturgy international and inclusive. There are several thousand young people present when we arrive as a family, and each year Taize welcomes hundreds of thousands of visitors and pilgrims.

In contrast, Anglo-Catholicism's equivalent is Walsingham: 'England's Nazareth', not far from Norwich. The liturgy is beautifully ornate, but in almost every other aspect conveys an ethos that reaches back to the past. The accent is firmly placed on recovering a tradition and maintaining it; there is little sense of innovation, inclusiveness and participation. There are young people and some young clergy; but in truth, it is the same script being performed every time. There is no sense of renewal, revival or of deep engagement with the world around. Compared to the Iona Community or to Corrymeela, coupled with a spirituality that the youth can actually help to shape and perform, Walsingham's lack of overt social and political engagement feels like a retreat into a mythic church. Whilst it is not entirely fair to compare Walsingham to Taize, visitors engaged in a comparative exercise would be instantly struck by the differences between the places. Both have a decidedly 'catholic' feel; but one is securely grounded in the present and has set its face confidently to the future; the other continues to hope and pray for the restoration of the past.

The decline of Anglo-Catholicism is relatively new.[4] Once a dominant party within the Church of England, its current membership (either taken as numbers of churches, clergy or laity) probably now only constitutes about 10 per cent of the Church – arguably less. These figures are also reflected in the numbers engaged in residential ordination training. In 2005/6, the total number of Anglo-Catholic ordinands in full-time residential training stood at about 45 – some 10 per cent of the national total of (an estimated) 450. Recent research has suggested that about half of the Anglo-Catholics in training are likely to be opposed to the ordination of women – some 5 per cent of the total number of ordinands in Colleges. Unlike Evangelicalism (which accounts for around 30 per cent of the Church of England), Anglo-Catholicism no longer enjoys the same breadth of appeal, and there are a number of reasons for this development since the post-war era.

First, the rapid erosion of class-based support for Anglo-Catholicism should be noted. It no longer enjoys an identity as a strong cultural body that offers upward social mobility to young working-class men. Middle-upper-class support for the movement (especially amongst women) has also waned. Evangelicalism, in contrast, is the dominant faith of the suburbs, backed by strong international and numerical support. Second, concepts of authority in the Church of England have been challenged, democratized (i.e., synods, etc.) and dispersed, marginalizing the mode of Anglo-Catholic understandings of priest-hood and power. Third, the traditional Anglo-Catholic investment in aesthetics and ambiguity (see Pickering, 1989, etc) has been challenged by the clarity reached on the ordination of women, and the continuing pressure for precision on sexuality, desired by other parts of the church. Fourth, Anglo-Catholic identity has been eroded by successive litur-gical and theological movements in recent years, most notably Liberal Catholics and Affirming Catholicism. Fifth, the constituency of Anglo-Catholicism is failing to recruit sufficient new blood to sustain its current numbers. There is little sign of emerging major and distinctive Anglo-Catholic theological voices beginning to make major contribu-tions within the church or in public life. Sixth, the movement appears to be unable to appeal to more central ground without compromising its ethos (e.g., on women priests). It has developed a kind of emasculated aloofness when it comes to engaging in debate: a body that stands for authority but cannot convince is forced to withdraw, for to continue

---

[4] Although some scholars argue that it has always exaggerated its strength, and is therefore suffering from the collapse of its own myths rather than engaging with a narrative of comparative continuity. Reed (*Glorious Battle*, pp. 158ff) points out that of the 4,290 seats available within Ritualist churches in East London in 1886 (an alleged heartland for Anglo-Catholicism), only 1,251 were used – attracting 29 per cent of capacity, and only accounting for 17 per cent of total Anglican churchgoing in the area. Reed cites St Columba as an example – seats for 1,000, but an attendance of only 132 – a very disappointing figure, especially by Victorian standards.

talking without convincing will threaten the very confidence that has been placed in that authority. Seventh, some of the sectarian demons that shaped the original Tractarian movement have returned to roost. Anglo-Catholicism has developed into a highly specious body with its own peculiar evolution. Like a small land mass that has begun to break away from a larger continent, the movement faces its biggest challenge. Should it stay engaged with the continent, and evolve with all the challenges that the environment and its predators will undoubtedly muster? Or should it break away, and in so doing guarantee both survival and exile, with little hope of impacting the wider world? All the signs are, at present, that Anglo-Catholics cannot decide between the two: so the movement hankers after the very thing it despises: compromise. It wants to be a state within a state; an ecological haven for a vulnerable species, that will only survive through gentle husbandry protected from its predators.

But it is likely that the potential advent of women bishops will undoubtedly throw such choices into further disarray. Whilst it is currently possible to easily identify male and female clergy (and then regard the women clergy as not being validly ordained priests), and therefore distinguish between 'real' and 'bogus' priests, women bishops will ensure that such distinctions become impossible from the moment of their consecration. Assuming that women bishops will ordain men and women to the priesthood, the nightmare scenario for Anglo-Catholics opposed to women priests and bishops will become all too real. It raises the question, for some male bishops, of conditionally re-ordaining any priest ordained by a woman bishop. Furthermore, it takes the church to the brink of a potentially troublesome obsession with the 'archaeology of orders'. Just how many generations does one go back in order to establish that the bishops that consecrated the bishops that consecrated your bishop, who then ordained you, actually had valid orders at the point of origin? In the interminable search for a pure church, which necessarily values a lineage of purity in priesthood and episcopacy, it is likely that there is little more to be gained than further schism, and denominations turning in on themselves in ever-decreasing circles.

With these remarks in mind, we now turn to our two main case studies in this chapter – Methodism and Revivalism. In considering them as environments or habitats, the reader is being invited to contemplate how the denomination forms the context that determines the fate, survival and identity of its own clergy. In both cases, I wish to suggest that it is *denominationalism* itself that poses the largest threat to the original movements. Ecclesiologies that were born to be disturbing, mobile and fissiparous do not settle well on the lush plains of denominationalism. In the case of Methodism, bureaucratization and routinization are having a pronounced and deleterious impact upon denominational identity. In the case of Revivalism, it finds itself caught between movement and ecclesial identity. Revivalism is now steering itself uneasily through this most delicate phase of evolution, as it considers its state and shape in relation to culture and the wider church.

Methodism: a case study in denominationalism

Arguably, and in order to grasp something of the originating spirit of Methodism, one really needs to begin from somewhere outside the movement as it is manifest today. Methodism, like so many denominations, did not begin on its path of spiritual enquiry with the thought of becoming a denomination. But nor was the movement intending to be sectarian. There is a world of difference between bodies that seek to reify a spiritual intensity and particularity in order to enrich a larger body, and those that set their heart on leaving an allegedly corrupt body in the often vain hope that they can somehow maintain their purity. One of the ironies of studying subspecies is that they often have more to tell about the state of the parent species than is immediately apparent. Consider, for example, the discreet culture of Independent Methodists, who, after almost two centuries of existence, have joined the Baptist Union.

In John Dolan's prescient study, we learn, as the author candidly admits, that the Independent Methodists have never been a large denomination.[5] Even in the northwest of England, which is their heartland, the history of the denomination is little known. Dolan's account begins with the formative influences of the movement in the first half of the nineteenth century, and in the wake of John Wesley's death. Shaped by primitive Methodism, Quakerism and Revivalism, the Independents developed a distinctive brand of ecclesiology and missiology that sought to resist the growing denominationalism within mainstream Methodism. Some of its features resemble early traits in Revivalism – 'the Kirkgate Screamers', for example, who formed a chapel in Leeds – were shaped by spiritual experiences that would find an echo in Pentecostalism and Charismatic Renewal. An early nineteenth-century report records that:

> The Revivalists are those Methodists who are more particularly partial to noisy meetings. They claim, as a Christian privilege, a right to indulge their propensities to prayer and praise, at all times and on all occasions. This liberty they will take during [*sic*] the minister is engaged in preaching; and indeed at any other time they think themselves called upon by the motions of the Spirit of God. They are a simple, harmless and well-meaning body; but enthusiastical and ungovernable to an extraordinary degree.[6]

[5] J. Dolan, *The Independent Methodists: A History* (Cambridge: James Clarke & Co., 2005).
[6] Ibid., p. 33.

However, other influences owe their shape to cultural and political factors such as the Peterloo massacre, Chartism and the Beerhouse Act, through which Independent Methodism took on a radical political hue that lasted well into the twentieth century. Part of the beauty of Dolan's writing is to be found in that skill shared by all great historians: resurrection. In Dolan's text, the dead come to life, striding across the pages, full of character, body and fissiparous charisma. Describing an early Independent Methodist preacher, Dolan notes the perceptions of one member of an eighteenth-century audience:

> His manners have been clownish in the extreme, his habit and appearance more filthy than a savage Indian; his public discourses as mere rhapsody, the substance often an insult upon the gospel. . . He has affected a recognizance of the secrets of men's hearts and lives, and even assumed the awful prerogative of prescience. . .pretending to foretell. . .the deaths or calamities of persons.[7]

The passionate enthusiasm that fanned the embers of Revivalism is faithfully recaptured, and the history of the movement bursts into life. And even when it come to the moments for speaking of decline and survival, with the inevitable litany of chapel closures chronicled, the author manages to find poignant accents of gratefulness and melancholy as the movement searches afresh for its meaning and mission in the twenty-first century.

The great strength of Dolan's prescient history is its empathetic narration of a fairly typical nineteenth-century ecclesial trend: charting the gradual but inexorable slide from being a radical sectarian movement to becoming a denomination. Independent Methodists began by attempting to offer free ministry to some of the north's poorest communities. Their identity has eventually settled on becoming a tiny denomination that aligned with the Baptist Union in 2004. For any emerging movement seeking to break the hegemonic mould of denominationalism today, Dolan's history offers a tonic laced with a salutary warning. It is relatively easy to begin a new religious movement, but they are invariably much harder to develop and continue. But if that is true (and perhaps obvious) for the evolution of Independent Methodism, what can be said of the mainstream denomination?

Some years ago I was invited to address a group of Methodist adult educators at a conference. I wanted to get a feel for the different theological outlooks that might be present in the group – about 25 in all – so I set them the task of completing the late James Hopewell's 'Worldview Test' which is published posthumously in his groundbreaking book, *Congregation: Stories and Structures* (1987). In this exercise, worldviews are assessed through a matrix of questions that discern the types of (faith) stories individuals and groups sense they have the most affinity with. According to Hopewell, who adapted his 'Worldview Test' from Northrop Frye's literary categorizations (*The Anatomy of Criticism*, 1951), there are four basic types of faith story: Tragedy (or Canonic), Comedy (or Gnostic), Romantic (or Charismatic) and Irony (or Empiric).

Normally when I have used this exercise before as a theological educator with other groups, there has always been a fair amount of variety to be noted amongst the respondents. Typically, Evangelicals will be mostly Canonic in their outlook; Charismatics are heavily disposed towards being Romantic; Quakers, and those who incline to Celtic spirituality or to the writings of mystics, will more usually be Gnostic; and those who are more liberal-minded in their theology tend to gravitate towards the Empiric worldview. So, for example, in any average Anglican congregation or gathering of clergy, there will be a considerable mixture of worldviews; a considerable variety of beliefs.

The Methodist group I was with completed the test, and we logged the results onto a screen. But what was surprising was the almost total homogeneity of the group, who in their worldviews, all expressed a marked Empiric/Ironic tendency, which can be broadly identified with a 'liberal' attitude to theology, faith and ethics. A few showed some secondary inclinations towards Gnostic worldviews, but there were no examples of advocates of the Tragic or Romantic worldviews to be found at all. I was puzzled by this. How, I asked, did the group ever have a disagreement or engage in strong debate? How did they generate discussion and dialogue if all the members of the group were roughly of the same mind?

The group looked at one another, and one eventually spoke: 'we hardly ever disagree with each other – that's why we like coming away together – we get on so well, and tend to see things in the same way'. And that was that. To be fair to the group, most could see that their cosiness with each other was potentially problematic. With no grit in the oyster, their discussions were of the comfortable and conformist variety. Moreover, there did not seem to be an obvious potential source of challenge to the worldviews that were in the ascendancy (indeed, it was a virtual monopoly).

'Monochrome' would be a kind of nomenclature for the dynamics I have described above. Not so much black and white, either, as several shades of grey. And certainly no hint of colour. Indeed, I have many Methodist friends and colleagues who speak openly about the state of the church: 'ageing and passionless' is a phrase that features in nearly every narration. Such descriptions are, of course, caricatures. I regularly encounter Methodists who are passionate. Some are fierce, earnest and even excitable about ecumenism. Others are ardent and animated about a variety of issues: social justice; equality – especially racial and sexual; the wickedness of the privilege invested in the 'established' church; the problem with the Church of England, and so forth. But as I reflect on the conversations I have with Methodists, I have begun to realize that I seldom hear individuals celebrating the Methodist church itself, or who are in touch with the kind of spiritual spark that lit Wesley's soul,[8] or ignited the Independent Methodists.

Granted, there may be several reasons for this. Methodism could rightly, from its very beginnings, profess to be more interested in the world than in its own interiority. The totemic Wesleyan mantra – 'the world is my parish' – has firmly fixed Methodist eyes on looking outwards for centuries. Equally, the Wesleyan core experience – 'my heart was strangely warmed' – confirms that the only major interiority that any self-respecting Methodist should be concerned with is the transformed self-before-God. The origins of Methodism lie in a connexional of two affinities: one of one heart, mind and experience of Christ and the grace of God, and the other united in the implications and outworkings of that for local and global praxis. Thus, early Methodism was not marked by the erection of grand buildings, or by the kind of theological aesthetics that helped shape the Oxford Movement. The Methodist Movement was true to its founders, who engaged in significant counter-cultural Christian praxis, and became a catalyst for radical social change that went hand-in-hand with preaching the gospel in word and deed. Wesley visited prisons; he worked for the relief of the poor; credit unions were set up; spiritual enthusiasm was inseparable from significant social witness. Put another way, the Christian religion of England began to be both a socially liberating and spiritually emotivating force in the lives of ordinary people.

Arguably, the search for contemporary Methodist identity should begin and end at this point. It would begin by recognizing that Methodism began primarily as a *movement*, and end by also recognizing that the movement eventually became a church. (Indeed, Methodism is arguably the largest 'Continuing Anglican Church' in the world.) But rather as the House Church Movement has discovered in the late 1990s, what begins as a radical movement can end up quickly becoming mired within the process of bureaucratization and routinzation. Attention soon shifts from changing the world to changing the fabric on the seat coverings; from a radical challenge to contemporary culture to the challenge posed by the treasurer at the AGM – to increase giving by 1 per cent so the leaking church hall roof can be fixed.

Of course, no church is immune from these dynamics, but it should not be forgotten just how deleterious such aspects tend to be upon the morale of ecclesial communities. And what a powerful disincentive such agendas are to younger generations contemplating joining their local Methodist congregation. Who wants to join an organization that is

---

[8] Although to be pedantic, Wesley only claimed that his heart was 'strangely warmed' – a rather Laodicean remark – but perhaps not surprising from one who was actually an Anglican.

characterized by maintenance and struggle? My point is that the Methodist journey – that from movement to church – is an uncomfortable one to contemplate at the best of times, and in the search for a Methodist ecclesiology that can successfully adapt (evolve) within modernity, it merits more attention than it usually gets. True, Methodism has managed the evolution from movement to church better than most. But I want to suggest that in the spiritually competitive, culturally diverse and socially secular society of the twenty-first century, Methodism probably has a more promising future as a movement than as a church.

If any evidence of this were needed, one need only turn to the Millennium edition of *The Constitution, Practice and Discipline of the Methodist Church*. As Angela Shier-Jones notes:

> Pythagoras' theorem can be stated in 24 words. The Lord's Prayer in traditional English form has only 70 words...the Ten Commandments can be listed using 179 words...[but] *The Constitution, Practice and Discipline of the Methodist Church* requires no less than 225,966 words – to tell us what?[9]

I suspect that Methodism has arrived at this soul-numbing point for a number of reasons, but there is time to mention just five.

First, and constitutionally, it has quickly positioned itself as a pre-eminent Protestant Church with a global ministry. So far, so good. But part of the baggage that goes with that mission is the (inevitable and accompanying) substantial industry in ecclesial civil service, which must then ensure continuity of identity and a degree of standardization in the delivery of mission, liturgy and service. The effect of this is to suffocate diversity (e.g., see my earlier vignette); the movement becomes monochrome – the church a gathering of the like-minded. (However, we must not forget that Episcopal Methodists, originating from the USA, make up half of the world's Methodist population. So there is a real sense in which Methodist ecclesiology – connexional or episcopal? – is actually quite schizophrenic.)

Second, the character and culture of British Methodism at a national and meta-organizational level appears to closely resemble the morphology of some sort of proto-retro-socialist organization. By that I mean political parties or trade unions, with Methodism as its sacred alternative. There seems to be a great deal of bureaucracy, coupled with an apparent sense of democracy. However, the all-powerful Conference appears, nonetheless, to operate in a classic 'hegemonic working-class' style, replete with ballots, motions and rulings. Nominations for the Conference President are carefully choreographed and almost entirely predictable: democracy has triumphed over

[9] A. Shier-Jones, 'Being Methodical', in *Unmasking Methodist Theology* (ed. C. Marsh *et al.*; London: Continuum, 2004), p. 29.

theocracy. In other words, it all seems about as far away from the *spirit* of the original Methodist movement as one could possibly be. (David Hare, the playwright, confessed that before he wrote *Racing Demon*, he had wanted to base his drama on the machinations of the Church of England's General Synod. He attended one session in London, and concluded that the three-day meeting was so absurd as to be beyond parody or satire. But the General Synod does not run the Church of England – it is merely one of several instruments of governance and politicking that thinks it does.)

Third, and locally, Methodist churches appear to be struggling with their identity as never before. There are many reasons why this is so. Temperance is not the issue it once was: I have yet to meet a Methodist that doesn't drink. Furthermore, few people care for the difference between conformity and non-conformity; today's religious consumers simply want to find a good local church – assuming they are looking at all. The distinction between a parish church and a congregational church will be mostly lost on the emerging generations of the twenty-first century. True, there is some residual awareness of the differences between Catholic and Protestant, and of the provision offered by an established, national church (Anglican in England); but a subtle public consciousness of the nuances and differences between denominations has otherwise dissipated. Ironically, ecumenism has had a double-edged effect on smaller nonconformist churches: in drawing denominations together, it has obviated their particularities. The ecclesial menu now available to the religious consumer is more standardized.

Fourth, Methodism has experienced a relatively recent collapse in its theological confidence. I do not mean by this that it lacks good, intelligent professional theologians. It has plenty of them, and their contribution to the wider theological firmament seems to be as strong and vibrant as ever. The crisis is more at local level. It is often said that Anglicans carry their theology in liturgy, and Methodists in their hymns. If that is true, then one would expect the rapid deterioration of corporate worship in schools and colleges to have had a deleterious impact on both denominations within a very short space of time. But strangely, the appetite for traditional liturgy has enjoyed a renaissance in recent decades, suggesting that 'operant' Anglican theology can survive quite well in the twenty-first century. Singing hymns, on the other hand, has enjoyed more mixed fortunes. In one way, through television (e.g., BBC *Songs of Praise*) and other large events (e.g., national memorials, etc.), their place in the public affection seems assured. On the other hand, singing hymns in any other context is now rare. Music for worship has also diversified immensely in the post-war era. The sheer range of resources and materials now available has broken the Methodist monopoly of 'singing theology'.

Fifth, and still at a local level, Methodist churches seem to be struggling to be particular – especially in their theology. Most of its public theological concerns seem to be caught up within a broad social agenda. Such engagement is, of course, to be applauded. But my question is this: does the church define the agenda, or the agenda define the church? Listening to some prominent Methodists speak recently, I have sometimes felt that I was hearing little more than a tired and fairly predictable set of socialist assertions, which are then honed with a fairly thin Christian gloss. Depth and substance in the argument, and in the character of engagement, have not been easy to discern. Equally, the places where a passionate Methodist missiology are expounded are all too few. This is ironic when one considers the totality of the legacy of the Wesley brothers.[10] As things stand at present, local Methodism clearly still attempts to embody the radical Christian social teaching of the Wesleys. But to be fully faithful to its movement identity and spiritual roots, Methodism needs to recover its head, heart and nerve for evangelism as well.

As we are concerned with evolution and survival in this chapter, I want to end this brief section by suggesting that the future of Methodism lies in articulating a spirituality, theology and ecclesiology that can re-engage with the public sphere. I offer three brief points by way of summing up. First, Methodism began as a movement and religious society that *supplemented* the church. Most of the original Methodists were also Anglicans. Now, the great advantage of movement identity over ecclesial identity is that the former can usually afford to be more sharply focused in its teaching and praxis. It can also venture beyond margins, and take risks that established institutions cannot normally afford. If Methodism can recover a sense of itself as movement, it might begin to shed some of the impedimentary ecclesial vestiges that it has acquired over the centuries. In a postmodern world, it might find that, as a movement, it is able to be reflexive and proactive. In a post-associational world, in which fewer and fewer people are committed to belonging to organizations (and yet demand higher levels of service for less commitment), a *movement* rather than a church might be a much better conveyor of the *spirit* of Methodism.

Second, the core identity of the Methodist movement lies in its origins, naturally enough. Put simply, that is, first, a commitment to radical, innovative and engaging Christian social teaching, with an accompanying praxis of corporate and individual discipline that is rooted in a committed and rigorous discipleship and centred on holiness. And second, an understanding that the overwhelming experience of transforming grace – the heart 'strangely warmed' – is what drives individuals and congregations to share the love of God poured out in Jesus Christ, so that others may also be transformed. Put

[10] Cliff College, for example, is one of the few Methodist training colleges that is devoted to missiology and the study and practice of evangelism. But I note with interest that its outstanding work is more off than on the edge of British Methodism, when it would surely be better for the church if it were closer to its centre.

succinctly, Methodism, as a movement, and at its best, is passionate evangelism wedded to a burning zeal for social action; it is the marriage between the Student Christian Movement (SCM) and the Christian Union (CU). It can be the fusion of the earnest concerns of the Urban Theology Unit and the exuberance and academic acuity of Cliff College. But it is the movement that must continually give birth to the church; the church must not presume to parent the movement.

Third, if Methodism didn't exist, it would probably have to be invented. The dynamic combination of Christian social action and intelligent evangelism is arguably a uniquely concentrated ecclesial embodiment within a single denomination. Furthermore, in a postmodern age, Methodism would do well to remember that insofar as its theology is expressed, its medium has always been its message. A movement that expresses its theology in the reflexive space and responsive arena of song has understood something fundamental about the work of the Holy Spirit. That, coupled with a spirituality that connects and transforms, stressing as it does the essential nature of inner conviction and necessity of outward signs, is arguably a movement already well-suited for the postmodern age. In an era that increasingly divorces feelings from dogma, and action from inner conviction, Methodism has a particular theological contribution to make.

Ultimately, it is my belief that Methodism, in its future, should focus and reflect on its core strength – those gifts and charisms that gave it a strong movement identity in the first place. It has a clear future as a movement, and it is also clear that an explicit ecclesiology can be developed from this (which began as 'Holiness Clubs'). But that does not necessarily mean that it need continue to be an independent denomination, or indeed even act as a 'church' *per se*. Perhaps Methodism is rather like Wales – you can see the point of it, granted. But it is a distinctive principality rather than a full-blown country: its future is only secure in a United Kingdom. To follow this analogy through, I see no reason why Methodism cannot function like Quakerism, with people either belonging exclusively to such movements, or belonging to a church or denomination *and* the movement: in effect, dual passports. In other words, we are back to the future. It should be possible to be an Anglican, and to be a Methodist, with Methodism no longer describing a denominational label, but rather a particular spirituality and form of 'methodical' discipleship.

Methodism, then, as an intelligible and vibrant movement, is more like the leaven in the lump than even it may ever have realized. I suspect that the future of Methodism – at least in Britain – might lie in the church saving itself from becoming too 'churchy': a poor cousin of modernity. Habitually, all churches recover something of their colour when they cease to be comfortable, and begin to look urgent. So instead of trying to operate like a modernist meta-organization, Methodism might need to revisit some of its primary and generative spiritual roots, in order to return to being a movement, and in so doing, renew not only itself, but also those other denominations around it that undoubtedly need to learn from the fusion of its dynamic evangelistic heritage and capacious social witness. To be sure, this would be a costly decision. To journey from being a movement to a church, and then back to being a movement, is not a development that many in Conference or Marylebone Road would welcome. But I wonder what the Wesley brothers would have had to say about it?

Revivalism: assessing the future of Charismatic Christianity

Sometime during January 1936, the Pentecostal preacher and revivalist Smith Wigglesworth from Bradford, Yorkshire, spoke to a young man named David Du Plessis, a fellow Pentecostal minister from the USA. According to Hocken, Du Plessis immediately knew that the words spoken to him were a 'prophecy':

> There is a revival coming that at present the world knows nothing about. It will come through the churches. It will come in a fresh way. When you see what God does in this revival you will then have to admit that all you have seen previously is a mere nothing in comparison to what is to come. It will eclipse anything that has been known in history. Empty churches, empty cathedrals, will be packed again with worshippers. Buildings will not be able to accommodate the multitudes. Then you will see fields of people worshipping and praising together...the Lord will use you if you remain faithful and humble – you will see the greatest events in Church history.[11]

Startling prophecies about the impact of revival are not new. Indeed, the latter half of the twentieth century may be said, in some sense, to have entirely borne out the predictions and prophecies of Pentecostals, Revivalists and Charismatics, who have seen their numbers steadily rise on a global scale. Estimates on numbers vary, but taken as a whole, the number of Christians *influenced* by Charismatic renewal, Pentecostalism or its variants (which is not to say that being influenced by these movements means that individuals identify themselves as being inside or part of any one movement) may run to 400 million people, which is something like 20 per cent of the world's Christian population. Charismatic Christianity has touched every part of the world, has significantly affected virtually every Christian denomination, as well as spawning its own seminaries, churches and exponents.

[11] P. Hocken, *Streams of Renewal: The Origins and Development of the Charismatic Movement in Britain* (Exeter: Paternoster, 1986), p. 19.

Broader than Pentecostalism, Charismatic Christianity has spread to the 'mainline churches' and the 'middle-class churches', and is allegedly 'flourishing in the contemporary world...a fluid culture that is seeping into numerous social contexts'.[12] Whereas Pentecostalism is a distinctive culture with a recognizable ecclesiology and doctrines (e.g., affirming the necessity of a 'second baptism' of the Holy Spirit, which may lead to a phenomenon such as the individual speaking in tongues), Charismatic renewal is more of a hybrid. It takes insights from revivals of previous eras, stresses the Pentecostal theme of empowerment through the Holy Spirit, but at the same time tends to influence and feed off mainstream denominations rather than creating its own.

Assessing the relative strength of Charismatic Christianity – and thereby testing the veracity of the prophecy – is a complex business. For example, do Roman Catholics or Anglicans, influenced by the teaching and ministry of recent exponents of revivalism such as John Wimber, count as 'Charismatic'? Some may, but many choose to remain within their denomination, and relate to an influential movement rather than joining it. Equally, Restorationists may not see themselves as 'renewing' churches in the sense that Du Plessis meant, but rather as a movement – not a church or new denomination – that is restoring God's kingdom and power in 'the last days'.[13] Then there are Pentecostals, an established denomination (or rather federation of denominations, bound together by their cultural morphology rather than any formal concordat) that is committed to maintaining and proclaiming the immanence of God, the gifts of the Spirit and the continuity of the miraculous.

To speak of Charismatic Christianity is to deploy an umbrella term that covers many different churches, movements, theologies, expressions of belief and modes of behaviour. It is impossible to generalize. For example, not all Charismatics speak in tongues. For some, if not many, this is a Pentecostal distinctive, as is the theology and epiphenomena of 'baptism in the Spirit'. Some Charismatics believe that the spiritual renewal they strive for will be reified in the churches; others, that it can only be truly manifested in movements that are beyond any recognized type of ecclesial structure. Some stress spiritual warfare – combating demons, principalities and powers – while others stress physical or 'inner' healing. Still for others, the combination of a conservative theological outlook plus a strong emphasis on the immediacy of spiritual encounter provides a powerful type of belief: 'fundamentalistic...not just a noetic phenomenon, but also a way of being in the world'.[14] For many, the major characteristic of Charismatic

---

[12] S. Coleman, *The Globalisation of Charismatic Christianity* (Cambridge: Cambridge University Press, 2000), pp. 22, 49.

[13] A. Walker, *Restoring the Kingdom: The Radical Christianity of the House Church Movement* (Guildford: Eagle Press, rev. and expanded edn., 1998 [orig. edn 1985]).

[14] Coleman, *Globalisation of Charismatic Christianity*, p. 27; M. Percy, *Power and the Church: Ecclesiology in an Age of Transition* (London: Cassell, 1998), pp. 62–66.

Christianity is its exuberant and dynamic worship, with many new songs written, a number of which have been adopted by historic denominations. It is now almost impossible to purchase a hymnal of any kind that does not contain several 'choruses' – short, pithy, affective worship songs that tend to be more expressive of sentiment to or from God than they are didactic.

Surveying the achievements of Charismatic Christianity over the last fifty years can leave the onlooker feeling a little breathless. The movement seems to have swept all before it. For many Charismatics, it seems that the mighty river of God's revival is flowing, and it looks to be unstoppable. But rivers have to flow somewhere, and indeed, they also have to be fed – by streams. And this simple observation, albeit based on a metaphor, raises some interesting questions. Are all the tributaries that have fed Charismatic Christianity sustainable as sources? And what of the river itself? Is it still flowing thick and fast, or has it now spread out so much into the wide compass of the denominationalist delta that its once intense and concentrated power has given way to an extensive and dissipated influence?

The signs point in somewhat different directions. We have already alluded to the phenomenal achievement of Charismatic Christianity in the twentieth century, and there is every reason to suppose that it will make a major contribution to Christian formation in the twenty-first. In the past twenty years, a number of academic studies have been positively smitten by Charismatic Christianity and its potential prospects.[15] However, Charismatic Christianity is, for many people, also becoming a *less* intense form of religion, a resource 'pool' in which to dip into, if you will, rather than a river that drives one in a particular direction. In a pluralist and postmodern world, believers increasingly behave like consumers; they *relate* to practices and doctrines, without necessarily believing in them entirely, or pursuing them wholesale. The initial experience of the 'rush' of the rivers of revival, so apparent in the post-war years, appears to have given way to a markedly calmer flow.

There may be many reasons for this. Cognitive dissonance – the psychological disassociation that occurs amongst believers when prophecies are not fulfilled[16] – tends to make successive generations of believers more cautious and circumspect about extravagant claims. Put simply, Charismatic Christianity has significantly influenced the churches, and, to an extent, the world, but the early visions of Charismatic Christianity coming to dominate denominations have not come to be; the prophecies of worldwide revival have not come to pass.

---

[15] H. Cox, *Fire from Heaven: The Rise of Pentecostalism, Spirituality and the Reshaping of Religion in the Twenty-first Century* (New York: Addison-Wesley, 1994); D. Martin and P. Mullen, *Strange Gifts? A Guide to Charismatic Renewal* (Oxford: Blackwell, 1984); S. Tugwell *et al. New Heaven? New Earth?* (London: Darton, Longman & Todd, 1976).

[16] L. Festinger, *When Prophecy Fails* (New York: Harper & Row, 1956).

Equally, charisma itself, over time, becomes routinized. What begins as fresh, authentic, groundbreaking and novel – all legitimate descriptions of Charismatic phenomena – can soon become ritualized, replicated, domesticated and fossilized.[17] The evidence for this can be seen in the leadership of English Charismatic churches; to a large extent, churches and movements are being led by the same people who were leading thirty years ago. Potential younger leaders are either still waiting in the wings – but lack the actual charisma of the founder leaders – or have left to join other churches. For some within Charismatic Christianity, the recognition that charisma becomes routinized over time has driven them out from the movement and back to the mainstream denominational churches. For others, it has driven them out of Charismatic Christianity and into other movements, including those that are communitarian (e.g., The Nine O'clock Community in Sheffield), spiritually diverse and novel (e.g., the 'Toronto Blessing') and the post-institutional (e.g. post-evangelicalism[18]). As one leading figure within British Charismatic Christianity confided to me recently:

> The sea is all rather flat at the moment... I sense that people are rather bored with Charismatic phenomenon, and a bit nervous of just jumping on to the next bandwagon, in case they get their fingers burned again. They've had Signs and Wonders, the Kansas City prophets, power evangelism, power healing, deliverance, the 'Toronto Blessing', and more besides... But where has it taken us? I think that people are just tired.[19]

Understanding the complexity of the contemporary situation in which Charismatic Christianity finds itself is vital if some predictions are to be made about its futures. What follows, then, are some remarks about the present that are suggestive of impending directions and developments. In offering these reflections, I am largely confining my comments to Charismatic renewal in Britain (rather than Restorationism or Pentecostalism), which represents a typical case study of how Charismatic Christianity has sought to distance yet embed itself within existing ecclesial traditions, accommodating them and resisting them by turns; to be distinct, yet related.[20] (Much of what I have to say does not necessarily apply to the Americas, Africa or to East Asia.) In saying this, I acknowledge that there can be no doubt that the 'new wine' of Charismatic Christianity has had a powerful effect on the Church of

[17] C. Smith, *The Quest of Charisma: Christianity and Persuasion* (Westport, CT: Praeger, 2000); Percy, *Power and the Church.*
[18] See D. Tomlinson, *The Post-Evangelical* (London: SPCK, 1995).
[19] Private correspondence, July 2000.
[20] D. Bridge and D. Phypers, *More than Tongues Can Tell: Reflections on Charismatic Renewal* (London: Hodder & Stoughton, 1982).

England in recent decades.[21] A once marginal movement has become mainstream; Charismatic renewal now has its own seat at the 'High Table' of ecclesiological expression. To the terms 'high', 'low', 'middle', 'evangelical' and 'catholic', 'Charismatic' can also now be added as a prefix.

As we have already noted, statistics appear to show that Charismatic Christianity, as an ecclesiological expression, is the only 'growth' area in the firmament of Christian expression, and is therefore, somehow, 'the future'.[22] Furthermore, the type of religion offered – tactile and immediate – is particularly and perfectly suited to a postmodern world, with its emphasis on fulfilment, healing, the individual and celebration. In contrast, I would express some cautionary notes on a number of fronts. These comments are based on general observations made of Britain. Again, it should be stressed that it is the future evolution of Charismatic renewal/Christianity that we shall be exploring, rather than Pentecostalism.

First, some commentators claim that the apparent growth-rate of Charismatic Christianity is highly questionable. Peter Brierley's statistical work, which is largely sympathetic to Charismatic Christianity, cannot decide if there were 20,000 people in 'New Churches' in 1980, or more than 50,000; or 95,000 in the year 2000 – or as many as 198,000 (compare his *UK Christian Handbook* of 1994/5 [p. 258] to that of 1998/9 [p. 212]). Brierley's national estimates for members of New Churches seem to grow with each new survey, even though most major regional independent Charismatic groups – such as Ichthus or Pioneer – report static or even declining numbers. Furthermore, the burgeoning post-evangelical movement (which includes many 'ex-Charismatics') suggests that whilst many have been influenced by Charismatic Christianity, just as many have left it. It may still be true that many continue to enter through the front door of revivalism[23], but the rate of attrition via the back door is not being properly attended to. There is a vast army of ex-Charismatics waiting to be researched.[24]

Second, Charismatic renewal remains a *movement* within the church: it is rarely a viable type of ecclesiology in its own right. Evidence to support this thesis comes from the sharp decline in numbers attending independent 'house churches'. Charismatic renewal must be a 'renewal' not just of the individual, but also of tradition, liturgy, sacramental worship, and the like. The 'movement' either drives people out of the church and into 'Restorationism', or deeper into the church itself.[25]

Third, Charismatic renewal is subject to the normative Weberian

---

[21] J. Gunstone, *Pentacostal Anglicans* (London: Hodder & Stoughton, 1982).
[22] See P. Brierley, *UK Christian Handbook* (London: Marc Europe, 1994–5, 1998–9).
[23] Tomlinson, *The Post-Evangelical*.
[24] Walker, *Restoring the Kingdom*, p. 303.
[25] Ibid., pp. 348–67.

constraints that apparently govern charisma, namely eventual routinization. New wine (rather like New Labour) can only be 'new' for a while. Eventually it becomes part of the establishment; subversion gives way to maturity and participation.[26]

There are also other reasons to be cautious about the future of Charismatic Christianity. Instances of schism in Charismatically-influenced churches are often high. David Martin has noted that neo-Pentecostal churches in South America have partly mushroomed because they operate and franchise in the high streets like any other shop, competing for the 'commerce' of belief.[27] This looks impressive and engaging, but Lesslie Newbigin[28] warns against judging quality of belief through quantity of adherents: 'the multiplication of cells unrelated to the body is what we call cancer'. This may seem a harsh judgement, but the divisiveness of Charismatic phenomena should not go un-remarked. The cancerous analogy is also helpful in suggesting that whatever growth is produced, it has frequently seemed to lack any purpose other than further growth and enthusiastic intensity.

One of the keys to understanding the past, present and future of Charismatic Christianity is to perceive its 'revivalist' identity. Revivals, of course, are no stranger to Christian history. Since the Reformation, there have been revivals of piety (seventeenth century, Puritan), holiness and its sociality (early eighteenth century, Methodist) and catholic ritualism (nineteenth century, the Oxford Movement), of 'speaking in tongues' (twentieth century, *glossolalia* in Pentecostalism), enthusiastic religion (late nineteenth century, Cane Ridge, Kentucky) and of Creation Spirituality (late twentieth century, and allegedly resonant with Celtic Christianity). There is almost no time in Christian history which cannot lay claim to its own revival. Each of these revivals, although different phenomenologically, shares a common 'genetic code'. This can be a complex agenda that at first sight looks simple. Yet it is far from that. So what are revivals? Why are they so often found breaking out in apparently ordinary, established churches? And how does this help us in assessing the future of Charismatic Christianity?

First, revivals are all attempting to reach back to the past, to restore 'something' that is deemed to have been 'lost' by the church. Revivals seldom offer something that is entirely new: their credibility depends on it being shown that this was somehow part of the *original* Christian message. Second, revivals arise out of their own distinctive social and cultural genres. They are partly produced by and are reactions against their own society, and are therefore necessarily relative; in effect, parasitic upon the culture they purport to reject. Third, revivals often occur during times of social upheaval. The end of an age, the passing of

[26] Ibid., pp. 310–15.
[27] D. Martin, *Tongues of Fire* (Oxford: Blackwell, 1990).
[28] L. Newbigin, 'On Being the Church for the World', in G. Ecclestone (ed.), *The Parish Church* (London: Mowbray, 1988), p. 35.

an era, or a particular calamity often produces religious fervour. In times of peace and security, a form of liberalism often thrives. But when, say, society moves *en masse* from an agrarian way of life to an urban one, revivalism can flourish.[29] Social uncertainty can make people flock to a rekindling of religious certainty, and the recovery of *communitas* for a church that is being lost in the world. Last, they stress the experience of revival as a key to self-knowledge. Revivalism is not taught but 'caught': in conferences and churches, the necessity of personal experience is brought home to believers in worship, teaching and ministry.

Contemporary Charismatic Christianity has been gestating within mainstream churches for almost fifty years. The main tributaries lie in Pentecostalism and fundamentalism, and, like all revivals, it seeks to exchange the perceived absence of God for a new sense of presence. Pentecostalism was an experiential response to modernity, in a similar way that fundamentalism was a sort of rational (or cognitive) response to the same. Both movements began within a decade of each other, and were reactions against theological and moral liberalism, besides being drives towards embodying a form of religious clarity that could provide an alternative to the muddied waters of increasing pluralism and relativism. Both movements sired their own denominations, seminaries and schisms, as well as developing their own distinctive cultures.

After the Second World War, the skeleton of the Smith Wigglesworth prophecy started to take on some flesh of its own. Charismatic Christianity began to emerge as a movement that was deeply syncretic, born out of a peculiar alliance. Lapsed fundamentalists were waking up to discover themselves as evangelicals, and those still in Pentecostalism were searching for new emphases on the immanent power of the Holy Spirit. The result was a new conflation that stressed revival. Rational religion and the certainty it brought was valuable: but many people wanted more than this – they wanted to *experience* something as well.[30] Faith was not just thinking about God, but feeling him too. This became the *sui generis* of contemporary Charismatic Christianity. Even those sympathetic to the movement agree that the drive for experience is a key to understanding its identity.

So in terms of theological coherence there is something of an irony. In spite of the millions involved in contemporary Charismatic Christianity, there is very little that could be classed as 'Charismatic theology'. Like Fundamentalism and Pentecostalism, the movement has spawned its own seminaries, notable preachers and exponents; but a theologian of national or global significance has yet to emerge. Charismatics tend to appeal to the work of theologians who feed their

[29] J. Butler, *Awash in a Sea of Faith: Christianizing the American People* (Cambridge, MA: Harvard University Press, 1990).
[30] J. Hopewell, *Congregation: Stories and Structures* (London: SCM, 1987), pp. 75–79.

theological outlook, without they themselves necessarily being paid-up revivalists. For example, just one work of James Dunn (*Baptism in the Spirit*, 1979) is widely read in almost all Charismatic churches and fellowships that I know of, although Dunn himself remains a sanguine Scottish Presbyterian. The works of George Eldon Ladd, James Kallas and Walter Wink are also highly esteemed within the movement.

There are some exceptions to this rule that we should note. Historians of the movement, such as Walter Hollenweger (1972) or Hocken (1986) have written about Charismatic thinking and praxis, but neither has constructed a 'Charismatic theology'. Gifted scholars such as Simon Tugwell (1976) or David Watson (1965), who clearly can be identified as Charismatic, have tended to produce popular 'testimony–teaching' type books, not serious works of scholarship that outline a theology. Edward O'Connor (1975), and Herbert Muhlen (1978) have produced accessible theological appraisals that have attempted to mediate the Charismatic or Pentecostal tradition *to* denominations. Suenens (1978 and 1979) has also attempted to show how Charismatic reflections can shape pastoral encounters or social action.

However, these contributions, which are slight in number, must be balanced by the obvious lack of theology in the mainstream of the Charismatic tradition. Indeed, in the *Dictionary of Pentecostal and Charismatic Movements*, by Burgess, McGee and Alexander (1988), there is no entry for 'Theology' at all. Naturally, this does not mean there are no 'doctrines' in Charismatic Christianity: ideas about the person and work of the Holy Spirit are critical to its identity. However, beyond this, there is unlikely to be a developed Christology, soteriology, doctrine of the church and the like.

This observation is important. Why is it that there can be so much schism in Charismatic Christianity? Answer: there is no doctrine of the church, and no theological template for tolerating plurality. (All that can be said to exist is a notion of gathered homogeneity, which emphasises size.) Why is evangelism so poor, numerical growth usually coming from 'converting' people who are already Christians? Answer: Charismatic Christianity has no soteriology of its own. Why does Charismatic Christianity apparently succeed so quickly where others have apparently failed for so long before? Answer: there is no real Christology, creeds, sacramental or Trinitarian theology and praxis to burden believers with. Adherents are offered an immediate form of spiritual experience – a kind of bathetic sentience through which one encounters quasi-numinous phenomena. Faith is nurtured not through knowledge, but through a community of feeling in which one learns to appreciate power, charisma and non-order – yet often within an authoritative structure. The opposite of movement is stability; the latter is the enemy of Charismatic Christianity.

The observation that contemporary Charismatic Christianity has no real systematic theology, as such, is not meant to be patronizing. There are actually good reasons why this is the case. But let me say something about how the movement attempts to compensate for the void. First and foremost, it has a strong background in biblical fundamentalism. Whilst not everyone who would identify themselves as Charismatic is a fundamentalist, most will be 'fundamentalistic'.[31] That is to say, they will use the Bible in a literalistic, pre-critical fashion, hold their beliefs in a similar way to classic fundamentalists (i.e., intolerant of plurality and liberalism, prone to schism, monologue, etc.), and yet be looking for spiritual power that is linked to, but beyond, a tightly defined biblical authority. As one author puts it, revivalism offers 'an eschatologically justified, power-added experiential enhancement'.[32]

Second, Charismatic Christianity purports to be, at least in part, a movement that has *distanced* itself from theology. Harvey Cox sees Charismatic Christianity as the major component in an 'experientialist' movement that is tired of the arid, over-rational religion of modernity, which was split between liberals and conservatives. Charismatic renewal is often a self-conscious religion of experience and feeling that deliberately pitches itself against too much 'thinking' about God.[33] Cox is at least partly right in his observation: whenever and wherever I have attended a revivalist gathering, believers are often encouraged to desist from rationalizing, to abandon critical faculties, and are instead to 'let God touch their heart'.

Third, the absence of a theological, doctrinal or ecclesiological basis makes Charismatic Christianity incredibly free in its reactions to and inculcation of contemporary culture. Indeed, social relevance is a trademark. Card-carrying Charismatics are not bogged down by centuries of tradition, nor do they have much of a past to justify or carry. Thus, they tend to use any theologians or aspect of Christian history selectively, to resource their beliefs,[34] but at the same time eschew a depth of participation in theological, ecclesiological, historical or sociological processes, for fear it will weigh them down. Charismatic Christianity is essentially a matter of the heart, and works best when it travels lightly.

With these theological considerations in mind, it must be acknowledged that most of the best appraisals of Charismatic Christianity are sociological. Here I think especially of Meredith McGuire (1988), David Martin (1990), Simon Coleman (2000) and Andrew Walker (1985 and 1998), to name but a few. However, a new voice must be added to these, namely that of Danielle Hervieu-Leger. Hervieu-Leger shows how movements like Charismatic Christianity appeal to social elements for whom self-realization and personal accomplishment

---

[31] Coleman, *Globalisation of Charismatic Christianity*, p. 27.
[32] Hopewell, *Congregation*, p. 76; cf. K. Poewe, *Charismatic Christianity as a Global Culture* (New York: Columbia University Press, 1994), pp. 103ff.
[33] Cox, *Fire from Heaven*.
[34] M. Percy, *Words, Wonders and Power* (London: SPCK, 1996), pp. 172ff..

particularly appeal. In her *Religion as a Chain of Memory* (2000), she suggests that such religious movements may be seen as a sign of protest against the establishment, and therefore parasitic upon it. Thus:

> One could ask whether the search within these communities for non-verbal forms of emotive communication does not also express a protest against the stereotype nature of approved religious language, something about the diminished quality of articulate religious quality in modern culture. The place taken in these groups by the gift of tongues raises the questions directly...tongues, defined by scholars as 'phonologically structured human expression without meaning, which the speaker takes to be a real language but which in fact bears no resemblance to any language living or dead', is not a vehicle for communication but for expression. The content is of little importance: tongues finds its meanings not in what is said but in the very fact of speaking and responding, in this form, to an immediate experience of great emotional intensity. In the emotive response there is a general sensation of the presence of the divine, profound joy, and inward well-being which finds the means of expressing itself.[35]

This is undoubtedly an interesting observation, but it raises a more intriguing question. If these forms of emotive and spiritual expression were originally protests against the establishment and the status quo – as they were in Pentecostalism and its nineteenth-century predecessors, such as the Irvingites – what happens to the identity of the movement that produces them when it too becomes part of the establishment? If the label 'Charismatic' now has a place at High Table with other respectable ecclesiastical prefixes, and can be part of a mainstream rather than a marginal spiritual diet, then how will the movement fare? Certainly, much can be said about the capacity of the Charismatic Movement to influence the wider church. But surely if the wider church has comparatively little difficulty in accepting that same movement, then we are only a few steps away from taming and domesticating a body of belief that was once at odds with the mainstream. In other words, in the very act of influencing the wider church, Charismatic Christianity has run the (necessary) risk of self-expenditure. (Such a position is, of course, entirely consonant with the parables of Jesus, and indeed, his own self-understanding.) For this reason, Hervieu-Leger comments:

> At the same time it has been seen that the absorption of Utopia into religion in the form of dogmatic glaciation or of innovative routinization secretes its own antibodies, paradoxically by allowing

---

[35] Hervieu-Leger, *Religion as a Chain of Memory*, p. 59.

the possibility of an alternative reading of the foundational stories to refrigerate the utopian dynamic of protest from within religion itself. From the radical movements of the Reformation to the efflorescence of leftist, there is no shortage of examples to illustrate the resurgence of Utopia, even when and to the extent that it loses strength by becoming institutionalised in a new religion. Such resurgence presents a religious character (or a religious feature) whenever it takes the form of radicalising demands based on devotion to an inspirational source for which the religion it is opposed to claims to provide the only legitimate reading. In [these] dialectics of religious conflict, Utopia constitutes the third term, as essential as it is destined for annihilation'.[36]

Destined for annihilation? Is that the evolving fate awaiting Charismatic Christianity, as it finally sits down at High Table? In one sense, yes. It does begin to lose its cutting edge and its *raison d'être* if it moves from being a marginal counter-cultural movement to something more mainstream. And yet it has little alternative. Apart from the church, and as a movement, it cannot survive as a complete culture without becoming a kind of spiritual ghetto. And as Tomlinson's study of post-evangelicals has already shown, Charismatic consumers will not be bound by doctrinal or ecclesial frontiers. The options appear to be communion and participation within mainstream denominations, which risks dilution and annihilation, but at least guarantees a kind of extensive influence – or, separatism, which might guarantee purity and power, but risks alienation, marginalization and ghettoization. Sociologically, we can say that Charismatic Christianity has largely chosen the former path; Restorationists in the more purist House Church Movement tradition have chosen the latter. At the risk of inverting a well-worn phrase of Jesus, it may be that the broad road leads to salvation, and the narrow path to annihilation. In evolutionary terms, Charismatic Christians, as a distinctive species, may risk losing their distinguishing and unique characteristics to a larger gene pool as they continue to inter-marry within multiple denominational partners.

Correspondingly, and in terms of ecclesiology, there are some additional problems that arise directly out of these observations that relate to the question of Charismatic theology and the sociological observations we have made. First, although some people claim Charismatic Christianity is an ecumenical, uniting movement, it tends to be anything but this. History shows that Charismatics tend to be highly divisive: each new revival within the movement brings fresh division and more schism. Contemporary Charismatic revivalism has no history of uniting denominations, although it sometimes brings together federations of like-minded people. The reason that ecumenism

[36] Ibid., p. 148.

and unity is difficult to achieve in revivalism is because of the subjective, individualistic nature of the religion.

Second, and linked to this point, the worship of contemporary Charismatic Christianity compounds the problem of persistent ecclesial fracture. Classic revival worship, such as under Wesley, Moody or Edwards, had a tendency to use hymns as didactic material. In the case of Wesley, his theology was actually taught in his hymns and sung by converts. The creeds, sacraments and traditions of the church were caught up in eighteenth- and nineteenth-century rhythm: people were partly bound together by shared doctrines. Contemporary Charismatic Christianity, in contrast, attempts no such thing. It does not supplement sacraments, but replaces them: it is in worship that you meet God, not bread, wine, word or creeds. Furthermore, the function of worship is not didactic but emotive: it is a vehicle to move people closer to God, to 'release' them, to stir the heart. Consequently, most songs in contemporary revivalism are devoid of serious doctrinal content: they express feelings about or to God. This, of course, is no basis for theological or ecclesial unity – it just creates a 'community of feeling' which is always open to the ravages of subjective individualism.[37]

Third, the fundamentalistic roots of Charismatic Christianity also guarantee ecclesial problems. In such communities, it is never the Bible that rules, but always the interpreter.[38] Consequently, some Charismatic churches can look quite totalitarian. Even here, there is a theological account for the lack of ecclesial breadth. Although Charismatics have done much to promote the Holy Spirit in recent years, there has been no move towards developing a Trinitarian doctrine that could give an ecclesial basis for openness, mutuality and plural forms of sociality. Ironically, the stress on experience in Charismatic Christianity means that there is no 'coping stone' to keep orthodox views together. Schism occurs in the movement precisely because one person of the Godhead is invariably promoted or ignored over another. There is never any agreement over the basis for ecclesial authority. It is nearly always driven by charisma, authority, power and emotion, and therefore always open to a charismatic counter-coup.

The future for an enthusiastic Christian movement without a real theology is potentially troubled. It has no way of preventing schism, lacks depth in discernment, colludes in social abrogation, and may well be a spent force in a new millennium. But a movement that stresses personal empowerment, intimacy and love, yet is 'doctrine-lite' (but still with all the fizz of new wine), innovative and novel, may actually turn out to be a highly popular *credo* for a third millennium. Many

---

[37] M. Percy, 'Sweet Rapture: Sublimated Eroticism in Contemporary Charismatic Worship', in J. Jobling (ed.), *Theology and the Body: Gender Text and Ideology* (Leominster: Fowler/Wright/Gracewing, 1999).
[38] K. Boone, *The Bible Tells Them So: The Discourse of Protestant Fundamentalism* (London: SCM, 1989).

mainstream denominations, for the moment at least, seem content to supplement their diets with the spice of enthusiastic, paranormal and esoteric religion. As one Anglican Charismatic Vicar explained to me recently, they have not 'sold out' to the consuming fire of total revivalism – they have just been 'warmed in a gentle way' (Percy, private correspondence, May 1996) – influenced, but not possessed. Passion and enthusism may be the dish of the day, but it is not the only item on the menu.

For a Western world that is increasingly privatized and individual-istic, a postmodern, enthusiastically-driven religion may be the one that proves to be the most popular at the dawn of a new millennium: yet that is no guarantee of ultimate longevity. Charismatic Christianity is often a fashion-led, consumerist religion; full of fads, a populist, culturally relative and relevant phenomena. We should learn to read the signs: the Charismatic crazes of today are often only destined to become tomorrow's footnote in the history of revivalism. In my view, the bright and beautiful plumage that once made up Charismatic Christianity is fading fast. A healthy and vibrant body of belief with a once lustrous skin is now showing signs of age: wrinkles, worry-lines, and some middle-age sagging have set in. But perhaps growing up isn't all bad? Ecclesial maturation and ultimately denominational inculcation may yet be the greatest achievement of British Charismatic Christianity. Yet some will resent this future, even though it was prophesied long ago:

> On the train, I took an old *Restoration* magazine out of my briefcase. In it, he [Bryn Jones, a prominent House Church Movement 'Apostle'] sets out the yardstick to measure all new movements of the Spirit of God... Let it determine its own future: 'The charismatic awakening that does not deal with the root of independence, individualism, sectarianism and denominationalism will be deficient as far as the heart of God and the need of our generation is concerned. It will inevitably follow the well-trodden path of decline back into the slough of spiritual paralysis and sectarian strife'.[39]

Here, then, is a prophetic prediction. So far as Charismatic Christianity is concerned, I think the party is largely over. The celebrations, the abundance and the optimism of the last quarter of the twentieth century have reached their peak, and whilst people are still crowding in through the front door, plenty have left through the back door too. The charisma that has driven the movement will be routinized, and the cognitive dissonance will ultimately settle on the corporate Charismatic psyche, ameliorating memories but also postponing (indefinitely) the realization of promises and prophecies for the future. Already,

---

[39] Walker, *Restoring the Kingdom*, p. 296.

'fellowships' that boldly proclaimed in the 1970s that they were not a new denomination,[40] but a restoration of God's kingdom, have quietly adopted the label 'new churches', and taken their small but significant place at the High Table of ecumenical dialogue. The journey from being a *movement* (which was originally against structures, stability and settlement) to being a *church* (which knows its place, values its order, and practices its rituals) is already well underway.

Yet this is not the end of the story. If I may be permitted to further indulge the 'High Table' metaphor once more, and extend the dietary analogy, the Charismatic Catering Corp. will continue. It has earned its place alongside those other ecclesiastical prefixes, and I predict it will keep it. However, scholars and researchers will be watching the next ten years with keen interest. In a postmodern climate, how will Charismatic Christianity maintain its market share within the ever-mutating Christian tradition? Is the growth that Charismatic Christianity has enjoyed in recent decades sustainable? Or has there been too much diversification and dissipation already? And what about identity – what exactly is it that will keep Charismatic Christians together, once the big tents of Spring Harvest and New Wine have been folded up and put away? In an increasingly post-institutional world, how will Charismatic Christianity, which once thought of itself as *the* future, cope with being just one option amongst many? Can you keep your customers without changing the menu? Will you lose clients if you do? Scholars will be watching to see who and how many continue to be fed by Charismatic Christianity – individuals and denominations – and asking how else, if at all, those spiritual diets are supplemented.

Conclusion

In this chapter we have considered three different types of Christian movement, and discussed the potentially problematic evolutionary process involved in developing a more concrete ecclesial identity. Anglo-Catholicism was considered briefly and, first, as a representative example of a movement that has attempted to possess an ecclesial identity that is in fact larger than itself. In failing to become a movement with broad appeal, it has slowly retreated into itself, and is now deeply engaged in an exercise of maintenance rather than mission. This is in sharp contrast to initiatives with a wider vision, such as Taize and Iona, which have managed to engage the political, cultural and spiritual inclinations of our current generation, and also demonstrated a real aptitude for 'catholic' liturgical innovation – something almost wholly lacking in most strains of Anglo-Catholicism.

[40] Walker, *Restoring the Kingdom*, p. 297.

Methodism was considered in more depth, because it represents a movement that is learning to live with its denominational identity, yet within a culture that increasingly disregards such ecclesial marques, and looks instead, ironically, for spirit and movement rather than structural symbolism. Methodism stands at something of a crossroads in evolutionary terms. Should it return to its roots, and in so doing risk neglecting its hard-won ecclesial identity? Or should it try to preserve its denominational distinctiveness, yet within a context that places less and less value on such branding?

Charismatic renewal and revivalist impulses were considered in most detail, as the movements represented within this tradition can be understood as evolution in process. A number of groups that began in the 1960s and 1970s now face a set of awkward questions in respect of their future. Should congregations that once set their face against becoming a denomination now be styling themselves as 'new churches'? How long can a church be 'new', exactly? And how do such churches begin to distinguish themselves from (or compete with?) more established denominations that copy their style, but might also offer more substance (i.e., tradition)?

What perhaps begins to become clearer in this type of analysis is that the story of 'evolutionary success' in ecclesiology is less to do with appearances, and much more about cellular structure, environmental 'fit' and the capacity to adapt. Put another way, a focus on denominations and movements risks ignoring the bigger driving forces and currents within the natural history of ecclesiology. And there are two major modes to note. First, it remains the case that the dominant ecclesial configuration, globally, is broadly liturgical. Whether that is Orthodox, Roman Catholic, Anglican or Lutheran, the vast majority of the world's two billion Christians exercise their spiritual lives through liturgy, which guarantees a degree of unity over and against the cultural and contextual differences that might surface if individual environments were allowed full rein. The second major mode to note is Evangelicalism – a tradition not bound together by performance (i.e., liturgy), but by belief (or more accurately, a kind of 'grammar' that encompasses both behaviour and belief). Here again, the unity over and against evolution that might be prompted by specific environmental factors can be guaranteed by creedal conformity, which in turn permits considerable performative diversity.

Both of these modes – a kind of ecclesial DNA, if you will – have triumphed in late modernity because they have managed to deliver both unity and diversity, together with homogeneity and plurality. This is the equivalent of the 'catholic gene' – permissive, adaptive, yet with clear generational continuity, and the capacity to both engage with and resist the predators and nutrients of contemporary culture. The survival of ecclesial species, and their clergy, depends on locating this catholicity; it allows the body to function within a larger environment. Independent Methodists have found that they can ensure something of their survival through 'inter-breeding' with Baptist herds. Leaders of new churches – who have long thought of themselves as unique and imperious beasts – have yet to discover who their main predators may be. And most strains of Anglo-Catholicism, once populous and proud, are fast becoming a protected species. Indeed, now that this most 'catholic' of species can choose its own bishops (i.e., parishes may elect to be under the authority of a 'Flying Bishop' they can trust, rather than taking a risk – dare one say it – on God), there is a serious risk of inter-breeding, and of its consequences. It is indeed ironic that of the three case studies we have discussed, this last example, of all ecclesial movements, should show the least trace of the 'catholic gene'.

The advent of late modernity – replete with secularism and pluralism – has seen many churches struggle to build and consolidate a concrete sense of (ecclesial) identity within an era of considerable cultural fluidity. In the face of such challenges, many churches are tempted to re-describe their histories in order to establish a sense of consistency and direction. Many have resorted to 'myths of continuity', in an attempt to re-narrate the church as a single and unambiguous line of development, beginning with the apostles and continuing to the present. Such theologies, so it is thought, guarantee clarity and governance. Correspondingly, many theologies of episcopacy, for example – and perhaps especially in Anglicanism – engage in a kind of complex theological idealization, which closely aligns itself to the varieties of theology more usually associated with Roman Catholicism. But in actual fact, the concept of episcopacy in Anglicanism owes just as much to functionalism, pragmatism and rather reactionary organizational dynamics over the course of history, as it does to any received or thought-through Catholic doctrine. Anglican bishops are (perhaps tellingly), consecrated for their role, rather than being ordained again, as it were. They are set apart for the task of oversight, but they remain as priests and deacons. Yet recent Anglican theology has invested more time and energy in deliberating and defining episcopacy than in any other generation. The challenges of contemporary culture and modernity appear to have pressurized Anglicanism into reconstructing itself (at least in its mind) around a more avowedly Roman Catholic theology of episcopacy, which (it assumes) might achieve greater clarity and control.

In this respect, it is perhaps worth recognizing that commonplace Anglican understandings of episcopacy are normally more aligned to those of say, United Methodists or Lutherans, than they are to those of Roman Catholicism. But interestingly, it is the latter model that remains more attractive for some Anglicans, since the myth of continuity and coherence has a more beguiling power than facing the awkward histories of pragmatism and disorganization that beset most denominations. In evolutionary terms, we could say that it remains preferable, perhaps, for some ecclesial groups to believe in a created and given order (established by God, long ago), in the midst of considerable cultural change. But in fact there has always been considerable ecclesial adaptation and modification in relation to the environment – which might, of course, be no less Godly. Arguably, the Catholic gene works best within ecclesial polity when it recognizes the latter; for that is when adjustment can be reasoned (again), and then grounded in tradition instead of myths. Rather than a mere change of perspective, a real acclimatization of the body can then occur. And to adapt like this is merely to contemplate the call to ongoing incarnation: to be the living body of Christ in God's world.

Chapter 6

On Ministry

The church has used criteria of one kind or another for setting aside ministers since earliest times. The New Testament records the standards and expectations that are required by those who have been set aside for ministry. Some of the earliest epistles wrestle with the type and quality of ministry that should normally characterize the church, and it is clear even from these documents that praxis and environmental adaptation were playing a part in ministerial formation as much as tradition and revelation. But the theological debate on the shaping of ministry is not so much about this relationship, as it is concerned with which element to privilege over the other. Richard Hooker questioned the Puritan habit of always prioritizing scripture over tradition. Reformers like Martin Luther, on the other hand, did precisely the opposite. Both sought to correct errors of emphasis, as they saw them, and return ministry to a more holistic foundation. We noted some of Hooker's observations in Chapter 2, but this seems an appropriate point to record some of Luther's protestations (taken from *The Babylonian Captivity of the Church*):

Which of the ancient Fathers has asserted that by these words priests were ordained? Whence this new interpretation? It is because it has been sought by this device to set up a source of implacable discord, by which clergy and laity might be placed farther asunder than heaven and earth, to the incredible injury of baptismal grace and confusion of evangelical communion. Hence has originated that detestable tyranny of the clergy over the laity, in which, trusting to the corporal unction by which their hands are consecrated, to their tonsure, and to their vestments, they not only set themselves above the body of lay Christians, who have been anointed with the Holy Spirit, but almost look upon them as dogs, unworthy to be numbered in the Church along with themselves. Hence it is that they dare to command, exact, threaten, drive, and oppress, at their will. In fine, the sacrament of orders has been and is a most admirable engine for the establishment of all those monstrous evils which have hitherto been wrought, and are yet being wrought, in the Church. In this way Christian brotherhood has perished; in this way shepherds have been turned into wolves, servants into tyrants, and ecclesiastics into more than earthly beings...thus all we who are Christians are priests; those whom we

call priests are ministers chosen from among us to do all things in
our name; and the priesthood is nothing else than a ministry.[1]

Luther's arguments against the distinctive privileging of ministry –
bound up in orders and sacraments – reminds us that the identity and
function of ministry has always been contested. Similarly, the study of
ministry is not simply an ecclesial task. It can benefit from a range of
disciplines that might be brought to bear upon the subject – theology,
anthropology and sociology – to name but a few. We have also noted
how the burgeoning field of 'professional studies' can be illuminating,
especially when set within a wider discussion centred on development,
which, in the context of this study, has been shaped by the analogical
use of evolutionary theory. But there is an additional factor in the study
of ministry that needs to be considered, namely the personal nature of a
vocation. This is one of the most delicate aspects of ministry; that sense
of call which requires proper discernment and sifting from the church,
and yet always remains personal and specific to each individual. To
have a vocation is not the same as a career: the former is rooted in
advancement, whilst the latter is grounded in service.[2]

To reflect personally, for a moment, I can vividly remember the first
strong inkling of a call to ordained ministry, shortly before my
seventeenth birthday. The sense of call came at a most unlikely time,
and was (to be honest) quite unwelcome. I had not thought of entering
the church, and had no particular ambitions in education. But the call –
manifest in both the promptings of others, and a kind of 'thud' in my
very being (soul) – was undeniable. Faced with what I knew to be real
(yet had not sought), I realized in the space of a very short time that to
do anything else with my life would be less than what the life was meant
for; less than what God wanted. It is possible to analyse such inklings
from a psychological perspective, to be sure. But the actual moment of
epiphany is a stark recognition of who and how one is in relation to
God. And in beginning to know your place before God, one begins to
appreciate the wonder of creation, redemption and of continual grace.
R.S. Thomas, in his poem 'The Bright Field', puts it well:

I have seen the sun break through
to illuminate a small field
for a while, and gone my way

---

[1] The edition cited is the *First Principles of the Reformation or The 95 Theses and the
Three Primary Works of Dr. Martin Luther*, ed. Henry Wace and C.A. Buchheim
(London: John Murray, 1883).
[2] However, some caution should be exercised in maintaining such exclusive
categories. Many philanthropists and social (capitalist) entrepreneurs (and therefore successful in career terms) will usually have deep vocational pulses that drive
their businesses for the purposes of wider social, religious and humanitarian benefit.
Equally, many who began with a fairly simple vocation can be surprised by the
development of that call in terms of responsibility, management and leadership.

and forgotten it. But that was the pearl
of great price, the one field that had
the treasure in it. I realize now
that I have to possess it. Life is not hurrying

on to a receding future, nor hankering after
an imagined past. It is the turning
aside like Moses to the miracle
of the lit bush, to a brightness
that seemed as transitory as your youth
once, but is the eternity that awaits you.

The call had an unmistakable spiritual velocity that I could not deny, but equally could not entirely understand. Because of this, I, like countless others, turned for advice, and was supported and nourished by others (a critical dimension in the process of discernment). It helped me, for example, to resolve to read theology at university – as both a test of the call, as well as means of gaining a deeper knowledge of the Christian tradition. That aside, however, I have been continually struck by how much that call was shaped by the example of others. The shaping of ministry is, in some profound and personal sense, a matter of praxis. It is a kind of learned behaviour. Whether that learned behaviour is something that is of nature or nurture, one cannot easily tell. But what is clear for many who enter ordained ministry is this: it is the praxis that inspires us first. Whilst we may ultimately test a call by reference to the tradition and other meta-theological criteria, clergy are often initially (and perhaps primarily?) formed by the environment in which they develop. 'Like breeds like' is a statement about both nature and nurture.

It is, of course, more subtle than that, since many vocations that begin in one tradition can then emerge and flourish in another. There are processes of change, conversion and confirmation. But this dynamic merely underlines the curious and special nature of a religious vocation. This is because in the sense of calling, which is to obedience and service, there is also liberty. And because it is God who calls, and because God is necessarily more than the partial or total sum of ecclesial expressions, individuals and communities regularly find that their sense of calling leads them to diversification (perhaps through inter-group or intra-denominational reaction), specialization and perhaps to individuation.[3] Sometimes this dynamic has a comically sectarian flavour to it. One thinks, for example, of Garrison Keillor's description of the Brethren in Lake Wobegon, who were divided on the issue of women wearing trousers (allegedly forbidden by Deuteronomy), or on whether warm baths were too sensual (not

---

[3] Wilson, *Darwin's Cathedral*, pp. 138ff.

explicitly discussed in either the Old or New Testaments). But more seriously, and as David Sloan Wilson points out, separation and diaspora produce new strains of identity within a religious species that may prompt problems when an opportunity for re-integration emerges. Under the conditions of diaspora, for example, several things may happen to the separated group. First, it maintains stricter boundary control of its religious identity within its new context. This may lead to a partial 'ghetto' mentality developing. Second, such a group has to re-negotiate its tradition in a new environment; what mattered before may not now seem significant. Third, the group has to relate to its new context, and co-operate with the environment. The kinds of accommodations made here may well have an impact on any re-integration of that group, resulting in the separated group only achieving partial recognition when the opportunity for full reunion presents itself.

But despite the emergence of differences here, it is likely that common traits will remain. Although clergy will differ in their theological outlooks and liturgical emphasis, and will express such differences in a variety of ecclesial modes, it is unsurprising that some of the basic tasks that shape the vocation are common across the 'species'.[4] Specifically, these include pastoral engagement with people at liminal stages of life (i.e., birth, marriage, death, etc.), teaching and applying the faith, the performance of rituals that have a variety of functions, and, in some deep and profound sense, representing God to the people and the people to God.

In my own ministry, and very much with the benefit of hindsight, I can now see that the examples of praxis that tended to make a deep impression on the shaping of my own vocation were centred on being with people at times of deep crisis and grief, in which there was little consolation. Peter, the first vicar that I really knew, told me about how he had sat with a grieving newly-wed husband, whose wife was killed on the way home from their honeymoon in a car crash. There is little to say in the midst of such tragedies, despite the clamour for answers to the question 'why?' But there is pastoral solidarity, support and comfort in the midst of this most searing and heartfelt pain. Peter's successor, David, also recounted a story – of going to see a mother who had lost her daughter in a car crash, only months after she had begun her new job following graduation. Her whole future was before her, and the death, therefore, was a pointless waste of a young life. But the comfort that comes in the midst of grief is often in the form of presence, empathy and holding; words are not enough. The priest does not visit with solutions and answers; at such times he or she comes with love, support and comfort. This is something I was to later witness as a

---

[4] For a more general perspective on evolution and religion in these respects, see S. Atran, *In Gods We Trust: The Evolutionary Landscape of Religion* (New York: Oxford University Press, 2002), and P. Boyer, *The Naturalness of Religious Ideas* (Berkeley, CA: University of California Press, 2002).

curate of a parish, working for an incumbent, where the apprenticeship relationship becomes even more explicit.

The behaviour learned at these times inevitably models a paradigm for ministerial praxis that continues to live on. I recall as a curate visiting a family who were losing their fit and healthy teenage son to a virulent strain of 'flu. We sat together in the hospital for the best part of a week, tending the young lad as one by one his basic and vital organs failed, and the fight for life was slowly but surely lost. Each day was flecked with hope and prayer, even to the end. But more than this, each day was a reminder of the power of love, and that the lengthening and darkening shadow of death could not extinguish the relationships that were formed and deepened by the shared pain that was all too abundant. In the midst of this, I became conscious of how vital and marginal the role of the priest can be. Just as at birth and baptism clergy hold the newborn, or join hands at a wedding, so at death there is another kind of holding, and a letting go. We prepared the young man's body for his final journey. We lit candles as a sign of hope for the resurrection. We sat together round the coffin, and I invited members of the family to talk, and to be still. Just like the clergy that helped to form and shape my own ministry, I discovered for myself that the words for such occasions are few, but there is much to be said for holding, comforting and presence. Later, when my wife became vicar of a parish, I was once again struck by the story of a young mother who started to come to our church. She had lost a child in the early years of her marriage. But her reason for coming to church was that Emma (my wife) did not have a neat answer to the question of suffering. She came because she was offered support and friendship in the midst of grief – not theological solutions to life's insoluble questions.

The idea of clergy being pivotal in 'holding' people at times of crisis or uncertainty can extend well beyond the obvious liminal phases of life. Quite recently I was invited to a house to perform an exorcism. If at once this sounds a little too dramatic, let me explain. Someone connected to the parish asked if the church could help with a matter that they were finding both puzzling and disturbing. A young couple with their two-year-old son had recently moved into the neighbourhood. But after a while the child had started to complain about 'seeing things' and had started to become disturbed and frightened. The boy reported seeing an elderly man wandering around the upstairs of the house, although no one else could see this. Added to which, the rooms where the appearances took place were unusually cold, in spite of central heating. The couple called the church, because they knew that I had worked with this sort of thing before.

What is one to make of this? I am well aware that there are potential social, psychological and psychotherapeutic angles that could be explored. However, after an interview in the home, it seemed that there were no obvious reasons for what one might call 'a lingering, disturbing and unexplained presence'. There were, for example, no deaths in the house reported by the previous occupants. Under such circumstances, I take the view that there are two priorities. First, take the presenting situation seriously as a point of pastoral need; the unexplained should not be over-dramatized, or talked-up as something to be feared unduly. Second, religious-type problems tend to be best addressed by religious rejoinders. Correspondingly, I sprinkle the rooms with holy water, saying the Lord's Prayer and various collects in all the rooms where there has been disturbance. After that, I have a cup of tea with the family, play with the child a little, and go home. Two weeks later, the mother mentions to me that the child slept soundly from that night, and there have been no further instances of disturbance. 'Fine', I said, 'and thanks for the tea.'

What are we to make of this? As a Christian priest within a broad Anglican tradition, my answer is unequivocal: nothing. The instance points nowhere in particular. It does not confirm or deny that there are (to quote St. Paul) 'powers and principalities' to deal with that we cannot see. It does not, to me at least, prove the insuperable power of Christ over and against malign spiritual forces that govern the world, unseen. This is not the world of Frank Perretti. So what does the encounter mean? Of course, I don't know what it means. But in my view, the encounter, and others like it that I have been part of, points in two contrary ways. First, it suggests a vernacular spiritual dimension to human and social existence that needs addressing by more than mere dismissal.[5] Second, it suggests that the grace of God, operative within imaginative *pastoralia*, elicits faith and trust, and creates a new environment of hope in which the presence of God, mediated through words and symbols, speaks and acts in fresh ways to reassure and reconfigure. There is nothing to be sure of here. But there is plenty to be thankful for, including the gift of an uncertain faith and religious practice that perceives it has been part of something bigger.

I realize that it is rare for theologians to speak like this, but it is important that those of us who are committed to 'faith seeking understanding' do not avoid the real spiritual questions and puzzles that absorb most people's lives. Part of the difficulty for theology is that, too often, it takes on the dogmatic whilst stressing the experiential, and yet is unwilling to scrutinize the experiential itself. Put more sharply, there are rules about frames of reference for one kind of Christian knowledge, and other rules (or none?) for other kinds of knowledge. As is so often the case in Christianity, fundaments find themselves exempted from appropriate critical enquiry.

Mention of frames of reference allows me to introduce a short analogy at this point, which might begin to articulate something about the compass and ambiguities of ministry and its attendant spirituality. As someone who was raised 'low church' in my childhood and gradually

[5] Cf. J. Reader, *Blurred Encounters: A Reasoned Practice of Faith* (Glamorgan: Aureus Books, 2005).

evangelicalized throughout my teens and twenties, I became very aware, even if uncritically at first, as to how many of the truths we held were controlled by prior frames of reference. For example, it is obvious that the Bible does not speak of itself at all, let alone as an infallible text. And yet 1 Timothy 3.16 would be regularly used to frame all debates about biblical reliability: 'all scripture is inspired by God...' was a frequently intoned mantra. But no one ever bothered to say where the Apocrypha fitted into this, let alone mentioning the synoptic problem. Similarly for debates on sexuality, where the Bible is confusing and reticent, key texts conditioned not only how we looked at the rest of the Bible, but also at the world. We were framed; and in turn we framed everything we saw.

Looking at life through a frame has its advantages; the picture remains in focus and frozen. The view never changes; only your view on the view alters. But for the curious, there are too many unanswered questions. Who made the frame? What lives and moves outside the frame? What aspects of the picture are obscured by the frame? It is at these junctures that an enquiring liberal mind and an accompanying spirituality start to take root. For myself, I soon realized that the frames of reference I was working with were too particular; to parody J.B. Phillips, 'your frame is too small'.[6] The realization that the portrait of faith I had been staring at for most of my life actually *surrounded* me, totally (but openly, not suffocatingly) changed not only my theology, but also my spirituality. Moreover, you begin to appreciate the ways in which you yourself are in the picture. The frames, suddenly, became almost redundant; they remain useful for capturing detail and focusing on issues, but their limits (as well as their relativity and selectivity) are recognized for what they are.

Put in a slightly more conventional way, ministry works with boundaries, not barriers. Many clergy find – in praxis rather than theory – that the borders of faith are open, because it is eventually recognized that God is both outside and inside those borders. This then assumes that the only acceptable frame of reference is an open frame, which allows the viewer to look beyond the immediate and catch a glimpse of the ultimate. The missiological dimension of this is explored in writings such as Vincent Donovan's *Christianity Rediscovered* and J.V. Taylor's *The Go-Between God*. Open frames of reference let God in, who is not the property of the church. Or, to paraphrase Sydney Carter, 'Jesus is *not* Copyright of the church'.[7] Simone Weil expresses this same dynamic better than most theologians:

> For it seemed to me certain, and I still think so today, that one can never wrestle enough with God if one does so out of pure regard for the truth. Christ likes us to prefer truth to him because, before

---

[6] J.B. Phillips, *Your God is too Small*, (London: Epworth Press, 1952).
[7] Sydney Carter, *Love More or Less: Poems*, (London: Stainer & Bell, 1971).

being Christ, he is truth. If one turns aside from him to go toward truth, one will not go far before falling into his arms.[8]

There are perhaps many ways of illustrating the potentially dependent nature of a vocation, but space permits just mention of one here. Some years ago, a top-selling Evangelical author penned a book called *Prayer Without Pretending*. The book was hugely influential within the cloistered circles of the Christian Union, and was regarded as essential reading. But the author, Anne Townsend, has another story to tell. Although a popular speaker on the student evangelical circuit, she became disillusioned with her own theology and its inability to engage with the complex realities of her own life. She began to suffer from bouts of depression, which eventually culminated in a suicide attempt. Whilst in hospital recovering, she was visited by a hospital chaplain. She knew about these people, or so she thought: 'Anglican – probably not even a real Christian', she surmised. Her fears were confirmed when he gave her some books by David Jenkins to read. But being bored and suicidal, she read them anyway, and a transformation began to take place. In the midst of this liberal theology, she found a faith that was, in her words, more mature, and one in which she felt she could move forward. She has subsequently become an Anglican priest herself – her vocation transformed.[9]

The idea that vocations are shaped and transformed by testing external forces is not wholly alien, when one begins to reflect on the ambivalence of ministerial encounters. Several years ago I was invited to be the honorary chaplain to a professional rugby club. I performed all the usual duties – occasionally burying some ashes on the pitch, celebrating (victory, not communion), counselling and consoling, drinking the odd pint...and even running a Christmas Carol service in the bar. Yet the most demanding aspect of being a rugby club chaplain was sitting with my fellow supporters. Inevitably, in all the fracas and fury of a game, it was the name of God that was frequently invoked by all who watched. ('Say one for us, Padre...' was the classic vernacular request.) So after a crucial-but-missed-kick, my neighbour would habitually turn to me and say, 'Blimey, I don't think your boss is helping us much today.' The retort, inevitably: 'Sorry. But I'm more marketing than sales...'. It was in such blurred pastoral encounters that one often discovered something of the art of ministry. This consisted of being present, but not imposing. Of being open and available to all. Of not standing on clerical dignity, or prescribing spirituality. Of being very much in the world, but not actually quite of it.

For most who are clergy, ministerial formation is a process of patience and growth. It is a marathon rather than a moment; a lifelong vocation rather than an instant (re-)creation. God is the potter; his

---

[8] S. Weil, *Waiting For God* (New York: Harper, 1973), p. 69.
[9] See M. Percy (ed.), *Previous Convictions* (London: SPCK, 2000).

people the clay. Formation comes through the dynamic interaction between faith and culture; between theology and context (environment); between reality and spirituality; between the prompting of the individual and the discernment of the community. Rather like the reasoning of this book, it is a correlative process. Correspondingly, almost every denomination makes some kind of clear distinction between the ministry of all of the people of God and the representative ministry of the clergy. For example, the Presbyterian Church (USA) *Book of Order* states:

> All ministry in the church is a gift from Jesus Christ. Members and officers alike serve mutually under the mandate of Christ who is the chief minister of all... One responsibility of membership in the church is the election of officers who are ordained to fulfil particular functions. The existence of these offices in no way diminishes the importance of the commitment of all members to the total ministry of the church. These ordained officers differ from other members in function only... When women and men, by God's providence and gracious gifts, are called by the church to undertake particular forms of ministry, the church shall help them to interpret their call and to be sensitive to the judgments and needs of others.[10]

Similarly, *The Book of Discipline of the United Methodist Church* records that:

> Ministry in the Christian church is derived from the ministry of Christ, who calls all persons to receive God's gift of salvation and follow in the way of love and service. The whole church receives and accepts this call, and all Christians participate in this continuing ministry. Within the church community, there are persons whose gifts, evidence of God's grace, and promise of future usefulness are affirmed by the community, and who respond to God's call by offering themselves in leadership as ordained ministers.[11]

Although such statements have a clarity and finality about them, which is arguably essential for the proper ordering and function of ecclesial polity, there is also a sense in which ministry is often better understood through some of the more inconclusive vignettes that were related earlier. Ministry is often about being with the unfinished. The Gospels, of course, rather understand this, and all four leave us with the

---

[10] The Presbyterian Church (USA), *Book of Order* (Louisville, KY: Office of the General Assembly, 1986), G-6.0101-102, G-6, 0105.
[11] *The Book of Discipline of the United Methodist Church* (Nashville, TN: United Methodist Publishing House, 1996), p. 301.

possibility of a sequel; so the loose ends are not tied up. Consider the Gospel of Mark, for example, who ends his narrative with these words – *ephobounto gar* – 'for they were afraid'. What kind of conclusion is that? The resurrection has apparently just happened, and the salvation of the world set in motion – but 'they were afraid' does not inspire confidence. Yet as the American writer Eugene Peterson points out, this word *gar* is transitional; no Greek writer would normally end a sentence with *gar*.[12] It is a word that gets you ready for the next part of the sentence – except that there isn't one. So the original end of Mark's Gospel is an end of sorts – but not a very good one – which is why other later revisions of the text soon began to supply their own, including the disciples running off into the sunset, happily believing and rejoicing.

But I prefer the original, director's cut, so to speak. Mark finishes mid-sentence, I think, deliberately. *Gar* leaves the reader off-balance, mid-stride; where will the next step be? This is artful reticence; a conclusion is *withheld* from the disciples and the reader. It is now up to the reader to say what happens next. In other words, the Christian faith cannot be wrapped up as a finished product. The frame is open; the picture not completed. As Peterson says: 'write a resurrection conclusion with your own life'. More often than not, it is that step that marks out the beginning of a ministry. It is a call that first catches us off-balance – and then invites us to take a step.

Calling and constraint

In describing ministry as partly a step into the unknown, we are again made aware of the delicate nature of the vocation in relation to environments. A range of external factors may have a direct bearing upon the fecundity of a specific denomination, which in turn will affect the range and reception of individual callings. Most denominations keep statistics about their clergy – the average age of ordination, the number deployed in a given district or diocese, and the numbers coming forward for ordination, for example. It remains the case that across the denominational spectra, there can be some surprising trends to note that point towards environmental factors in the shaping of vocations. Mention has already been made of Anglo-Catholicism, Methodism and Independent Charismatic churches in the previous chapter. But are trends of decline and growth traceable in other denominations? And if so, what are the likely causes?

The Roman Catholic Church in eighteenth-century France was able to boast 130,000 clergy to serve a population of 25 million – that is about one priest for every 200 people. In today's figures for Britain, that would mean an army of 300,000 clergy, or 1.5 million clergy for

---

[12] E. Peterson, *Under the Unpredictable Plant* (Grand Rapids, MI: Eerdmans, 1994).

America. But the number of French clergy declined significantly after the Revolution, since the church was perceived to be aligned with the monarchy. The Republic of Ireland, once the Roman Catholic 'priest factory' of Europe, now only has one theological college open for its seminarians. In 2005, the Church of Ireland (Anglican) had more ordinands in its college than its Roman Catholic counterpart. Irish Roman Catholic religious orders, together with the clergy and the congregations of the wider church, are reeling from successive scandals of a financial and sexual nature. In turn, pressure to democratize the church has grown, to establish greater accountability and transparency between clergy and laity. More generally, consistent polling and surveys have shown a marked deterioration in the respect for and confidence placed in the clergy. What was once a 'profession' that was surrounded in awe and mystique, and seen as irreproachable, is now treated with suspicion – and even contempt. The same dynamics can be traced in the Archdiocese of Boston, where church property has had to be sold to pay legal compensation to victims of clergy sexual abuse, and also to balance the books as a result of a marked decrease in the financial giving of the laity. All of this, in turn, has led to a serious decline in the numbers coming forward to test their vocation for ordination. The clerical economy has switched from one of fecundity to infertility in the space of only a few decades, and it is difficult to see how such trends will easily be reversed.

Other denominations struggle for new clergy for entirely different reasons. Currently, the United Reform Church of England (a hybrid of Congregationalists and Presbyterians) cannot find enough trainee clergy to fill any of its theological colleges. The dissenting tradition, which for so long was partially parasitic upon the comparative health and hegemony of a privileged established church, has gradually lost its rationale as the Church of England's own prestige and power has declined. (Indeed, the size of the pilot fish is entirely related to the success of the shark.) Moreover, the older dissenting traditions of Victorian and Edwardian eras have been replaced in the post-war years with new Charismatic independent churches and Pentecostalism, which has increased the range of religious competition, and, ironically, hit the historic non-conformist denominations the hardest.

Other environmental factors also contribute to the health of vocations within denominations. After both the Great War and the Second World War, the numbers of men offering themselves for ministry in the Church of England and entering the priesthood rose sharply, only for these figures to tail off within five years. No reliable analysis of this data exists, although one can perhaps speculate that after the horrors of both wars, many who returned to civilian life wished to offer their lives with a renewed sense of purpose, which in turn led to the rise in vocations. Thirty years ago, around two-thirds of ordinands training in Church of England theological colleges were under the age of 30. That figure is currently 13 per cent within colleges, with two-thirds of ordinands now in the 30–50 age range. And because less than half the number of ordinands now train in colleges (something approaching 60 per cent train on part-time courses, which do not admit students under the age of 30), the true figure for ordinands under the age of 30 is closer to 5 per cent. Again, no reliable analysis on this data exists, although one could speculate that professional ministry is now becoming, for many people, something more akin to a second career than a lifelong commitment that perhaps began at school. This is, of course, to take nothing away from vocations that are formed and shaped in later life; it is merely to note that the clergy are not as young as they were. But on the other hand, one can equally say that wisdom, maturity and life experience are more present in the arena of formation than might have been the case even twenty years ago.

There is, however, a possible undercurrent to these statistics that may be worth exploring. Urban Holmes suggests that despite clergy remaining well educated (In 1967, 90 per cent of Episcopal clergy in the USA had a seminary degree, and a significant percentage had a masters-level degree), the status of the clerical profession has continued to decline.[13] He notes that a Gallup Poll in 1967 showed that only 8 per cent of the population recommended the role of a clergyperson as a preferred profession. This would indicate, possibly, that the deferred entry into ministry and priesthood (and therefore the relatively recent but rapid rise in the average age of ordination) is bound up with potential clergy discerning a need (possibly subconsciously) to have an alternative or supplementary professional identity and role that is in addition to being a clergyperson. This is often compounded by denominations, which place an emphasis on the value of life experience and careers prior to ordination – or even, sometimes, as a condition. Denominations, of course, in their defence, are doing no more than reading the signs of the times and discerning the work of the Holy Spirit, and are therefore acting as though they realize that the person who has only ever been a clergyperson, and has only ever wanted to be that since they can remember, is perhaps less deployable than someone with, say, a ten-year career in industry behind them. The assumption of churches, in other words, is that for clergy to relate to their environments, they need to draw on the resources of the world in which the denomination is set. If that world values professional careers in other spheres, it is likely that the church will absorb some of that same value system, which will in turn shape its vocations.

This sounds fine in theory. From an evolutionary perspective, clergy need to be both 'fit' for their environment as well as apart from it, in order to maintain an appropriate distinctiveness. But if society has become more complex in the late modern and postmodern era, it follows that the very environment that supports clergy will also be more

[13] Holmes, *Future Shape of Ministry*, p. 139.

fragmented and specialized. Holmes points out that clerical identity and roles have shifted markedly in the post-war era:

> From one or two clearly defined ideas of what it is to be a clergyman, depending on whether the emphasis is Catholic or Protestant – the representative of the authority of God's Church or the preacher of the Word – to a different and poorly defined role...no longer does the clergyman operate *primarily* from the altar or the pulpit...but from his study.'[14]

With such changes come the apparent accoutrements of professionalism: perhaps a staffed office at church and 'office hours' rather than a study at home, or other quasi-work-based practices that borrow unselfconsciously from the world of business or the professions. A hospital chaplain recently related a story to me of a woman dying in hospital, who had asked to see her vicar. The church had quite a large congregation, at least by British standards, so one might have expected there to be some delay in the vicar's visit. However, the woman was eventually visited by a volunteer lay-pastor from the congregation – neither person knew the other. The woman with the terminal illness asked why she was not worthy of a visit from the vicar? It was explained to her that the vicar 'did not do pastoral visits of this kind', as his ministry was mainly centred on running this large congregation. The hospital chaplain attempted to telephone the vicar, but could only get through to the parish secretary to begin with, and although he did eventually speak to the vicar's personal assistant, no conversation with the vicar was possible; his home phone number was not given out to anyone, and he was only available during office hours. What is interesting in this vignette is that members of the vicar's congregation saw nothing strange or untoward in this. For them, the vicar was like a CEO of a major company; he made big decisions and presided over a big (Godly) business. It was quite unreasonable to expect a man with such responsibilities to visit a terminally ill person at hospital who was on the margins of the congregation. There were volunteers and employees who could carry out these functions.

Whilst some clergy in certain ecclesial traditions adapt very easily to the kind of cultural shift described above – one where the church inculcates 'professional' business habits, and invests a new kind of mystique in clergy that become chief executives – Holmes detects an underlying problem in clerical roles and identity which merits further consideration. Leaving aside the fact that very few clergy will have the resources to develop ministries which mirror the world of business, Holmes suggests that the problem many clergy now face is multi-tasking: administration, pastoral counselling and visiting, and fund-

[14] Holmes, *Future Shape of Ministry*, pp. 140–41.

raising all point to a role that is poorly defined. Clergy find that the work they entered ministry for – serving, helping, relating, preaching and liturgical – is increasingly squeezed out by other demands. The role can suffer from poor definition, which in turn is often compounded by a lack of support resources. This then leads to a loss of morale, and, in some cases, clergy leaving the ministry to find 'more definite' careers. Interestingly, in David Osborne's recent critique of rural ministry, he homes in on this issue, and shows how the lack of a properly prescribed role for clergy results in a slow haemorrhaging of morale and energy, leading eventually to clergy leaving full-time ministry to return to a more manageable profession or vocation.[15] This dynamic is something that Towler and Coxon's survey of English Anglican clergy in the 1970s also picked up on, where they showed that the drop-out rate of clergy from full-time ministry was at least 6 per cent – a figure that has since increased to more than 10 per cent, and remains worryingly above average if compared to other professions or vocational work.[16]

Hoge and Wenger's[17] study of clergy in the USA suggests that the main reasons for clergy leaving ministry are constant, and that these factors also point to the absence of a clearly defined role in the midst of pressure and demands. The five main reasons are (1) clergy experiencing the denomination as not being supportive, or conflict with the denomination; (2) clergy who become burned out, stressed and overworked; (3) clergy who suffer through marital or family breakdowns, or who are threatened by the fracture of close relationships; (4) conflict with staff or church members; (5) moral or doctrinal conflict, including sexuality, gender and ethical issues.

In the Church of England, the numbers of clergy leaving full-time paid ministry each year is estimated to be around 220 – about 4–5 clergy per diocese per year. These statistics, of course, should be read against the more general cultural trends that affect ministry that we have previously identified. First, the evolution of clerical identity has led to its compression and specialization. But this has also led to marginalization; religion is not as 'public' as it once was. Second, many tasks previously performed by clergy/churches were lost in the industrial revolution and through emerging secularization. Third, creeping professional identity did not keep pace with developments in other professions. (Is ministry a hobby or a career?) The rise of voluntary and lay ministry suggests that a vocational identity crisis exists for some clergy. Fourth, ministry sits uneasily between the matrix of being and doing, although in this respect, it is rather counter-cultural. As we noted earlier, ministry is not a 'job' in the same sense that many other professions and forms of labour would recognize. Fifth, modern-

---

[15] D. Osborne, *The Country Vicar* (London: Darton, Longman & Todd, 2005).

[16] Towler and Coxon, *Fate of the Anglican Clergy*, p. 180.

[17] Dean R. Hoge and Jacqueline E. Wenger, *Pastors in Transition: Why Clergy Leave Local Church Ministry* (Grand Rapids, MI: Eerdmans, 2005).

ity poses an array of threatening afflictions: consumerism and choice, the erosion of cultures of duty and obligation, patterns of social liberalization, the rise in religious pluralism, together with the commodification of spirituality, are all competing with formal religious identity and belonging.

In the midst of this, however, clergy can often find that their roles and tasks are rooted in the expectations of the communities in which they serve, and these expectations are, in turn, rooted in patterns of performance that have been established long ago. And because religion tends to value both continuity and charisma, it can therefore be difficult to adapt churches and ministries to environments and contexts that have turned hostile. A recent experiment run by a television company has followed a newly appointed priest to a run-down urban parish (Lundwood) on the edge of Barnsley, South Yorkshire.[18] Subsequent television programmes have charted some significant success in outreach and community development, much to the surprise of the locals. But what is perhaps most remarkable about the programme is the way in which expectations of the community have been shaped by the presence and engagement of the priest and a reinvigorated church community. The traditional script of despair and pessimism that pervades the community has now been challenged, and there is a fresh voice that is flecked with hope. This is, of course, not what was expected, because the parish of Lundwood are working with a local cultural meta-narrative that anticipates continuing decay and hopelessness. But this is something that the Christian story, in the form of a newly arrived vicar and a more inspired congregation, is now questioning.

The idea that ministries and churches will in some sense correspond to the context of local narratives is not so surprising. For some time the discipline of congregational studies has been drawing attention to the ways in which local implicit theologies are cultivated in discrete contexts that can then shape the theological, spiritual and ecclesial horizons of Christian communities. However, it is also possible to establish some common aspects of ecclesial dynamics and clergy roles which reflect a commonality in performance and behaviour that is not grounded in explicit shared theological outlooks. Many clergy will, for example, recognize that there is a sense in which (analogically) their role is akin to conducting an orchestra. They are drawing out the appropriate sounds from instruments, but in such a way that contributes to a symphonic whole. But the public nature of conducting means that the conductor is both performing and performed. Rather like script-ure itself, the clergyperson finds that their dynamic interaction with tradition, revelation and a grounded context, means that they become part of the script that they are writing, performing and

[18] 'Priest Idol', Channel 4 (2005) follows Fr James McCaskill, an American Anglican priest from Pennsylvania.

orchestrating. Put another way, and to briefly turn to the work of James Scott, their public work is a combination of improvisation and compliance.

> The public performance required of those subject to elaborate and systematic forms of social subordination: the worker to the boss, the tenant or sharecropper to the landlord, the serf to the lord, the slave to the master, the untouchable to the Brahmin, a member of a subject race to one of the dominant race. With rare, but significant exceptions the public performance of the subordinate will, out of prudence, fear, and the desire to curry favour, be shaped to appeal to the expectations of the powerful... The dominant never control the stage absolutely, but their wishes normally prevail. In the short run, it is in the interest of the subordinate to produce more or less credible performance, speaking the lines and making the gestures he knows are expected of him.[19]

If this in some sense maps the day-to-day power dynamics of clergy in role (and with tasks) performing their duties with others who are performing within that same ecclesial context, we ought to be aware that there is often a hidden or private transcript that merits attention. In some regards, this may connect to some of our earlier observations on why clergy might leave full-time paid ministry, or why parishes suffer breakdowns in relationships. Again, James Scott's work is illuminating here, in helping to identify the 'hidden transcript' in organizations, which he says:

> Consists of those offstage speeches, gestures and practices that confirm, contradict or inflect what appears in the public transcript... [It] is produced for a different audience and under different constraints of power than the public transcript... [T]hese are the forms that political struggle takes when frontal assaults are precluded by the realities of power... [T]he aggregation of thousands upon thousands of such 'petty' acts of resistance have dramatic economic and political effects. Poaching and squatting on a large scale can restructure the control of property. Peasant tax evasion on a large scale has brought about crises of appropriation that threaten the state. Massive desertion by serf or peasant conscripts has helped bring down more than one ancient regime. Under the appropriate conditions, the accumulation of petty acts can, rather like snowflakes on a steep mountainside, set off an avalanche.[20]

So, Hoge and Wenger suggest that clerical extra-marital affairs might be

---

[19] James C. Scott, *Domination and the Art of Resistance: Hidden Transcripts* (New Haven, CT: Yale University Press, 1990), pp. 198–99.
[20] Scott, *Domination and the Art of Resistance*, p. 18.

seen as a kind of cry for help: 'a sick way of relieving stress...to shoot yourself in the foot is the only way to get out of a terribly stressful situation... "I can't handle this, but I can't say that" [so]...'.[21] For some this may appear to be a way of transferring blame, but in the light of Scott's observations, we can perhaps begin to see how 'petty acts of rebellion' in ministry (or other organizations) are really attempts to reify resistance to a dominant script. Small acts of resistance may begin to accumulate and occur when clergy feel that they are no longer themselves; that they have become 'lost' in the expectations, demands, projections, desires and routines of others. There may never need to be a decisive moment when this point has been reached – the Rubicon crossed, as it were. It is more like the steady accumulation of snowflakes; eventually, something gives.

Part of the difficulty for most clergy is that, unlike the conductor of an orchestra, or the CEO of a major corporation, they lack the power-base to execute decisive initiatives or decisions. This is because the Christian faith is already scripted, and can be performed in a variety of ways. Even the office of the Archbishop of Canterbury is not analogous to being the chairman of a large company. Any archbishop may venture to suggest what the missiological priorities of the Church of England could or should be. But it is entirely a matter of choice and interpretation as to how such directives are taken up by other bishops, clergy and laity. There is no relationship of compulsion between the leader of the church and the led. Some understanding of this dynamic is important for the study of ministry and its development. Clergy very seldom have the privilege of being able to be strategic; they only have the possibility of being tactical and pragmatic. Moreover, even when clergy think they are being strategic in leadership, no assumptions can be made about the tactics and pragmatism of the laity in the congregation. Christianity is a contested faith, even in the most homogenous communities of discipleship. What is proclaimed from the pulpit or declared to be a fundamental article can always be assented to – but it must also be interpreted and applied. There is nearly always a gap between 'official' and 'operant' religion. Michael de Certeau offers a helpful distinction that further aids our reflections here:

> I call a *strategy* the calculation (or manipulation) of power relationships that becomes possible as soon as a subject with will and power (a business, an army, a city, a scientific institution) can be isolated. It postulates a place that can be delimited as its own and serve as a base from which relations with an *exteriority* composed of targets and threats (customers or competitors, enemies, the country surrounding the city, objectives and objects of research, etc.) can be managed. As in management, every 'strategic' rationalization seeks

[21] Hoge and Wenger, *Pastors in Transition*, pp. 130ff.

first of all to distinguish its 'own' place, that is, the place of its own power and will, from an 'environment.' ... It is also the typical attitude of modem science, politics, and military strategy.[22]

But most ministers working in pastoral practice operate from a (well-informed and theoretically shaped) *tactical* base, where it is not possible to directly impose one's will:

A *tactic* is a calculated action determined by the absence of a proper locus. No delimitation of an exteriority, then, provides it with the condition necessary for autonomy. The space of a tactic is the space of the other. Thus it must play on and with a terrain imposed on it and organized by the law of a foreign power. It does not have the means to *keep to itself*: at a distance, in a position of withdrawal, foresight, and self-collection... It does not, therefore, have the options of planning general strategy and viewing the adversary as a whole within a distinct, visible, and objectifiable space. It operates in isolated actions, blow by blow. It takes advantage of 'opportunities' and depends on them, being without any base where it could stockpile its winnings, build up its own position, and plan raids. What it wins it cannot keep... It must vigilantly make use of the cracks that particular conjunctions open in the surveillance of the proprietary powers. It poaches in them. It creates surprises in them. It can be where it is least expected. It is a guileful ruse.[23]

It is possible that this is what Jesus had in mind when he exhorted his disciples to be as wise as serpents and innocent as doves. It is a call to shrewdness that recognizes that the power-base from which clergy serve is composed of such ambivalence (i.e., servant–leader, etc.) so as to make it almost impossible to have deep and resolved clarity about the nature of the tasks and roles. This is, of course, precisely what draws many people into ministry. They do not come seeking power, but merely to influence in the name of a higher power.

The notion that ambivalence somehow faithfully captures an aspect of clerical roles and identity is something that can be tested in a variety of distinct arenas of ministry. For example, many clergy can be used (formally or informally) by their congregations and communities to guard certain kinds of knowledge, and to keep confidence on certain kinds of information (cf. Malachi 2.7). But there are all kinds of issues of protocol here, which deserve some closer scrutiny. For example, a recent Church of England report on episcopal appointments made an intriguing observation, namely that bishops-elect should be able to keep their appointments secret, but not confidential – an interesting

[22] Michael de Certeau, *The Practice of Everyday Life* (trans. Stephen Rendall; Berkeley, CA: University of California Press, 1984), pp. 35ff.
[23] De Certeau, *Practice of Everyday Life*, pp. 37ff.

distinction. In some pastoral situations, perhaps involving confiding or confession, there will be clashes of interest and values in maintaining confidentiality: against the public interest, and against natural justice, to sometimes maintain confidentiality in the face of the information that has been disclosed or received. And yet, the public confidence in confidentiality could not possibly be maintained if confession, in whatever discipline it is deemed to operate, was routinely breached every time the public interest appeared to be threatened by the withholding of that information. Clergy mostly find themselves operating tactically here, rather than strategically.

To reflect on confidentiality more generally for the moment, the word comes from two Latin roots: *con* – completeness, and *fidere* – to trust. To confide is to trust wholly; to impart knowledge with reliance on secrecy. A confidence is a secret communication: but what are secrets, and what rights do we have with them? On one level, the rights to secrecy are closely connected with the rights to privacy – to be let alone. However, there are occasions when the right to secrecy may be an infringement of a greater autonomy – in which case the clergy may face a moral dilemma at this point. More problematic is the sharing of secrets or knowledge in the interests of wider consultation or collegiality. Just as one accepts some loss of autonomy on joining society, so one might be expected to accept loss of privacy over health matters (for example), when accepting medical care provided by a hospital, or perhaps social care provided by a particular service.

It therefore follows that the boundaries of confidentiality can be rather elastic – ones in which secrets can be imparted and shared, but not abused – and only ever discussed with the interests of the individual and society at large in mind. But more particularly, and as an ecclesial and spiritual discipline, the art of private confession is regarded as sacramental. Everything revealed under the seal of confession (or, as it is sometimes called, the sacrament of reconciliation) for the specific purposes of receiving absolution is deemed to be 'under the seal', and kept secret by the priest. Nothing may be revealed to a third party, or to the penitent outside of the sacrament, and, by action or remission on the part of the priest, to the disadvantage of the penitent.

This absolutist approach to confession is, interestingly, a degree above confidentiality, suggesting once again that there are aspects to clerical roles and identity that are ultimately sacred and secure in ways that resonate with other professions, but that have evolved in distinctive ways to become reified as concrete practices. John Shelton Reed's (1996) work on Victorian Anglo-Catholicism suggests that the practice of private confession quickly evolved for two reasons. First, it was counter-cultural, and therefore akin to other practices that occur within a new religious movement: it is a mark of rebellion against established values. Second, and more tellingly, the practice was especially taken up by younger women to escape the patriarchal domination of domestic life. The relatively rapid rise of private confession in the late nineteenth century prompted letters of outrage to *The Times*, and critical tracts being written by Protestant clergy who sought to defend the integrity and privacy of the family, which was held to be compromised by the possibility of young women (i.e., allegedly vulnerable and suggestible) imparting secrets about their family life and personal lives to third parties (i.e., Anglo-Catholic priests). Of course, the more the practice was opposed, the more it grew and evolved, since it became an accepted (if rebellious) means by which young women could assert their emerging independence, but under the protection of religion. The theological 'myths' surrounding private confession tend to begin in such complex evolutionary tales. The priestly order, finding the practice cast as a task that contributes to the role of liberator and saviour, quickly acquires an accent of apotheosis. In turn, those practising the art reach for the highest sacred language they can find to account for the mystery they find themselves entwined in, quickly resorting to a range of linguistic tautologies: the clergy are, like Christ, 'both priest and victim'. The priesthood is pre-eminently Christ's, but shared with those called 'only by courtesy of heaven'.

However, and despite the cautionary remarks on the evolution of private confession here, there is still something fundamental to the nature of confession that is deeply linked to the clerical profession. As I have already been hinting, even though confidentiality is regarded as being a degree above secrecy, it remains the case that secrets may be widely shared and known. To some extent, one aspect of the clerical profession is discerning the difference between the two. The socially and legally accepted right of any person to the privacy of their thoughts, feelings, writings and other personal effects is something that goes to the very heart of the values and virtues of many of our societies, and this is anticipated in religion as much as anywhere else. Similarly, the New Testament offers an unusual perspective on secrecy. We might say that revelation partly depends on concealment, disclosure, breaches of confidence and confession. The birth narratives relating to Jesus silence those who won't confess, give voice to those who will, invite witnesses to be secret, but then reveal to others. The stories of Zechariah, Anna, Simeon, the Wise Men, Joseph and Mary are all suggestive in this respect. For Christians, the salvation story depends on a degree of concealment and confidentiality – and yet, 'that which is hidden shall be revealed'. The light that comes in to the world is here to reveal the secrets of the heart, to make the blind see, and to bring illumination to the dark. In other words, there may be a place for the secret and the confidential – but in Christianity, these are contingent, for we shall one day know fully – 'even as we are fully known'.

This reflective excursion suggests three final points about confidentiality in relation to clergy roles and identity. First, that being secretive can be very important for maintaining professional boundaries, and is suggestive of confidence in confidentiality. Clergy, in the very act of being called, are schooled at an early stage of their development in the skills of disclosure, discernment and refinement. It is only by revealing what is happening to them on the inside that a call can be tested.

Second, however, clergy also learn that being discreet and secretive is important for the craft of ministry. Secrets are only shared in order that the knowledge one carries can be re-appropriated, re-apportioned and sometimes shared as part of a more liberating tactic. A striking example of this appears in the Gospel according to St Luke. A woman of apparently dubious repute interrupts a party given by Simon the Pharisee to honour Jesus of Nazareth (Luke 7). The woman, according to the gospel text, is widely known as a 'sinner'. But Jesus receives her warmly and allows her to touch him and caress him in ways that many would have regarded as defiling. Interestingly, the woman at no point gets to speak to Jesus (according to the text), but is nonetheless, at the end of this strange encounter, assured that her sins are forgiven.

Third, and as some of my colleagues in psychotherapy occasionally remark, you cannot truly confess until you have first heard the words of absolution. True absolution depends on the cartouche of confidentiality being responsibly unlocked – of secrets being sifted, but in ways that are respectful, healing, professional and thoughtful. Closely linked to the notion of confidentiality is the notion of confession, and to confess is to acknowledge something fully – especially something wrong; to own or admit, and to make known. Just as confidentiality is *complete trust*, so is confession a kind of *complete speaking*. And while the act itself may be private, or secluded, it nearly always has public consequences. It is on this very cusp that clergy often find themselves being formed, and yet also discover this dynamic as part of their deeper ministry.

The purpose of this all too brief section on calling and constraint has been to reflect on some of the ambivalence of the clerical role and tasks in relation to vocations. As we have already observed, becoming a clergyperson is not like entering the ranks of any other profession. The evolution of expectation in relation to tasks and roles will vary across the theological and ecclesial spectra. For most denominations, there are no formal, academic minimal requirements for ordination. There is of course an expectation that a standard of competence in the ordering and orchestration of public worship will have been attained. There will be a requirement that the minister both understands and can articulate the Christian tradition.

Yet beyond that, there is a great deal of fluidity about how time is spent and what should chiefly occupy the mind and time of a minister. For some clergy, the actual absence of precision and definition in role and tasks is problematic, and may lead them to leave full-time paid ministry. Clergy, in entering ministry, find that they are being performed as much as they are the conductors and orchestrators of Godly performance. Yet at the same time, and at some deeper level, there are a range of qualities, attributes and habits that seem to bind the variety of the clerical species together. These will include pastoral care in liminal moments, discretion and confidence in situations of counselling or confession, and a capacity to represent the people to God and God to the people. In the final section that follows, therefore, we will turn to look at the clergy as agents of transformation within the communities and congregations that they serve.

Knowledge, transformation and service

One of the advantages of using evolutionary theory to reflect upon clerical identity and ministerial formation is that it invites us to ponder the organic nature of spiritual growth. It points us away from an illusory world of immediate ecclesial growth, which is often predicated on a distorted understanding of the relationship between the being of God and the actuality of the church. In the imagination of some, the pattern for ecclesial growth is simply disclosed (or at worst, coded) in Scripture – a kind of recipe, if you will – in which all that is required is for the faithful minister to discern and follow the 'instructions'. However, and despite a perfectly understandable human desire for such clarity, the Christian tradition does not offer such knowledge. Whilst there can be plenty of agreement on what Scripture says, it is in the nature of the tradition that its meaning is not so plain; it must be worked out in the mature environs of a reflective Christian community, guided by the Holy Spirit. So there is plenty to be said for scriptural reasoning, whereby the church wrestles with the texts that eventually come to be embodied within the community, transforming them more and more into the likeness of Christ. It is in becoming the body of Christ that the church begins to draw in those who are outside. It is by developing into an organic expression of the revelation of the love of God, uniquely embodied in Jesus, that the church begins to be the body of Christ for the world. Such incarnation suggests patience, wisdom, hospitality, costly discipleship and mature reflection. And if the fruit that is to be borne will be fruit that lasts, then there will be very few easy or quick routes to productivity and growth. Karl Barth understands something of this theological and ecclesial dynamic when he remarks that:

> The true growth which is the secret of the up-building of the community is not extensive but intensive; its vertical growth in height and depth... It is not the case that its intensive increase necessarily involves an extensive. We cannot, therefore, strive for vertical renewal merely to produce greater horizontal extension and a wider audience... If it [the Church and its mission] is used only as a means of extensive renewal, the internal will at once lose its meaning and power. It can be fulfilled only for its own sake, and then – unplanned and unarranged – it will bear its own fruits.[24]

[24] K. Barth, *Church Dogmatics* (Edinburgh: T & T Clark, 1958), IV, ii, chapter 15, p. 648.

Here Barth is saying something very simple: true growth can only come through the quality of our relationship with God. And sometimes, in terms of extensive growth, that will appear to be fruitless. But this is precisely the point where we are called to contemplative persistence rather than pragmatism, and to question ourselves before we embark on a headlong rush into a search for new formulae or another strategy for our churches or diocese. Barth steers us away from this by reminding ministers and churches that first and foremost they are to be for God, before they are busy for clarity, success and ambition for the kingdom.

In a similar vein, David Martin reminds us that the division between maintenance and mission is essentially a false one. As any dean knows, a beautifully kept cathedral (or greater parish church) is, de facto, a sign of mission and a pointer to the kingdom. Active maintenance through gradual renewal is a form of mission, just as letting church buildings decline, collapse or simply appear shabby in the public sphere constitutes a very poor advert, suggesting that the church cannot take care of itself. Churches, in other words, can represent our being before God. Martin writes:

> Not only are they [i.e. churches] markers and anchors, but also the only repositories of all-embracing meanings pointing beyond the immediate to the ultimate. They are the only institutions that deal in tears and concern themselves with the breaking points of human existence. They provide frames of reference and narratives and signs to live by and offer persistent points of reference…they celebrate and commemorate; they are islands of quietness; they are places in which unique gestures occur of blessing, distribution and obeisance; they offer spaces in which solemnly to gather, to sing, to lay flowers, and light candles. They are – in Philip Larkin's phrase – serious places on serious earth.[25]

This, of course, raises some intriguing questions for ministers in the process of formation, and in their own participative formation of Christian communities. How is one to be 'a persistent point of reference'? How do churches adapt and survive in contemporary culture? Can ministers and their churches really risk a focus that concentrates more on being than doing? To some extent, the answer to these questions will depend on the distinctive ecclesiological and missiological outlook of a denomination. For those where innovation and certain types of energy and activity are highly valued, there is likely to be more emphasis on the sense of action and direction rather than reflection and presence. For other traditions, however, slow, reflective growth will be valued more than a sense of immediacy and speedy

---

[25] D. Martin, 'Believing without belonging: a commentary on English religion', *Crucible*, April–June 1994, pp. 59–64, p. 1, quoted in G. Davie, *Religion in Britain Since 1945* (Oxford: Blackwell, 1994), p. 191.

reification. Put another way, some traditions have evolved to value continuity, whilst others prefer change; some will prefer the potential and risks of charisma to the clarity of carefully patterned order and authority. And in the midst of these competing convictions, the minister is both the formed and the shaper. But interestingly, I suspect that there is some kind of common 'genetic heritage' for ministers which is arguably detectable beneath the presenting accoutrements of ecclesial and denominational distinctiveness, which in turn is contributing to the formation (or perhaps programming?) of clergy at a deeper level than many will be consciously aware of. Three brief suggestions are offered.

First, it is probably the case that most churches are easier to identify through persons rather than systems: examples of faith and polity rather than theories of it. In view of this, I am be inclined to say that the practice of faith is more of an art than a science, and most especially in relation to problem-solving. Here, the 'management' of the church within the context of the challenges of contemporary culture is much more like a 'knack' than a skill; organizing or shaping the church is about learned habits of wisdom more than it is about rules and theories.[26] It is for this reason that gatherings of clergy are enormously significant, for in such contexts they share stories and experiences, and build up a bank of knowledge that affirms their distinctive roles and identity. The generation of this 'spiritual capital' becomes a means of both confirming and shaping clerical identity.

Second, those charged with the ministry of oversight, whether as parish clergy, bishops, ministers or college principals (to choose but a few examples) often speak of intuition rather than extended calculation or analysis when dealing with 'unique situations to which they must respond under conditions of stress and limited time'. This 'knack' or 'wisdom' depends, as Polanyi might say, on 'tacit knowing', where overseers seldom turn to theories or methods in managing situations, but instead realize that their own effectiveness depends on having learnt (and continuing to learn) through the 'long and varied practice in the analysis of...problems, which builds up a generic, essentially un-analyzable capacity for problem-solving'. In other words, ministers learn by experience in the field.[27] Moreover, this knowledge continues to be held and dwelt upon, and in the process of reflection is slowly transformed into vital spiritual capital.

Third, it is in sharing how problems are addressed and resolved, and how individuals and organizations fare in this, and what reflections or analysis one may have about such situations, that 'tacit knowledge' begins to be built up – and within relationships based on trust – so that the organization may then experience both stability and a degree of transcendence. What seldom works in ecclesial contexts is the devolving

---

[26] See D. Schon, *The Reflective Practitioner: How Professionals Think in Action* (London: Ashgate, 1991).
[27] Schon, *The Reflective Practioner*, p. 239.

of more power and authority to semi-detached 'systems' of governance or theories of leadership, no matter how worthy or novel. Granted, these may have their uses, but it is worth remembering that the most ecclesial communities remain stubbornly identifiable through persons rather than systems. Correspondingly, it is how churches and ministers actually 'hold' issues – the character clergy exhibit under pressure, and how they might continue to embody being the very best kinds of 'reflective practitioner' – that normally enables the church most as it seeks to address the multiple complexities of being within contemporary culture.

With these comments in mind, let me offer some more focused reflections on the role of clergy in relation to the formation within the Anglican tradition. It would be quite possible here to talk at length about explicit theological identity. But I prefer instead to address a few aspects of what I take to be anthropological identity, which in turn suggests a nascent value-based implicit theological shape. It is said that Henry Scott Holland once stood on the hill at Garsington shortly before his death, and gazed over the valley to Cuddesdon College and parish church, where he had asked to be buried. He noticed a flock of starlings flying past, and remarked how like the Anglican Church they were. Nothing, it seemed, kept the flock together – and yet the birds moved as one, even though they were all apart and retained their individual identity. In an increasingly diverse and cosmopolitan world, of which the Anglican Communion is a part, birds of a feather still need to flock together, even though each creature is individual.

Holland's observation allows us to develop another analogy here, centred once again on the identity of the species. The Anglicanism of the twenty-first century is recognizably different from that of the end of the nineteenth century. The flock, if you like, is no longer one type of bird. Evolution – through cultural and theological diversity – has meant that many Anglican provinces have evolved to 'fit' their contexts, and the ultimate diversity of the species clearly threatens its unity. But to extend the analogy just a little further, is it possible to still speak of a connecting DNA – some of the deep, core but hidden, constituents of identity which relate churches and clergy, even though they may not be immediately apparent? The question is a timely one, especially when cast within the broader debates that are often presented by ecumenism, intra-denominational ecclesial recognition, and any eventual reception. For example, the Anglican Communion has a long-standing tradition of being 'in communion' with churches that are not distinctively Anglican: the United Churches of South India and the Portugese Lisitanian churches come to mind. The churches encompassed by the Porvoo Agreement might also be mentioned. There is general agreement that the Old Catholic Churches of the Union of Utrecht share more than a passing affinity with Anglican polity and praxis, and that it is just an accident of history (i.e., those shifting tectonic plates again) that has kept the Portugese Lisitanian church closer to the bosom of

Anglicanism than their relatives in Northern Europe. So beneath the presenting exteriority of denominations and their clergy, what kinds of reflexes, programming and organic structuring might be said to bind the species together? Several remarks can be made here.

First, ordained ministry is (with very rare exceptions) a public matter rather than a private affair. The discernment of vocations is something that is sifted through conversation, testing and probing; it cannot be about the assertion of the will of the individual. There is no 'selfish gene' to uncover, for the ministry is concerned with costly service and sacrifice. Moreover, the 'activity' of ministry is both about being and doing; the performative is deeply related to the contemplative. It has a character of its own that corresponds to the call of the Spirit and to the example of Christ. It is, at the same time, a peculiarly embodied kind of existence, being both for and apart from the community. In that sense, it is profoundly shaped by the missionary call – God's invitation to the neglected and lost to become part of the kingdom. Ministry is, in other words, across the denominational spectrum, shaped by the congregations' sense of what mission is; but is at the same time challenged on that shape by the very people it chooses or discerns to embody that witness for them.[28]

Second, there is a traceable trajectory within the development of ministerial formation that closely corresponds to the development of churches. In the first instance, there are roots (or origins) that need to be present for the vocation to be born: calling, a sense of 'being for others and otherness', and being for God. Without this 'mystery' (which is seldom open to reductionist accounts or analyses), there can be no formation. This leads to the process of formation itself, which is, of course, essentially a kind of shaping. It is here that the analogy of evolution can be of value, providing illumination and critique in equal measure. The formation will express itself in particular and dynamic ways: worship, doctrinal emphases, spirituality and ecclesial particularity. Finally, the shaping is purposeful, and gives rise to particular fruit or outcomes. These will undoubtedly encompass and echo some of the virtues that gave birth to the call in the first place – holiness, blessing and service, to name but a few – which then find their way into congregations and communities, thereby enabling replenishment and renewal, which in turn will inspire further growth and vocations. There is, in other words, a kind of 'life cycle' to vocations; those that are born, grow and gift will 'seed' the next generation.[29] In turn, of course, the interruption of this cycle, caused by disputes or uncertainty (for whatever reason) can result in a decline in vocations which will be closely matched by a disintegration of the denomination.

---

[28] On this, see P. Avis, *A Ministry Shaped by Mission* (London: Continuum, 2005).
[29] See C. Cocksworth and R. Brown, *Being a Priest Today* (Norwich: Canterbury Press, 2002).

Third, there is a profound sense in which clergy either become or are regarded as being 'sacramental material'. The very nature of the vocation – in all its ambivalence – points to the possibility of transformation and renewal. Clergy find themselves embodying the values of their congregations, which in turn commits them to challenge (not just maintenance), and to a wider public (not just the gathering of the faithful). This calling is very much about the public expression of truths and values that have, for many, become increasingly private. So it is not the case that clergy are required to embody a greater degree of professionalism. It is that the clergy, as material, are required to participate in the social resonance of their contexts, and yet point to a sociality that is yet to come. In this regard, clergy (paradoxically) live as both central and marginal to their constituencies.[30] This is a role that is both prophetic and pastoral; it shakes the very foundations it also supports. The role is elided with society, but also set apart.

Fourth, the clerical role is one that embodies a necessary incompleteness. The idea of a full and total process of formation is contrary to the spirit of a calling. All clergy are 'work in progress'; learning individuals within a learning church. The knowledge that informs the craft of priesthood is not one that can be 'banked' and ultimately totalized.[31] To be a clergyperson – no matter what denomination – is to enter into a commitment that involves a continuous and open process of formation that involves each stage of life, each fresh encounter, each new prompting of the Spirit. There is a sense, therefore, in which the very ontology of clerical identity is a confirmation of both fulfilment and incompleteness. In the act of ordination (or its equivalents), clergy are entering into a lifelong commitment to be transformed; to not control the trajectory of their development, but to enter into the mystery of God which may shape an individual in ways that they would prefer not to own. Unlike other professions, an entry into clerical life is not about the slow and steady construction of expertise (although this can be part of the shaping). It is rather, offering: material that is malleable in the hands of God. The heart of a vocation is being clay in the hands of the potter; surrendering to the sublime.

Fifth, and finally, the nature of ministry is, as we discovered, evolving. In this respect, the clergypersons find themselves being called to a life of inward and outward transformation, whilst operating in a particular vocation that is at the same time being transformed by the environment in which it operates. As all 'species' discover, there is something deeply relational about being, and the very nature of ministry requires clergy to develop a habit of wisdom that is both receptive and resistant to change.[32] In the midst of this, the priest-like

---

[30] See K. Mason, *Priesthood and Society* (Norwich: Canterbury Press, 1992).

[31] See S. Croft and R. Walton, *Learning for Ministry* (London: Church House Publishing, 2005).

[32] See R. Greenwood, *Transforming Priesthood* (London: SPCK, 1994).

task, or the work of ordained ministry more generally, is about nothing more and nothing less than being for God. A popular story from World War II tells of a Romanian Christian who found himself imprisoned at Belsen, and deprived of all he needed to sustain his faith: no crucifix, bible, icons, devotional books, corporate worship or knotted prayer beads. So he prayed in secret – that he might respond to the call of love. He found himself spending time in the camp with the sick, the starving, the diseased, the dying and the betrayers – all those who were shunned by others. One day, as the camp drew close to liberation, an atheist – a priest, in fact, who had his faith shattered by the experience of war – came to see the Romanian and said, 'I see how you live here. Tell me about the God you worship.' And the Romanian replied: 'He is like me'.

Few Christians could ever reply: 'he is like me'. Yet it is the motto of the minister – a phrase to live by and aspire to. As the Gospels regularly hint, it is the example of faith that makes the difference, not the ideas; the praxis, not the theories. The call to discipleship remains compellingly simple: to be like him. To love one another as he loves us; to bear fruit that will last; and to love those who have no one to love them. As Jesus says: 'truly I say to you, as you did it to one of the least of these, you did it to me'. The story from Romania reminds us that all Christian discipleship is dedicated to the transformation of lives. The shaping of vocations is not merely education; it is also about formation, in which worship, reflection, contemplation and practice play a vital and necessary role in the shaping of identity. Such vocations speak of a church that is striving to become not only life-enhancing, but also life-changing. In a culture that all too easily consumes religion and spirituality on its own terms, ministers seek to deeply embody a form of discipleship that is both challenging and engaging.

Conclusion: the nature of ministry

In part, this study has been prompted by some profound misgivings in relation to the three dominant theological streams that primarily inform the shaping of clerical identity. The first of these is a kind of biblical functionalism, which assumes that the ministerial task can be easily and directly deduced through relatively plain hermeneutics. There are significant amounts of Christian literature that make the presumption that by understanding biblical characters such as Moses, David or Abraham, their pattern and style of leadership can be excavated, distilled and applied to today's church leaders. For reasons that will be obvious to most readers, such theological and hermeneutical man-oeuvres should be treated with deep suspicion. The second kind of stream is to invest conceptualizations of ministry in a kind of pietistic mystique, shaping the actual construction of reality with such abstruse sacred rhetoric as to remove it from any kind of concrete analysis.

The third kind aligns ministry with secular models at work, including the rationalization of corporations and planned growth in business. In contrast, this study has sought to show how ministry is grounded not only in notions of revelation, but is also related to the environment in which that ministry functions. The purpose of deploying evolution as an analogical lens has been to draw the attention of theological reflectors to the concrete reality of the church, and its practice and shaping as having a social and environmental dimension that needs to be accounted for. It is perhaps important to repeat that by engaging with clerical identity and ministry in this way, we are not capitulating to a kind of vapid reductionism. As with contemporary evolutionary theory itself, there is an in-built recognition that there is something extraordinary and special about each species. The role of genes can be grossly misrepresented; the genome is more of a 'library of recipes' than a blueprint, whereby cells and DNA will influence which recipe might be chosen, and what path might be followed.[33]

In some respects, this argument is less of a sociological strategy than it is a theological one. It remains the case that a doctrine of the incarnation requires the theologian to contemplate just how the person of Jesus is rooted in a particular time, context and place. To ponder on the gift of God in Jesus Christ is also to meditate upon the risk God takes in giving himself in a particular and embodied way to a particular time and culture, such that the very disclosure of God is bound up in the evolving understanding of revelation and humanity, and the progressive shaping of the environment. And just as God gives in such a way, so, likewise, is ministry both linked to the temporal and the eternal.

---

[33] See J. Dupre, *Darwin's Legacy: What Evolution Means Today* (Oxford: Oxford University Press, 2005).

Coda

To say that ministry [today] is going through a period of change sounds something of a cliché; but like many clichés, it needs saying.[1]

A study of clergy today seems specialised almost to the point of being esoteric. It may interest the clergy themselves to consider the observations of others, but it may well be thought to be of no wider interest or significance. This in itself is an observation about the clergy at the present time, and in itself is something remarkable, signifying the arrival of a wholly new era for religion and for religion's place in the life of a society.[2]

Although this monograph has primarily preoccupied itself with ordained ministry as its overt subject, readers will be aware that there is also a subtext. The more covert agenda of the book has been concerned with interrogating the types of theology that often support ecclesiology. In this respect, the work has sought to expose some of the more purist assumptions that underpin theologies of ministry, and to invite some fundamental questions about the nature of divine action in relation to human nature and the environment. We have not, of course, been able (or particularly willing) to resolve the issue of whether ministers, clergy or priests are the product of evolution or creation. From the outset, any potential resolution (e.g., 'intelligent design') has been set aside in order to address the book's more fundamental focus: the shaping of ministry and ministers in relation to their environment. In turn, that issue has, as its foundation, some more profound theological questions that briefly merit attention.

The question of ecclesial ancestry, for example – a theme that has been continually surfacing in the book – is something that many denominations frequently need to resolve. Taken one way, it is possible to argue that a number of denominations have their roots in accidents: 'the Methodists were never intended by the Wesleys', or 'the Church of England is just a historical consequence of Henry VIII's division with

---

[1] R. Towler and A. Coxon, *The Fate of the Anglican Clergy* (London: Macmillan, 1979), p. 151. For a more recent Methodist perspective on clerical change, see P. Luscombe and E. Shreeve, *What is a Minister?* (Peterborough: Epworth Press, 2002).

[2] Towler and Coxon, *Fate of the Anglican Clergy*, p. 1.

Rome' are typical if superficial assertions. Read like this, such denominational origins would be subject to the most reductive kind of evolutionary theory: merely the products and accidents of their environments. But ecclesial ancestry does not only lie in pragmatism. It is also the product of willed spiritual reasoning and deep theological searching; of wisdom before God in specific times and places. The development of denominations may well involve the negotiation of pragmatic responses to change. But they also emerge because individuals and communities have sought a particular kind of spiritual nourishment, which in turn has shaped and fashioned a new kind of ecclesial order that, in itself, is as capable of tracing its origins back to God as any other expression may. This is a kind of inductive theological reasoning, in which the denomination comes to express and reify its experience of God within the contours of a layered Christian tradition that builds up over time. It is a delicate ecology, yet one that knows (or ought to know) that its ancestry is authentic, as much as it may be complicated by history and environment.

That said, it remains the case that the majority of theologies that inform studies of ministry are primarily deductive in character. That is to say, Christianity's uniqueness and validity are treated as being simply given, a priori. The assumption is that revelation has already determined a detailed blueprint or formula for the present, which simply has to be discovered and applied. The actual application is the only part of the process that is deemed in any way to be hermeneutical; the actual status and origin of the tradition are not questioned. Correspondingly, a deductive theological manoeuvre creates the possibility of novel propositions being grounded in 'given' tradition. As we have argued earlier, this is a kind 'creationism' that can either ignore evidence from the environment, or, alternatively, narrate the development of contextuality as a strategy within a wider (but established) divine ordering. The biblical functionalism of ultra-Protestantism and the romantic idealism of ultra-Catholicism both collude with such a strategy, in which the corpus of the tradition is held to be concrete, and putatively applicable across cultures and time.

The difficulty of this theological strategy, as we have seen, is that it ignores the messy contingencies that often shape ecclesial order and identity: to say nothing of the unique character of local contexts which inevitably prompt and orchestrate fresh expressions of ministerial distinctiveness. So Towler and Coxon, from a strictly sociological perspective, are quite right: 'ministry is going through a period of change'. It inevitably adapts to its environments. But thus was it ever so: 'change' was always here to stay – it is a permanent resident in life, not an occasional guest. That said, a key question inevitably arises from the critique that has been offered: what kinds of theologies should inform the patterning and order of ministry, ecclesiology and the like? Clearly, the theological stratagem that will be best-placed to help the church come to terms with its identity-in-context are those that are practical in orientation, such that the concrete experience of Christian discipleship is allowed to inform the very shaping of theological discourse. Seward Hiltner, for example, recognizes that theologies emerge from a complex process of correlation in the midst of what we might term 'thick cultural traffic', in rich intra-dialogue with the faith tradition's core commitments. Developing the traffic analogy, he writes:

> We believe that a full two-way street is necessary in order to describe theological method. If we hold that theology is always the assimilation of faith, not just the abstract idea of faith apart from its reception, then it becomes necessary to say that culture may find answers to questions raised by faith as well as to assert that faith has answers to questions raised by culture.[3]

The advantage of this kind of theological strategy is that it gives more than adequate licence for a theology in which reflection emerges as a correlative exercise in which the inherent hybridity of Christian tradition is both recognized and affirmed. In such thinking, the very nature of divine action is therefore understood to be something that takes place within (and also gives itself to) situations and contexts that do not lend themselves to the easy separation of the sacred and the profane. Writers such as Schreiter recognize that the gospel never enters culture in a pure form – it is always incarnated: 'it is already embedded in the less-than-pure culture of the speaker, the treasure carried in vessels of clay'.[4]

The recognition of hybridity in formation is as important vocationally as it is theologically. We have already drawn attention to the problems encountered in theologies of ministry that produce a (false) idealism – one that encourages ecclesial expressions to imagine that their origin and trajectory lies in a protected and unbroken thoroughbred lineage. Whereas in reality, all ministers are mongrels: just as all ministries are ultimately complex negotiations between tradition, culture, time and environment. They emerge through contextual engagement and congress, rather than a putative purity that hermetically seals them off from any development other than that which is determined by the tradition. Ministry and ministers, in other words, emerge from syncretism.

In that respect, the idea of 'treasure carried in vessels of clay' is a far from perfect analogy, since the gold and the dirt are not yet separated in ministerial identity. The nuggets are deep in the rock, or lie in tiny shards buried in the gravel and the sand. The task for the theological interpreter of ministry is to mine, pan and sift for these within themselves in the continual testing of discernment, so that the people of God can also ultimately 'come forth as gold.' (Granted, this is a task

---

[3] S. Hiltner, *Preface to Pastoral Theology* (Nashville: Abingdon, 1958), p. 223.
[4] R. Schreiter, *The New Catholicity: Theology Between the Global and the Local* (Maryknoll, NY: Orbis, 1997), p. 71.

that can only be fulfilled eschatologically, even as it must be strived for hermeneutically.) Similarly, our earlier notion of the minister as conductor (within an orchestra) is also problematic. The implied gap between the producer (or director) and the cast, or perhaps the conductor, orchestra and audience, fails to perceive that the Christian message is inherently part of the process of syncretism. The listener, like the performer, is always synthesizing. Ministry and ministers are part of the process of synthesis – a unique and fresh expression of hybridity that resonates with the past, but also chimes with the present. Even familiar biblical imagery stumbles at this point.

For example, the widespread usage of the sheep–shepherd paradigm (cf. John 10, etc.) to explain the particularity of ordained ministry – which has a comforting pastoral resonance, implying that congregations are led like sheep by a kindly shepherd – should be cautiously retired for its inadequacy. Leaving aside the problematizing of power relations that this paradigm always achieves, one is also aware that all shepherds are, in reality, drawn from the flock; they are not alien beings. Clearly the analogy fails as one that connotes any kind of ordering for ecclesial or pastoral polity. Unlike real life and ministry, the shepherd has never been a sheep, and the sheep cannot become a shepherd. Yet ministerial identity so often imagines itself to be of a different *species* to the laity. However, as we have pointed out earlier, the shaping of ministerial identity is a matter of apprenticeship; it is something learned in the field. You can learn *about* ministry in the classroom. But you can only learn *to be* a minister in the process of practice and mentoring. The correlation that needs to shape ministry is the very same kind of process that ought to shape theologies of ministry: one that takes account of experience, environment and tradition as they are encountered in practice.

We have already made mention of the work of Urban Holmes and others, and drawn attention to the refreshing realism that such writers bring to bear upon the identity and shaping of ministry. Holmes is clearly identifiable as a practical theologian working within the correlative paradigm; a kind of Christian realism that is rooted in the legacy of Tillich, the Niebuhrs and others. Similarly, James and Evelyn Whitehead's practical theological treatment of ministry offers a corrective to some of the paradigms we have been seeking to address in this critique, in which theological reflection emerges as a 'process of bringing to bear in the practical decisions of ministry the resources of the Christian faith'.[5] This correlative methodology recognizes that the sources which inform theological reflection include Christian tradition, experience (individual and corporate) and culture. These sources are multiple, competing, intra-penetrative and also ambiguous, such that the task of theological reflection emerges as a process of distillation,

[5] J. Whitehead and E. Whitehead, *Method in Ministry: Theological Reflection and Christian Ministry* (San Francisco: Harper & Row, 1980), p. 6.

refinement and interpretation. This 'dynamic trilateral' (i.e., tradition, experience and culture) leads the Whiteheads to suggest that a correlative practical theology recognizes that ecclesial change and adaptation rather than concreteness is the more usual *modus operandi* for the church:

> On a complex pastoral question no ready-made answer is lying in wait in the tradition or in our experience. But in a truly assertive dialogue a solution – tentative, debatable, reversible – will be generated. This is more than a confidence in educational technique; it is a theological conviction about how the Spirit generates a historical tradition.[6]

The insights of the Whiteheads have important resonances for our thesis as a whole. The argument presented in this book has been positioned and pivoted in such a way that it can tilt in two particular directions. On the one hand, it reaches for a kind of 'natural theology' of ministry, or at least one that takes a more serious account of the work of the Spirit in contextuality and the environment as part of the shaping of tradition. On the other hand, the thesis has consistently critiqued idealized accounts of the church that are often solely creatures of the (theological) imagination, but represented as revelation. The idea that concepts of ministry are rooted more in the imagination (and perhaps fantasies) than they are in tradition is not so strange. The very nature of public ministry means that the 'clerical creature' will feature in the dreams and projections of the congregation, and in turn this suggests that clergy will continually re-imagine themselves within role and amidst their tasks. The advantage of a dynamic correlative theological approach to ministry is that it continually draws the church out of idealized paradigms and into a richer form of dialogue in which ministerial identity can be owned and assessed more honestly. To consider the messy contingencies of contextuality is, therefore, merely to ponder the variety of ways in which God both forms and speaks to his creation. It is done through both revelation and reality; indeed, the two, though distinguishable, are not to be separated.

If the correlative theological approach can help us to adopt a more nuanced view of revealed truth in relation to reality, then it might also assist in the task of reading and interpreting contextuality. Some of the most decisive splits in Christianity appear to be grounded solely in doctrinal disputes. However, when inspected more closely, the cultural aspects of separation can also emerge to give a richer account of the shifting tectonic plates of denominationalism. For example, the first great schism in Christianity is not only doctrinal; it is also between the centres of powers and culture in both the East and West. The second

---

[6] Whitehead and Whitehead, *Method in Ministry*, p.39.

great schism – the Reformation – owes much of its energy to theological disputes. But the Reformation must also be read as a symptom of emerging nationalism and states within Europe, which increasingly wish to order their own temporal and spiritual affairs, and develop a genuinely vernacular religious expression of Christianity. These sizeable paradigm shifts have led to the creation of the great continents of Christendom – Protestant, Roman Catholic and Orthodox – and their evolution since the sixteenth century tells an important story about their capacity to develop in places beyond their original context. In that respect, South America remains one of the most fascinating arenas of study that focuses on the development of religion, as both Roman Catholicism and Protestantism vie for pre-eminence within a highly variegated ecology.

The twentieth century has, of course, seen the seedlings of a third schism, namely that between conservatives and liberals, or between traditionalists and radicals. The fault lines in this scenario are complex to trace, but the early indications are that this is less about the creation of a further continent than it is about the emergence of new ecclesial islands caused by denominational erosion and more local ecological calamities or geological catastrophes. To some extent, the emergence of the Southern Baptists – as distinct from (North) American Baptists – serves as some kind of paradigm that warns ecclesiastical communities about the price of failing to cohere. Such divisions, when they emerge, produce fresh expressions of ministry which are then traced inductively to some (mythic) point of origin. This theological 'result' is then, typically, adopted as a point of departure for deductive theological reasoning, thereby allowing the 'new' church to imagine itself as the 'original'. The fact that the two strains deriving from the single breed are likely to still remain very closely related in both structure and form can be a cause of acute anxiety for future generations of ministers and believers. (Just witness the amount of distance Mormons try to put between themselves and Reformed Latter Day Saints: the actual differences are lost on all but the shrewdest observer with an eye for detail.)

A correlative theological reading of ecclesial polity and ministerial praxis can also throw some light on how theological divisions are in fact symptoms rather than causes of ecclesial fracture. Consider, for example, the worldwide Anglican Communion, and its current difficulties in holding together as a meaningful and purposeful body. On the surface, the manifest difficulties appear to be centred on issues such as sexuality (i.e., the place of lesbian and gay people, whether as ordained or laity), gender (i.e., women bishops and women priests), the right use of the Bible (i.e., are ethical issues resolved principally by reference to Scripture, or does reason, culture and experience have a part to play in ethical decisions?) and the appropriate interpretation of Scripture (i.e., does it have one plain meaning, or several possible competing meanings?). It is therefore possible to narrate the schismatic tendencies in Anglicanism with reference to authority, theology and ecclesial power. But on its own, as a thesis, this is clearly inadequate, as such tensions have existed within Anglicanism from the outset. There has not been a single century in which Anglicanism has not wrestled with its identity; it is by nature a polity that draws in a variety of competing theological traditions. Its very appeal lies in its own distinctive hybridity.

Another way of reading the current difficulties is to register that the polity itself is expressive of competing but covert cultural convictions. We might say, for example, that current Anglican difficulties begin with the American Revolution (or War of Independence), which caused American Anglicans to reconceive their faith as Republicans rather than Royalists. The emergence of Samuel Seabury as the first American Anglican bishop (consecrated, incidentally, by Scottish bishops rather than by the Archbishop of Canterbury or any other English bishop) marks a seminal moment in the identity of Anglicanism. Although the gesture itself, at least on the surface, is not significant, it comes to represent the emergence of two competing streams of ecclesial and cultural polity within a single communion. The first is Royalist, and therefore bound to a culture that is aligned with hierarchy and obedience that is at least linked to divine right and ordering. But the second, which is Republican, is essentially democratic in orientation, and therefore about the rights of the people more than the princes and prelates. Moreover, there is a modification to the Royalist paradigm that needs factoring in here, for it is not a quasi-feudal system, but rather that which emerged out of the seventeenth-century English revolution (i.e., Civil War), which had deposed outright notions of kingship, but had then restored kingly power, albeit checked by new forms of democratic and parliamentary power.

There is some sense in which a range of current Anglican difficulties can be read against these deep underground cultural streams that eventually cause the apparent seismic doctrinal shifts. For example, the election of Gene Robinson (a genial, gay clergyman) as Bishop of New Hampshire is an expression of North American faith in the gift of democracy (from God) and the inalienable right to choose. A people who were chosen – liberated, as it were, from the yoke of colonial patrimony – are now themselves called upon by God to continue exercising their God-given right to choose. The will of a foreign power – even a friendly Archbishop of Canterbury – will be seen as an act of hostility and demotic feudalism. These two streams of power, deeply embedded in their respective cultures (not unlike Churchill's notion of two nations divided by a common language) is all it takes to produce two kinds of very different theological grammars within the same communion. Moreover, when such differences are mapped on to the worldwide Anglican Communion, and emerging post-colonial identity is taken account of within developing nations, which are suspicious of both the old ordering of kingly power and the apparent 'consumerism' of the democratic stream, the stage is set for some major divisions to emerge, which will inevitably manifest themselves in doctrinal and ecclesial difference. But such differences are, clearly, at least partially the product of their environments.

However, there is no need to conclude this Coda on a such a cautious note. Part of the purpose of utilizing the analogy of evolution as an analytical and critical lens for the study of ministry has been to account not only for the differences, but also to map the commonality across the clerical species. It is at this point that something of the purposes of a Creator might be said to be manifest in the variegated patterning of clerical identity and roles. What, after all, are the clergy for? Whilst a variety of theologies of ministry may entertain romantic fantasies about their point of origin and purity, it is in the tasks and life of ministry that clergy – perhaps uniquely – begin to express something of the correspondence between the Creator and the created. The 'set-apart-ness' that guarantees both centrality and marginality in any community is fundamental to the distinctiveness of the species and the particularity of the vocation. Moreover, it is frequently in the marginality of life and death that the office and the calling becomes grounded and apparent. It is here that the clergyperson connects with the enchantment of the Christian story, and, hopefully, becomes one who can in turn enchant with their ministry, by helping congregations find fresh meaning and substance in familiar materials.

One writer, a funeral director who constantly witnesses the ministry of clergy in death and bereavement, reflects upon this:

> I remember the priest I called to bury one of our town's indigents – a man without family or friends or finances. He, the grave-diggers, and I carried the casket to the grave. The priest incensed the body, blessed it with holy water, and read from the liturgy for twenty minutes, then sang *In Paradisum* – that gorgeous Latin for 'May the angels lead you into Paradise' – as we lowered the poor man's body into the ground. When I asked him why he'd gone to such trouble, he said these are the most important funerals – even if only God is watching – because it affirms the agreement between 'all God's children' that we will witness and remember and take care of each other.[7]

This vignette, as if one needed reminding, illustrates how there is an emotional bond between the minister and those beyond the congregation. The bond, no matter how faint, is an expression of Christ's own for those who are beyond the immediate horizon of social or ecclesial communities. The calling of the clergy is, in other words, an extension of God's love that must surpass any interest in the protection or the

---

[7] Thomas Lynch, 'Good Grief', *Christian Century*, 26 July 2003.

interests of the species itself. It is inherently costly and sacrificial in its orientation, seeking not its own security, but rather expressing the continual risk of incarnation. The same writer notes how, even at apparently formulaic funerals, clergy frequently step across their own proscribed lines of denominational belief and liturgical behaviour to form a bond with the deceased or the grieving, thereby expressing a commonality that is traceable throughout the clerical species. In so doing, ministers improvise and perform the love of God, holding souls and bodies in contested and ambiguous territory that is itself on the very edge of human existence and understanding:

> I remember the Presbyterian pastor, a woman of strength and compassion who assisted a young mother, whose baby had died, in placing the infant's body into a tiny casket. She held the young woman as she placed a cross in the baby's hands and a teddy bear at the baby's side and then, because the mother couldn't, the pastor carefully closed the casket lid. They stood and prayed together – 'God grant us the serenity to accept the things we cannot change' – then drove with me to the crematory.

> Or the Baptist preacher called to preach [at] the funeral of one of our famously imperfect citizens who drank and smoked and ran a little wild, contrary to how his born-again parents had raised him. Instead of damnation and altar calls, the pastor turned the service into a lesson in God's love and mercy and forgiveness. After speaking about the man's Christian youth, he allowed as how he had 'gone astray' after he'd left home and joined the army. 'It seems he couldn't keep his body and his soul aligned,' the young pastor said, and seemed a little lost for words until he left the pulpit, walked over and opened the casket, took out a harmonica, and began to play 'Just As I Am' while everyone in the congregation nodded and wept and smiled, some of them mouthing the words of promise and comfort to themselves.[8]

Whilst one can speculate on the ultimate origin of this type of ministry, most ministers will understand its purpose, and ultimately identify themselves within such stories. They will know that in this there is some spiritual comfort for one of the deepest human pains. They will understand they are expressing something of that divine balm for that most earthly of anguish. They will know that they have been called into a relationship with their environment that is flecked with certainties and ambiguities, coupled with insecurity and status. And in the midst of that, and perhaps pondering the origin of their own vocation, ministers

[8] Lynch, 'Good Grief'.

will reflect on how they have been drawn into something deep and mysterious that can be lived, but seldom understood and articulated:

> In each case these holy people treated the bodies of the dead neither as a bother or embarrassment, nor an idol or icon, nor just a shell. They treated the dead like one of our own, precious to the people who loved them, temples of the Holy Spirit, neighbours, family, fellow pilgrims. They stand – these local heroes, these saints and sinners, these men and women of God – in that difficult space between the living and the dead, between faith and fear, between humanity and Christianity and say out loud, 'Behold, I show you a mystery.'[9]

In ending on this note, I am conscious that there is more than something of an irony here. We began these essays by noting Russell's observation (as well as those of others such as Towler and Coxon) that clergy had been facing a growing problem of marginalization since the Victorian era, and had through various means, not least the 'invention' of professionalism, attempted to combat this in the nineteenth and twentieth centuries. However, this marginality is, it seems, part of the character and construct of being a minister. Clergy, to function as effective ministers, often discover their role and tasks to be about becoming central in the more marginal and ambiguous moments of life. Clergy occupy that strange hinterland between the secular and the sacred, the temporal and the eternal, acting as interpreters and mediators, embodying and signifying faith, hope and love. They are both distant and immediate, remote yet intimate. And in occupying this most marginal and transitory ground, and sometimes helping to close the gaps between these worlds, they become humanly and spiritually necessary even as they live out their (party willed, partly imposed) social marginality. It is a unique yet evolving paradigm. It is nothing less than to follow the call of Jesus: to belong both to the wilderness, but also to the city. To be a citizen of some place; but also of heaven. To be of the people; but also for their sake, to be wholly other. And it is possible that even Darwin understood something of the complexity of this conundrum for the study of ministry, as he reflected on the role of the Creator, and the struggle for life within the environments he had studied. He concludes the 6th edition of *Origin* with these words:

> There is grandeur in this view of life, with its several powers, having been originally breathed by the Creator into a few forms or into one; and that, whilst this planet has gone circling on according to the fixed law of gravity, from so simple a beginning endless forms most beautiful and most wonderful have been, and are being evolved.

[9] Lynch, 'Good Grief'.

Bibliography

Albrecht, P. 1961, *The Churches and Rapid Social Change*. London: SCM Press.

—— 2001, *An Anglican-Methodist Covenant*. Peterborough: Methodist Publishing House and Church House Publishing.

Advisory Board of Ministry. 1998, *Stranger in the Wings. A Report on Local Non-Stipendiary Ministry*. London: Church House Publishing.

Anglican–Roman Catholic International Commission (ARCIC). 1973, 'Ministry and Ordination'. London: Church House Publishing.

Atran, S. 2002, *In Gods We Trust: The Evolutionary Landscape of Religion*. New York: Oxford University Press.

Avis, P. 2005, *A Ministry Shaped by Mission*. London: Continuum.

Barnett, J.M. 1979, *The Diaconate: A Full and Equal Order*. Harrisburg, PA: Trinity Press.

Barsley, M. 1963, *How to Become Archbishop*. London: Anthony Blond.

Barth, K. 1958, *Church Dogmatics*. Edinburgh: T & T Clark.

Baum, W. 2005, *Understanding Behaviourism: Behaviour, Culture and Evolution*. Oxford: Blackwell.

Bear, G. 1999, *Darwin's Radio: The Next Great War will Start Inside Us*. London: HarperCollins.

—— *Darwin's Children: The Next Stage of Human Evolution*. London: HarperCollins.

Beer, G. 1983, *Darwin's Plots*. London: Routledge and Kegan Paul.

Beeson, T. 2002, *The Bishops*. London: SCM Press.

Beresford, J. (ed.), 1997, *James Woodforde: The Diary of a Country Parson*. Norwich: Canterbury Press.

Berger, P. 1969, *A Rumour of Angels*. Garden City, NY: Doubleday.

Berra, T. 1990, *Evolution and the Myth of Creationism*. Stanford, CA: Stanford University Press.

Boone, K. 1989, *The Bible Tells Them So: The Discourse of Protestant Fundamentalism*. London: SCM.

Boyer, P. 2002, *The Naturalness of Religious Ideas*. Berkeley, CA: University of California Press.

Bridge, D. and Phypers, D. 1982. *More than Tongues Can Tell: Reflections on Charismatic Renewal*. London: Hodder & Stoughton.

Brierley, P. 1992, *Act on the Facts*. London: Marc Europe.

—— 1994/5 and 1998/9, *UK Christian Handbook*. London: Marc Europe.

Broom, D.M. 2003, *The Evolution of Morality and Religion*. Cambridge: Cambridge University Press.

Brown, C. 2000, *The Death of Christian Britain: Understanding Secularisation 1800–2000*. London: Routledge.

Browning, D. 1991, *A Fundamental Practical Theology*. Philadelphia: Westminster.

Bruce, S. 1997, *Religion in Modern Britain*. Oxford: Oxford University Press.

Burge, T. 2005, *Science and the Bible*. Philadelphia: Templeton Foundation Press.

Burgess, S. McGee, G. and A. Patrick (eds), 1988, *A Dictionary of Pentecostal and Charismatic Movements*. Grand Rapids, MI: Zondervan.

Burnet, T. 1719, *The Sacred Theory of the Earth*. London: John Hooke.

Butler, J. 1990, *Awash in a Sea of Faith: Christianizing the American People*. Cambridge, MA: Harvard University Press.

Bynum, C. 1992, *Fragmentation and Redemption: Essays on Gender and the Body in Medieval Religion*. New York: Zone Books.

Carey, K.M. 1954, *The Historic Episcopate in the Fullness of the Church*. London: Dacre Press.

Carr, E. 1963, *What is History?* London: Penguin.

Carter, S. 1971, *Love More or Less: Poems*. London: Stainer & Bell.

Certeau, M. 1984, *The Practice of Everyday Life*. Trans. S. Randall. Berkeley, CA: University of California Press.

Chadwick, O. 1954, *The Founding of Cuddesdon*. Oxford: Oxford University Press.

—— 1975, *The Secularization of the European Mind in the Nineteenth Century*. Cambridge: Cambridge University Press.

Chapman, A. and Kent, P. 2005. *Robert Hooke and the English Renaissance*. Leominster: Gracewing.

Chapman, M. 2004, *Ambassadors of Christ: Commemorating 150 Years of Theological Education in Cuddesdon, 1854–2004*. Hampshire: Ashgate.

—— 2004, *God's Holy Hill: A History of Christianity in Cuddesdon*. Oxford: Wychwood Press.

—— 2006, *Anglicanism: A Very Brief Introduction*. Oxford: Oxford University Press.

Chapman, R. 2002, *Godly and Righteous, Peevish and Perverse: Clergy and Religious in Literature and Letters: An Anthology*. Norwich: Canterbury Press.

Charley, J.W. 1973, *Agreement on the Doctrine of the Ministry*. London: SPCK.

Church of England. 2003, *For Such a Time as This: A Renewed Diaconate in the Church of England*. London: Church Publishing House.

Clark, D. 1982, *Between Pulpit and Pew: Folk Religion in a North Yorkshire Fishing Village*. Cambridge: Cambridge University Press.

Cocksworth, C. and Brown, R. 2002, *Being a Priest Today*. Norwich: Canterbury Press.

Coleman, S. 2000, *The Globalisation of Charismatic Christianity*. Cambridge: Cambridge University Press.

Collins, S. 2000, 'Spirituality and Youth' in M. Percy (ed.), *Calling Time: Religion and Change at the Turn of the Millennium*. Sheffield: Sheffield Academic Press.

Cox, H. 1994, *Fire from Heaven: The Rise of, Pentecostalism, Spirituality and the Reshaping of Religion in the Twenty-first Century*. New York: Addison-Wesley.

Craig, G. and Jones, E. 1982, *A Geological Miscellany*. Princeton, NJ: Princeton University Press.

Croft, S. and Walton, R. 2005, *Learning for Ministry*. London: Church Publishing House.

Cunningham, H. 1980, *Leisure in the Industrial Revolution*. Beckenham, UK: Croom Helm.

Darwin, C. 1981, *The Origin of Species*. London: Penguin.

Davie, G. 1994, *Religion in Britain Since 1945*. Oxford: Blackwell.

Davies, D. 1995, *Observations of a Clipston Curate: The Rev Evan Williams 1752 to 1824*. Northants: Dorothy Davies.

Dawkins, R. 1995, *River Out of Eden: A Darwinian View of Life*. London: Weidenfeld and Nicolson.

Dearmer, P. 1932, *The Parson's Handbook*. London: Henry Milford.

Desmond, A. and Moore, J. 1991, *Darwin*. Harmondsworth: Penguin.

Dolan, J. 2005, *The Independent Methodists: A History*. Cambridge: James Clarke & Co.

Donovan, V. 1982, *Christianity Rediscovered: An Epistle to the Masai*. London: SCM Press.

Dunn, J. 1979, *Baptism in the Spirit: A Study of the Religious and Charismatic Experience of Jesus and the First Christians*. London: SCM.

Dupre, J. 2005, *Darwin's Legacy: What Evolution Means Today*. Oxford: Oxford University Press.

Eldredge, N. 2000, *The Triumph of Evolution and the Failure of Creationism*. New York: WH Freeman.

Elton, G. 1969, *The Practice of History*. London: Fontana.

Eysenck, H. 1954, *Manual of the Eysenck Personality Inventory*. London: London University Press.

Festinger, L. 1956, *When Prophecy Fails*. New York: Harper & Row.

Fichter, J. 1961, *Religion as an Occupation: A Study in the Sociology of Professions*. Notre Dame, IN: University of Notre Dame.

Fletcher, A. 1997, *The Barbarian Conversion*. New York: Holt.

Fox, K. 2004, *Watching the English: The Hidden Rules of English Behaviour*. London: Hodder & Stoughton.

Francis, L. and Kay, W. 1995, *Teenage Religion and Values*. Leominster: Gracewing.

Frye, N. 1951, *The Anatomy of Criticism*. Princeton: Princeton University Press.

Gasquet, F.A. 1906, *Parish Life in Medieval England*. London: Methuen and Co.

Gilbert, A. 1976, *Religion and Society in Industrial England*. London: Darton, Longman & Todd.

Gill, R. 1992, *The Myth of the Empty Church*, London: SCM Press.

Glasse, J. 1968, *Profession: Minister*. Nashville, TN: Abingdon Press.

Goldscheider, F.K. and C. 1993, *Leaving Home Before Marriage: Ethnicity, Familism and Generational Relationships*. Wisconsin: University of Wisconsin.

Gordon-Taylor, B. 2001, 'The Priest and the Mystery: A Case of Identity', in George Guiver (ed.), *Priests in a People's Church*. London: SPCK.

Gould, S.J. 1990, *Wonderful Life: The Burgess Shale and the Nature of History*. London: Vintage.

Gowers, T. 2002, *Mathematics: A Very Short Introduction*. Oxford: Oxford University Press.

Greenwood, R. 1994, *Transforming Priesthood*. London: SPCK.

Guiver, G. 2001, *Priests in a People's Church*. London: SPCK.

Gunstone, J. 1982, *Pentecostal Anglicans*. London: Hodder & Stoughton.

Haig, A. 1984, *The Victorian Clergy*. Kent: Croom Helm.

Hall, J. 1987, *Congregation: Stories and Structures*. London: SCM.

Hall, J. and Neitz, M. 1993, *Culture: Sociological Perspectives*. New Jersey: Prentice Hall.

Hardy, D. 1996, *God's Ways with the World*. Edinburgh: T&T Clark.

Hare, D. 1990, *Racing Demon*. London: Faber & Faber.

Harris, C. and Startup, R. 1999, *The Church in Wales*. Cardiff: University of Wales Press.

Harris, M. 1998, *Organizing God's Work: Challenges for Churches and Synagogues*. Hampshire: Macmillan Press Ltd.

Healy, N. *Church, World and Christian Life: Practical Prophetic Ecclesiology*. 2000, Cambridge: Cambridge University Press.

Hervieu-Leger, D. 2000, *Religion as a Chain of Memory*. Cambridge: Polity.

Heywood, C. 2001, *A History of Childhood: Children and Childhood in the West from Medieval to Modern Times*. Cambridge: Polity.

Hillel, D. 2005, *The Natural History of the Bible: An Environmental Exploration of the Hebrew Scriptures*. New York: Columbia University Press.

Hiltner, S. 1958, *Preface to Pastoral Theology*. Nashville: Abingdon Press.

Hinde, T. 1983, *A Field Guide to the English Country Parson*. London: Heinemann.

Hinton, M. 1994, *The Anglican Parochial Clergy: A Celebration*. London: SCM Press.

Hocken, P. 1986, *Streams of Renewal: The Origins and Development of the Charismatic Movement in Britain*. Exeter: Paternoster.

Hoge, D.R. and Wenger, J.E. 2005, *Pastors in Transition: Why Clergy Leave Local Church Ministry*. Grand Rapids, MI: Eerdmans.

Hollenweger, W. 1972, *The Pentecostals*. London: SCM.

Holmes, U.T. 1971, *The Future Shape of Ministry*. New York: The Seabury Press.

Hooker, R. 1907, *The Laws of Ecclesiastical Polity*. London: J.M. Dent.

Hopewell, J. 1987, *Congregation: Stories and Structures*. London: SCM.

Hummel, C. 1975, *Fire in the Fireplace: Contemporary Charismatic Renewal*. London: Mowbray.

Hunter, C. 2003, *Darwin's Proof: The Triumph of Religion over Science*. Grand Rapids, MI: Brazos Press.

Hunter, L. 1931, *A Parson's Job: Aspects of Work in the English Church*. London: SCM Press.

James, E. (ed.), 1979, *Stewards of the Mysteries of God*. London: Darton, Longman & Todd.

Jenkins, K. 1991, *Re-Thinking History*. London: Routledge.

Jenkins, S. 1999, *England's One Thousand Best Churches*. London: Allen Lane.

Jones, I. 2004, *Women and the Priesthood in the Church of England: Ten Years on*. London: Church House Publishing.

Jones, S. 1999, *Darwin's Ghost: The Origin of Species Updated*. New York: Ballantine Books.

Keillor, G. 1985, *Lake Wobegon Days*. London: Faber & Faber.

Kelly, T. 1970, *A History of Adult Education in Liverpool*. Liverpool: Liverpool University Press.

Kett, J. 1977, *Rites of Passage: Adolescence in America, 1790 to the Present*. New York: Basic Books.

Kirby, W. William Spence. 1815–26, *An Introduction to Entomology: Or Elements of the Natural History of Insects*. Four volumes. London: Watts.

Kirk, K.E. 1946, *The Apostolic Ministry: Essays on the History and the Doctrine of Episcopacy*. London: Hodder & Stoughton.

Küng, H. 1971, *Why Priests?* Glasgow: William Collins Sons & Co.

Laqueur, T. 1976, *Religion and Respectability: Sunday Schools and Working Class Culture*. New Haven: Yale University Press.

Larsen, T. 1967, *Contested Christianity: The Political and Social Contexts of Victorian Theology*. Waco, TX: Baylor University Press.

Lewis, C.S. 1954, *English Literature in the Sixteenth Century Excluding Drama*. Oxford: Clarendon Press.

Lodge, D. 1989, *Nice Work*. London: Penguin Books.

Louden, S.H. and Francis, L.J. 2003, *The Naked Parish Priest: What Priests Really Think they're Doing*. London: Continuum.

Lowe, E.C. 1898, *The Country Parson*. London: John Murray.

—— 1867, *The Temple*. London: John Murray.

Luscombe, P. and Shreeve, E. 2002, *What is a Minister?* Peterborough: Epworth Press.

Lyell, C. 1873[1830–33], *Geological Evidence of the Antiquity of Man.* New York: Appleton.

—— 1873[1863], *Principles of Geology*. New York: Appleton.

Lynch, T. 2003, 'Good Grief', *Christian Century*, 26 July.

MacDonnell, K. 1970, 'Ways of Validating Ministry', *Journal of Ecumenical Studies* 7:17–30.

Maitland, F. 1897, *Domesday Book and Beyond*. Cambridge: Cambridge University Press.

Martin, D. 1978, *A General Theory of Secularization*. Oxford: Blackwell.

—— 1990, *Tongues of Fire*. Oxford: Blackwell.

—— 1994, 'Believing Without Belonging: A Commentary on English Religion' *Crucible*, April–June 1994, pp. 59–64.

Martin, D. and Mullen, P. 1984, *Strange Gifts? A Guide to Charismatic Renewal*. Oxford: Blackwell.

Marwick, A. 1970, *The Nature of History*. London: Macmillan.

Mason, K. 1992, *Priesthood and Society*. Norwich: Canterbury Press.

Massey, D. 1994, *Space, Place and Gender*. Cambridge: Polity.

Mayr, E. 2001, *What Evolution is*. New York: Basic Books.

McGrath, A. 2005, *Dawkins' God: Genes, Memes and the Meaning of Life*. Oxford: Blackwell.

McGuire, M. 1988, *Ritual Healing in Suburban America*. New Brunswick: Rutgers University Press.

McLeod, H. 2000, *Secularisation in Western Europe 1848–1914*. London: Macmillan/Palgrave,.

Mead, M. 1978, *Culture and Commitment: The New Relationships Between the Generations in the 1970s*. New York: Doubleday.

Methodist Publishing House. 1996, *The Book of Discipline of the United Methodist Church*. Nashville: Methodist Publishing House.

Midgley, M. 1985, *Evolution as a Religion*. London: Methuen & Co.

Moody, C. 1992, *Eccentric Ministry*. London: Darton, Longman & Todd.

Moorman, J. 1945, *Church Life in England in the Thirteenth Century*. Cambridge: Cambridge University Press.

Muhlen, H. 1978, *A Charismatic Theology*. London: Burns & Oates.

Murray, A. 1972, 'Piety and Impiety', *Studies in Church History* 8: 110–22.

Myers, D. & Scanzoni, L. 2005, *What God Has Joined Together?* San Francisco: Harper.

Nesbitt, P. 2001, *Religion and Social Policy*. Lanham, MD: AltaMira Press.

Newbigin, L. 1988, 'On Being the Church for the World', in G. Ecclestone, (ed.), *The Parish Church*. London: Mowbray.

Newman, J.H. 1851, *Lectures on Certain Difficulties Felt by Anglicans in Catholic Teaching Considered*. London: Longmans, Green & Co. 2nd edn.

—— 1895, *A Grammar of Assent*. London: Longmans, Green & Co.

—— 1895, *Essay on the Development of Doctrine*. London: Longmans, Green & co.

Newsome, D. 1961, *Godliness and God Learning: Four Studies of a Victorian Ideal*. London: John Murray.

O'Connor, E. 1975, *Perspectives on Charismatic Renewal*. Notre Dame, IN: University of Notre Dame Press.

O'Leary, D. 2004, *By Design or By Chance?* Minneapolis: Augsburg Books.

Odom, W. 1917, *Fifty Years of Sheffield Church Life 1866–1916*. London: Home Words.

Osborne, D. 2005, *The Country Vicar*. London: Darton, Longman & Todd.

Paley, W. 1802, *Natural Theology; or Evidences of the Existence and Attributes of the Deity Collected from the Appearances of Nature*. London: A Faulder.

Parks, S. 2000, *Big Questions, Worthy Dreams: Mentoring Young Adults in Their Search for Meaning, Purpose and Faith*. San Francisco: Jossey-Bass.

Parsons, G. 1988, *Religion in Victorian Britain*, vol. IV. Manchester: Manchester University Press.

Pattison, Stephen & James Woodward (eds). 2000, *A Reader in Practical Theology*. Oxford: Blackwell.

Percy, M. (ed.), 2000, *Previous Convictions*. London: SPCK.

Percy, M. 1996, *Words, Wonders and Power*. London: SPCK.

—— 1998, *Power and the Church: Ecclesiology in an Age of Transition*. London: Cassell.

—— 1999, 'Sweet Rapture: Sublimated Erotisicm in Contemporary Charismatic Worship', in J. Jobling (ed.), *Theology and the Body: Gender Text and Ideology*. Leominster: Fowler Wright/Gracewing.

—— 2000, *Calling Time: Religion and Change at the Turn of the Millennium*. Sheffield: Sheffield Academic Press.

—— 2002, *Salt of the Earth: Religious Resilience in a Secular Age*. Sheffield: Sheffield Academic Press.

Pesarchick, R. 2000, *The Trinitarian Foundation of Human Sexuality as Revealed by Christ According to Hans Urs von Balthasar: The Revelatory Significance of the Male Christ and the Male Ministerial Priesthood*. The Vatican: Editrice Pontificia University Gregoriana.

Peters, T. and Hewlett, M. 2003, *Evolution: From Creation to New Creation*. Nashville, TN: Abingdon Press.

Peterson, E. 1994, *Under the Unpredictable Plant*. Grand Rapids, MI: Eerdmands.

Phillips, J.B. 1952, *Your God is Too Small*. London: Epworth Press.

Pickering, W. 1989, *Anglo-Catholicism: A Study in Religious Ambiguity*. London: Routledge.

Plomer W. (ed.), *The Diary of Francis Kilvert 1840–1879*. London: Penguin, 1987.

Poewe, K. (ed.), 1994, *Charismatic Christianity as a Global Culture*. New York: Columbia University Press.

Pounds, N.J.G. 2000, *A History of the English Parish*. Cambridge: Cambridge University Press.

The Presbyterian Church (USA). 1986, *Book of Order*. Louisville, KY: Office of the General Assembly.

Prickett, S. 2002, *Narrative, Religion and Science: Fundamentalism versus Irony, 1700–1999*. Cambridge: Cambridge University Press.

Putnam, R. 2000, *Bowling Alone: The Collapse and Revival of American Community*. New York and London: Simon & Schuster.

Ramsey, M. 1972, *The Christian Priest Today*. London: Fount.

Randall, K. 2005, *Evangelicals Etcetera: Conflict and Conviction in the Church of England's Parties*. Hampshire: Ashgate Publishing.

Ranson, S. Bryman, A. and Hinnings, R. 1977, *Clergy, Ministers and Priests*. London: Routledge & Kegan Paul.

Reader, J. 2005, *Blurred Encounters: A Reasoned Practice of Faith*. Glamorgan: Aureus Books.

Reed, J. 1996, *Glorious Battle: The Cultural Politics of Victorian Anglo-Catholicism*. Nashville: Vanderbilt University Press.

Religious Research Association. December 2002. *Review of Religious Research*. Indiana: Indiana University Printing Services.

Rokeach, M. 1979, *Understanding Human Values: Individual and Societal*. New York: Free Press.

Roof, W. & McKinney, W. 1987, *American Mainline Religion: Its Changing Shape and Form*. New Jersey: Rutgers University Press.

Roof, W.C. 1993, *A Generation of Seekers: The Spiritual Journeys of the Baby Boom Generation*. San Francisco: Harper Collins.

Russell, A. 1980, *The Clerical Profession*. London: SPCK.

—— 1986, *The Country Parish*. London: SPCK.

—— 1993, *The Country Parson*. London: SPCK.

Schon, D. 1991, *The Reflective Practitioner: How Professionals Think in Action*. London: Ashgate.

Schreiter, R. 1997, *The New Catholicity: Theology Between the Global and the Local*. Maryknoll, NY: Orbis.

Scott, D. 1978, *From Office to Profession: The New England Ministry 1750–1850*. Pennsylvania: University of Pennsylvania Press.

Scott, J. 1990, *Domination and the Art of Resistance: Hidden Transcripts*. New Haven, CT: Yale University Press.

Shier-Jones, A. 2004, 'Being Methodical', in *Unmasking Methodist Theology* (ed. C. Marsh, *et al*); London: Continuum.

Sibley, D. 1995, *Geographies of Exclusion*. London: Routledge.

Smith, C. 2000, *The Quest for Charisma: Christianity and Persuasion*. Westport, CT: Praeger.

Stevens, W. 1955, 'Description Without Place', from *The Collected Poems of Wallace Stevens*. London: Faber & Faber.

Strinati, D. 1995, *Popular Culture: An Introduction to Theories*. New York: Routledge.

Suenens, C. 1978, *Ecumenism and Charismatic Renewal: Theological and Pastoral Orientations*. London: Darton, Longman & Todd.

Suennes, C. and Dom Helder, C. 1979, *Charismatic Renewal and Social Action: A Dialogue*. London: Darton, Longman & Todd.

Sweet, M. 2001, *Inventing the Victorians*. London: Faber & Faber.

Thomas, K. 1971, *Religion and the Decline of Magic*. London: Weidenfeld & Nicolson.

Thomas, R.S. 1995, *Collected Poems 1945–1990*. London: Weidenfield & Nicolson.

Thompson, E. (ed.), 1990, *Cultural Theory*. Boulder: Westview Press.

Tillard, J.M.R. 1973, *What Priesthood has the Ministry?* Nottinghamshire: Grove Books.

Tomlinson, D. 1995, *The Post-Evangelical*. London: SPCK.

Torry, M. 2004, *The Parish People, Place and Ministry: A Theological and Practical Exploration*. Norwich: Canterbury Press.

—— 2005, *Managing God's Business: Religious and Faith-Based Organizations and their Management*. London: Ashgate.

Towler, R. and Coxon, A. 1979, *The Fate of the Anglican Clergy: A Sociological Study*. London: Macmillan.

Tugwell, S. Hocken, P. Every, G. and Mills, J. 1976, *New Heaven? New Earth?* London: Darton, Longman & Todd.

Ussher, J. 1658, *The Annals of the World*, vol. IV. New York: Master Books.

Van Der Ven, J.A. 1998, *Education for Reflective Ministry*. Belgium: Peeters.

Vanstone, W.H. 1977, *Love's Endeavour, Love's Expense: The Response of Being to the Love of God*. London: Darton, Longman & Todd.

Visser, M. 2000, *The Geometry of Love: Space, Time, Mystery and Meaning in and Ordinary Church*. London: Penguin Books.

Wace, H. and Buchheim, C. (ed.). 1883, *First Principles of the Reformation or The 95 Theses and the Three Primary Works of Dr. Martin Luther*. London: John Murray.

Walker, A. 1985, *Restoring the Kingdom: The Radical Christianity of the House Church Movement*. Guildford: Eagle Press. Revised and expanded edition, 1998.

—— 1996, *Telling the Story*. London: SPCK.

Walton, M. 1981, *A History of the Diocese of Sheffield 1914–1979*. Sheffield: Sheffield Board of Finance.

Ward, G. 2005, *Cultural Transformation and Religious Practice*. Cambridge: Cambridge University Press.

Watson, D. 1965, *Towards Tomorrow's Church*. London: Falcon Books.

Watt, T. 1991, *Cheap Print and Popular Piety, 1550–1640*. Cambridge: Cambridge University Press.

Webster, A. 2002, *Reaching for Reality: Sketches from the Life of the Church*. London: SPCK.

Weil, S. 1973, *Waiting for God*. New York: Harper.

Wells, R. 1992, Victorian Village. *The Diaries of the Reverend John Coker Egerton of Burwash 1857–1888.* Stroud: Alan Sutton Publishing.

Wells, S. 2004, *Improvisation: The Drama of Christian Ethics.* Grand Rapids, MI: Brazos Press.

—— 2005, *An Anglican Critique of Establishment.* Suffolk: *Crucible*, G J Palmer and Sons.

Wesley, J. 1976, *The Works of John Wesley*, IX. Ed. R. Davies. Nashville: Abingdon Press.

Whiston, William. 1696, *A New Theory of the Earth.* London William Whiston.

White, A. 1897, *A History of the Warfare of Science with Theology in Christendom.* London: Appleton and Co.

White, G. 1788, *The Natural History of Selborne.* London: Penguin Books.

Whitehead, J. and E. 1980, *Method in Ministry: Theological Reflection and Christian Ministry.* San Franscisco: Harper & Row.

Wickham, E. 1957, *Church and People in an Industrial City.* London: Lutterworth Press.

Wieland, C. 2005, 'Darwin's Eden', *Creation* 27.3, (June–August, 2005) 1:16–20.

Wigley, J. 1980, *The Rise and Fall of the Victorian Sunday.* Manchester: Manchester University Press.

Williams, A. and Davidson, J. 1996, 'Catholic Conceptions of Faith: A Generational Analysis', *Sociology of Religion*, 57.3:35–52.

Williams, R. 2005, *Why Study the Past?* London: Darton, Longman & Todd.

Wilson, A.N. 1992, *The Faber Book of Church and Clergy.* London: Faber & Faber.

Wilson, B. 1966, *Religion in Secular Society.* London: Watts and Co.

Wilson, D.S. 2002, *Darwin's Cathedral: Evolution, Religion, and the Nature of Society.* Chicago: University of Chicago Press.

Wilson, E. 1998, *Consilience: The Unity of Knowledge.* London: Little, Brown and Co.

Woodward, J. 1695, *An Essay Towards the Natural History of the Earth.* London Richard Wilkin.

Woodward, T. 2003, *Doubts About Darwin: A History of Intelligent Design.* Grand Rapids, MI: Baker Books.

Yates, N. 1991, *Anglican Ritualism in Victorian Britain: 1830–1910.* Oxford: Oxford University Press.

Zoltman, G. 1973, *Processes and Phenomena of Social Change.* New York: Wiley.

Index